LIBRARY OF HEBREW BIBLE/
OLD TESTAMENT STUDIES

541

Formerly Journal for the Study of the Old Testament Supplement Series

ECCLESIASTES AND SCEPTICISM

Stuart Weeks

t & t clark

Published by T & T Clark International
A Continuum imprint
80 Maiden Lane, New York, NY 10038
The Tower Building, 11 York Road, London SE1 7NX

www.continuumbooks.com

Visit the T & T Clark blog at www.tandtclarkblog.com

Library of Congress Cataloging-in-Publication Data

Weeks, Stuart.
Ecclesiastes and scepticism / by Stuart Weeks.
    p. cm.
Includes bibliographical references (p. --) and index.
ISBN-13: 978-0-567-25288-3 (hardcover : alk. paper)
ISBN-10: 0-567-25288-4 (hardcover : alk. paper) 1. Bible. O.T. Ecclesiastes--Criticism, interpretation, etc. I. Title.
BS1475.52.W44 2011
  223'.806--dc23

                        2011021532

ISBN: HB: 978-0-567-25288-3

Typeset by Forthcoming Publications Ltd (www.forthpub.com)
Printed and bound in the United States

For David Weeks

CONTENTS

PREFACE

After some years of preparing a commentary on Ecclesiastes—which may yet take a few years to finish—I undertook this monograph largely as a way to escape the *minutiae* of the text, and to try to clarify for myself some of the bigger issues. My awareness that this book was being written at the same time as I prepared a more detailed treatment of Ecclesiastes has led me to impose certain constraints. In particular, I have tried to avoid engagement here with the many philological and text-critical issues raised by the text, beyond the extent necessary to indicate the reasons for my own interpretation. I have also tried not to take on every proposal with which I disagree on every topic: the interpretation of Ecclesiastes can rapidly come to resemble a bar-room brawl in a western, and I have been anxious in this context to prioritize what I think, not what I reject.

The idea for the book arose initially in conversation with Andrew Mein (when I was wondering how to wangle an invitation to the excellent LHBOTS receptions at SBL), and I am grateful both to him and to Claudia Camp for accepting my proposal to publish it in the series. I am grateful also to all those patient acquaintances and I-hope-not-ex-friends who have had to put up with my absorption and occasional irritation whilst I have been writing it: Qohelet is a demanding companion. My children, more than anyone, are owed apologies—not least, for some late and seriously over-cooked dinners—but also gratitude for their good-natured acceptance of it all. My colleagues at Durham have been supportive as ever, and I am especially grateful both to Robert Hayward and Walter Moberly for many helpful conversations, and to Robert Song for picking up the various administrative balls dropped along the way as this neared completion.

ABBREVIATIONS

ACCS	*Ancient Christian Commentary on Scripture: Old Testament IX: Proverbs, Ecclesiastes, Song of Solomon.* Edited by J. Robert Wright. Ancient Christian Commentary on Scripture. Downers Grove, 2005
AfO	*Archiv für Orientforschung*
AJSLL	*American Journal of Semitic Languages and Literature*
AS	*Aramaic Studies*
BETL	Bibliotheca ephemeridum theologicarum lovaniensium
BZ	*Biblische Zeitschrift*
BZAW	Beihefte zur Zeitschrift für die alttestamentliche Wissenschaft
CBQ	*Catholic Biblical Quarterly*
CBQMS	*Catholic Biblical Quarterly* Monograph Series
CEJL	Commentaries on Early Jewish Literature
de Rossi	de Rossi, J. B. *Variae lectiones Veteris Testamenti ex immensa MSS. editorumq. codicum congerie haustae et ad Samar. textum, ad vetustiss. versiones, ad accuratiores sacrae criticae fontes ac leges examinatae.* 4 vols. Parma, 1784–88
DJD	Discoveries in the Judaean Desert
ET	English translation
HAR	*Hebrew Annual Review*
HAT	Handbuch zum Alten Testament
HUCA	*Hebrew Union College Annual*
ICC	International Critical Commentary
JAAR	*Journal of the American Academy of Religion*
JARCE	*Journal of the American Research Center in Egypt*
Jastrow	Jastrow, M. *Dictionary of the Targumim, the Talmud Babli and Yerushalmi, and the Midrashic Literature.* 2 vols. London, 1886–1903
JBL	*Journal of Biblical Literature*
JEA	*Journal of Egyptian Archaeology*
JNES	*Journal of Near Eastern Studies*
JNSL	*Journal of Northwest Semitic Languages*
JQR	*Jewish Quarterly Review*
JSOT	*Journal for the Study of the Old Testament*
JSOTSup	Journal for the Study of the Old Testament: Supplement Series
JSS	*Journal of Semitic Studies*
JTS	*Journal of Theological Studies*

Kennicott	Kennicott, B. *Vetus Testamentum Hebraicum cum variis lectioni-bus*. 2 vols. Oxford, 1776–80
Levy	Levy, J. *Neuhebräisches und chaldäisches Wörterbuch über die Talmudim und Midraschim*. 4 vols. Leipzig, 1876–89
LHBOTS	Library of Hebrew Bible/Old Testament Studies
NICOT	New International Commentary on the Old Testament
OBO	Orbis biblicus et orientalis
OLA	Orientalia Lovaniensia Analecta
OTE	*Old Testament Essays*
PAAJR	*Proceedings of the American Academy of Jewish Research*
RB	*Revue biblique*
RThPh	*Revue de théologie et de philosophie*
SBL	Society of Biblical Literature
SJOT	*Scandinavian Journal of the Old Testament*
TDOT	*Theological Dictionary of the Old Testament*. Edited by G. J. Botterweck and H. Ringgren. Translated by J. T. Willis, G. W. Bromiley, and D. E. Green. 8 vols. Grand Rapids, 1974–
TZ	*Theologische Zeitschrift*
UF	*Ugarit Forschungen*
VT	*Vetus Testamentum*
VTSup	Vetus Testamentum Supplements
ZAH	*Zeitschrift für Althebraistik*
ZAW	*Zeitschrift für die alttestamentliche Wissenschaft*
ZDPV	*Zeitschrift des deutschen Palastina-Vereins*

INTRODUCTION

There are as many interpretations of Ecclesiastes as there are interpreters—perhaps more, indeed, since some interpreters have changed
their minds. There is nothing very novel, therefore, in offering a new
interpretation of the book, and I do so with the rather humbling expectation that no other interpreter will agree with it. I do hope, however, that
this study will draw attention to some aspects of the text which have
received less attention than they deserve, and perhaps also correct some
assumptions which have, I believe, been allowed to stand unchallenged
for far too long.

To put my interpretation in a nutshell, and to over-simplify it a little, I
believe that the sort of pessimistic statements and calls to pleasure which
the book makes were probably nothing very new in their day, and that
similar statements are so widespread in ancient literature that they barely
constitute scepticism in any meaningful way. On the other hand, the book
finds a way to integrate these sentiments into a more profound separation
between human life and the world in which it is lived: all that humans do
contributes to plans and processes beyond their comprehension, and all
that is really theirs can be found only at the level of feeling and sensation. This scheme is presented initially through a narrative, in which the
book's protagonist comes to realize that all that he has accomplished for
himself is not really his to own or control, and in which an intellectual
acknowledgment becomes a personal grievance. His speech, though,
is shaped by his own concerns in such a way that readers may find
themselves as critical of his motives as they are sympathetic to his
conclusions.

1. *Content*

Nothing in the study of Ecclesiastes is straightforward, and this monograph covers a lot of different issues, so it may be helpful to offer a road
map by summarizing my more detailed conclusions here in advance. Of
course, those who prefer to wait may look away now. My starting-point,

in the first chapter, is the figure of Qohelet himself, whose monologue forms the main part of the book.[1] After affirming that, for practical purposes at least, Qohelet should be thought of as a character rather than as the author of the book, I argue that important aspects of his characterization have been overshadowed by attempts to identify him with King Solomon, which also obscure the significance of the experiences that he describes early in the book.

The second chapter attempts to follow the connections between these experiences and Qohelet's portrayal of the world in Eccl 1–3. Where many commentators have been inclined to see in his prologue an analogy between passing human generations and natural cycles, I argue that Qohelet in fact intends a sharp contrast between the transience of humans and the permanence of the world in which they live. In this world, nothing ever has a beginning or a true end, but everything is part of a continuing process, which humans are too short-lived to comprehend. In the memoir that follows, Qohelet offers an explanation for this understanding in terms of his personal experience. Exercising his considerable wisdom in a quest for profit and purpose in human life, he was led to build up a business which was itself stable and self-perpetuating, but he then came to the devastating realization that it would pass to someone else on his death: the world would go on without him, and his business as part of it, so that nothing he had done for himself was really his. Indeed, since the business could pass to almost anybody, he could not even claim that his own possession of it was a mark of his own merit. This led him to consider the pleasure that he had achieved in his work to be the only thing that really was his, and to suggest that the enjoyment of such pleasure is the best that humans can hope to achieve for themselves. Following this account, 3:1–15 then explores the consequence that human activities are implicated in much greater processes, and that humans, perhaps by God's design, are therefore incapable of understanding the true significance of whatever they are doing.

In the third chapter, I explore Qohelet's ideas about how humans should actually live in this world, beginning with his commendations of pleasure. These set pleasure, as a certain and attainable good, against the unreality of material possessions and the problem of the human inability

---

1.   Qohelet, or strictly, perhaps, Qoheleth—the aspiration of the final *t* is omitted in conventional Jewish pronunciation—is, of course, the Hebrew name of the book, although it is better known in Christian circles by the attempted Greek translation of that name, Ecclesiastes. To save confusion between the book and the speaker, I shall use "Ecclesiastes" and "Qohelet" respectively for each.

to know the future. Qohelet also views pleasure, however, as something which is offered by God, potentially as a form of reward, so that not all humans may achieve it, whatever outward prosperity they may possess. More generally, the certainty of divine judgment means that humans must conform to certain expectations, most importantly in their attitude to God; they must not, however, expect righteousness to protect them from their own actions, and must deal with a world in which it may be difficult either to discern what God wants, or to predict what they can achieve. At the very least they must do wholeheartedly whatever it is that they do, because there is no possibility of finding joy or anything else through inaction, and they can only act for so long as they are alive. The chapter closes with an examination of Qohelet's attitude to wisdom, which he regards as important and useful, but also as limited, and—since it reveals the realities of the human situation—as a source of pain.

Qohelet himself famously describes much of what he sees as *hebel*, traditionally translated as "vanity," and the fourth chapter examines the meaning of this term in his usage. I suggest that he employs it as a way of characterizing not the failure of the world to meet reasonable human expectations, but the problem that humans face in their encounter with the world. What confronts them is *hebel* because it is illusory, and their reactions to it are *hebel* because they are deluded: the metaphor conveys an idea of something that can be felt but not be held, and that can touch but leave no impression. This is a problem of perception, and the chapter goes on to look at the more particular ways in which Qohelet believes human understanding to be constrained. He is not himself exempt from such constraints, but claims an authority to pronounce on the world which is rooted in his own exceptional experience and wisdom. His appeals to observation and experience, indeed, have led to descriptions of him as an empiricist, and he certainly does not rely on tradition or the views of others. Against such an idea of Qohelet as an empiricist, though, we have to set both his attachment to certain dogmatic positions and his suspicions about the reliability of human perception: he is not ultimately concerned to present or to embody an epistemology.

Chapter 5 turns to look beyond the book, taking as its starting-point the common claim that Qohelet is a sceptic, and asking what, in that case, he is sceptical about. Beginning with the observation that many of its themes and ideas are individually attested elsewhere in ancient literature, and that the monologue may be to some extent a re-working of existing materials, I examine several aspects of its broader, distinctive presentation. Qohelet is introduced not as a tradent of tradition, but as a lone voice, while his discourse, although disjointed in many ways and sometimes marked more by poetic than argumentative intent, makes an unusual attempt to extrapolate a general conclusion from its individual observations. Such features are understood as an attempt to present the character as radical and different, even though much of what he was saying may have seemed familiar to the original readers, and I suggest that they should warn us against taking the self-presentation of this very literary work at face value. Turning to some of the key themes in the monologue, I argue that Qohelet's views on divine sovereignty and determinism are given a particular twist by his distinctive separation of material prosperity from actual wellbeing and of human intention from the actual significance of human actions in the broader context of the world's processes. Essentially, though, they stand in continuity with ideas already expressed widely in ancient literature. His ideas about the limitations of human knowledge also correspond to well-established notions, although they are quite different from the Greek scepticism with which they are sometimes compared. Again, however, he has an apparently original contribution to make in his focus on human misperception; this is rooted in his similarly distinctive ideas about the nature of the world, as are his ideas about the need to seek pleasure. In all, where Qohelet is sceptical, he is usually expressing a scepticism so widely shared in ancient literature that it might be considered conventional; where his views appear to be distinctive, on the other hand, they are not usually sceptical. I doubt, therefore, that it is useful to describe him in these terms, and suggest that his own emphasis on illusion and disillusion may be a better way to approach his themes and motives.

Because this study is not intended to address a single question, I have not tried to distil the interpretation into some single conclusion. I do, however, offer at the end some observations on the way in which the book may have been supposed to be read. In the light of the subsequent discussions, these go back to questions raised in the first chapter about the characterization of Qohelet, and about the relationship between this character and the author of the book. There are reasons to suppose, I suggest, that Qohelet is not simply a mouthpiece for the opinions of the author: rather, the character is depicted as unusually materialistic, with a way of looking at the world that would probably not have been shared by readers of the book. The fact that such a character is forced to reject the value of material prosperity serves a literary purpose, but also suggests that we are supposed to engage with Qohelet's ideas, not necessarily to identify with his priorities and concerns.

2. *Method and Assumptions*

I have not attempted to argue the case below, but I share the general belief of commentators that Ecclesiastes was written no earlier than the Persian period, and is more probably a product of the Hellenistic period.[2] A very few scholars prefer an earlier date for the book,[3] and although I

2. In view of its many peculiarities, I doubt that such a dating can be sustained solely on the basis of the book's language in general, which has been a key criterion for many commentators. Commenting on Grotius' observations that much of its vocabulary was found only in late works, Franz Delitzsch famously commented in his *Biblischer Commentar über die poetischen Bücher des Alten Testaments*. Vol. 4, *Hoheslied und Koheleth. Mit Excursen von Consul D. Wetzstein* (Leipzig: Dörffling & Franke, 1875), 197, that, "Wenn das B. Koheleth altsalomonisch wäre, so gäbe es keine Geschichte der hebräischen Sprache." The history of no language is straightforward, however, and although the character of the book's language certainly suits a late date better than an early one, complications of register and dialect make it difficult to regard its character overall as probative. I do think, however, that the presence of loanwords from Persian in the text (פרדס in 2:5 and פתגם in 8:11) would be much harder to explain were the book earlier than the Persian period, and that may be the only reasonably solid evidence that we have; see C. L. Seow, "Linguistic Evidence and the Dating of Qohelet," *JBL* 115 (1996): 643–66, esp. 646–50, on this issue. Other criteria for dating present their own difficulties. Attempts to find specific, datable references in the book, or at least references to particular socio-political conditions, are generally not so much implausible as, essentially, speculative: our knowledge of the Persian and Hellenistic periods is far too incomplete, and it is generally hard to exclude other possible contexts. Addressing himself to Seow's "The Socioeconomic Context of 'The Preacher's' Hermeneutic," *Princeton Seminary Bulletin* 17 (1996): 168–95, James Crenshaw rightly asks, "Apart from the problem presented by any literary work…how many eras of the past are distinctive enough to be recognizable millennia later?"; see his "Qoheleth's Understanding of Intellectual Inquiry," in *Qohelet in the Context of Wisdom* (ed. A. Schoors; BETL 136; University Press and Uitgeverij Peeters: Leuven, 1998), 205–24, esp. 210. More particular questions of influence and the development of thought will be addressed to some extent below. It must be borne in mind, however, that we possess only a very small fraction of the literature that circulated in the ancient world, and that our attempts to reconstruct the development and spread of thought and literature can rarely be more than hypothetical.

3. So, for example, Martin Shields, *The End of Wisdom: A Reappraisal of the Historical and Canonical Function of Ecclesiastes* (Winona Lake: Eisenbrauns, 2007). For Shields, the references to the Jerusalem monarchy are decisive. Daniel C. Fredericks, *Qoheleth's Language: Re-evaluating Its Nature and Date* (Ancient Near Eastern Texts and Studies 3; Lewiston: Edwin Mellen, 1988), places the language of the book in the pre-exilic period, and although Fredericks claims not to be settling the question of date, his Chapter 7, "Implications for Qoheleth Research" (pp. 269–78), challenges hypotheses about the book which assume a later date, and looks at the significance of dating it alongside earlier wisdom literature.

doubt the originality of the Solomonic attribution that sometimes under-
lies such a dating,[4] let alone its accuracy, I have tried to take account
where appropriate of the possibility that the book might be from such an
earlier period. We know very little about the context of its composition,
although there are no compelling grounds to reject an origin within
Palestinian Judaism. Suggestions that the book was originally written in
a language other than Hebrew have been made from time to time, but, for
good reason, won little acceptance.[5] If it is indeed a Hebrew composition,

4.　See, for example, Gleason L. Archer, "The Linguistic Evidence for the Date of
Ecclesiastes," *Journal of Evangelical Theological Society* 12 (1969): 167–81, who
declares (p. 167) that "It is not true that the Solomonic authorship of *Ecclesiastes* has
been universally abandoned, at least in some Conservative circles. Aside from the
theological problems arising from the denial of the genuineness of even one book of
the Bible, there are very solid linguistic grounds for rejecting the verdict of spurious-
ness." It is not clear that Archer's view would be shared now even by any significant
number of conservative scholars, although (not surprisingly, given the context of
publication) similar views were expressed later in Larry L. Walker, "Notes on
Higher Criticism and the Dating of Biblical Hebrew," in *A Tribute to Gleason
Archer* (ed. Walter C. Kaiser, Jr. and Ronald F. Youngblood; Chicago: Moody,
1986), 35–52.

5.　David Margoliouth noted more than a century ago that "The Israelitish name
for God is nowhere employed, nor does there appear to be any reference to Judaic
matters; hence there seems to be a possibility that the book is an adaptation of a
work in some other language." That much is fair comment, but he went on to
observe that "This supposition would agree with the fact that certain of the idioms
found in it are not so much late Hebrew as foreign Hebrew… If this be so, the
character of the idioms noticed…renders it probable that the language of the model
was Indo-Germanic; and the introduction of the names 'David,' 'Israel,' and
'Jerusalem,' as well as the concealment of all names in the case of the anecdotes
which the author introduces…, is with the view of accommodating the work to
Jewish taste." See Margoliouth's article, "Ecclesiastes," in *The Jewish Encyclopedia: A Descriptive Record of the History, Religion, Literature, and Customs of the
Jewish People from the Earliest Times to the Present Day*. Vol. 5, *Dreyfus-Brisac-
Goat* (ed. Cyrus Adler et al.; New York: Funk & Wagnalls, 1903), 32–34, esp. 33b.
Apart from some attempts to view particular expressions as Greek in origin, this has
not really been followed up, and the principal candidate as a source-language for
Ecclesiastes has been Aramaic. This was proposed in a short note by F. C. Burkitt,
"Is Ecclesiastes a Translation?," *JTS* (Old Series) 23 (1921): 22–28, and adopted
with alacrity by A. Fernández, "Es Ecclesiastes una Versión?," *Biblica* 3 (1922):
45–50, who proposed that further evidence was to be found in the difficulties
surrounding השני in 4:15. Frank Zimmerman much later made a more wide-ranging
case in two articles, "The Aramaic Provenance of Qohelet," *JQR* 36 (1945–46):
17–45, and "The Question of Hebrew in Qohelet," *JQR* 40 (1949–50): 79–102, and
was supported by Charles Torrey, "The Question of the Original Language of
Qoheleth," *JQR* 39 (1948–49): 151–60. The best-known statement of the position,

an origin in the diaspora cannot be excluded, but is suggested by nothing in the text itself.[6]

There is much less consensus when it comes to matters of redaction. The text of Ecclesiastes is not marked by any dramatic shifts in style, and the structure, such as it is, seems too loose for us to identify additions or changes on the basis of disruption. The early translations of the book, furthermore, raise many text-critical problems for the reading of individual verses, but show a substantial coherence with the standard Masoretic text (MT), as do the small fragments of Ecclesiastes found at Qumran.[7] There are no strictly objective grounds, in other words, to suppose that the book has been extensively altered or supplemented since its composition, and if there were any significant alterations, they must have occurred very early in the history of its transmission. Nevertheless, many modern scholars have proposed that the book contains significant amounts of secondary material, either just in its epilogue or throughout, with some putting forward extremely complicated theories of multiple redactors.[8]

though, has probably been that of H. L. Ginsberg, stated in *Studies in Koheleth* (Texts and Studies of the Jewish Theological Seminary of America 17; New York: Jewish Theological Seminary of America, 1950), and defended in "Supplementary Studies in Kohelet," *PAAJR* 21 (1952): 35–62. See also "The Quintessence of Koheleth," in *Biblical and Other Studies* (ed. Alexander Altmann; Philip W. Lown Institute of Advanced Judaic Studies, Studies and Texts 1; Cambridge, Mass.: Harvard University Press, 1963), 47–59. Robert Gordis was an early and vehement critic of the theory: see especially his "The Original Language of Qohelet," *JQR* 37 (1946–47): 67–84; "The Translation Theory of Qohelet Re-Examined," *JQR* 40 (1949–50): 103–16; "Koheleth: Hebrew or Aramaic?," *JBL* 71 (1952): 93–109. It has now seemingly been discarded, and Charles Whitley's substantial examination in *Koheleth: His Language and Thought* (BZAW 148; Berlin: de Gruyter, 1979) demonstrates the considerable obstacles that lie in the way of any attempt to resurrect it; see especially his summary on pp. 106–10.

6. See H. W. Hertzberg, "Palästinische Bezüge im Buche Kohelet," *ZDPV* 73 (1957): 113–24. Paul Humbert, *Recherches sur les sources égyptiennes de la littérature sapientiale d'Israël* (Mémoires de l'Université de Neuchâtel 7; Neuchâtel: Secrétariat de l'Université, 1929), 113, suggests that the reference to the wind in 1:6 suggests an Egyptian origin, since north/south winds are typical of the Nile valley, not Palestine, but see my discussion of that reference in Chapter 2, below.

7. See Eugene Ulrich et al., *Qumran Cave 4 XI Psalms to Chronicles* (DJD 16; Oxford: Clarendon, 2000), 221–27, pls. XXV, XXVI; Philip Alexander et al., *Qumran Cave 4 XXVI Miscellanea, Part 1* (DJD 36; Oxford: Clarendon, 2000), 422, pl. XXIX. If the palaeographical dating is accurate, 4QQoh[a] provides a *terminus ad quem* for the book's composition in about 175–150 B.C.E.; 4QQoh[b] is somewhat later.

8. Perhaps the best known of the older theories was that proposed by D. C. Siegfried, *Prediger und Hoheslied. Übersetzt und erklärt* (HAT II/3/2; Göttingen:

Some older theories along these lines were based on other suppositions, such as an idea that Ecclesiastes was originally written in the form
of metric verse, which could be restored by the appropriate reversal or
deletion of secondary changes.[9] In general, however, redactional theories
about the book have been motivated by a perception that it contains more
than one viewpoint, and that the viewpoints which can be discerned are
incompatible. They are a reaction, in other words, to a belief that the text
as it stands is contradictory and incoherent.[10] Other scholars have

Vandenhoeck & Ruprecht, 1898). Siegfried held that the original book (composed
by "Q1") was extensively supplemented by four further writers or glossators
(Q2–5), with two epilogists (E1,2) and two editors (R1,2) subsequently inserting
additional material at the beginning and end. George Barton, *A Critical and
Exegetical Commentary on the Book of Ecclesiastes* (ICC; Edinburgh: T. & T. Clark,
1908), 28, comments on the theory that, "It is built upon the supposition that
absolutely but one type of thought can be harbored by a human mind while it is
composing a book." Among recent commentators, Martin Rose, *Rien de nouveau:
nouvelles approches du livre de Qohéleth. Avec une bibliographie (1988–1998)
élaborée par Béatrice Perregaux Allisson* (OBO 168; Göttingen: Vandenhoeck &
Ruprecht; Fribourg: Editions Universitaires, 1999), furnishes the most notable
example of this approach. He reconstructs an original "livret" of only about 20
verses, which has been progressively supplemented by a disciple, and a "Theolo-
gian-Redactor," the former tending to make the book more radical, the latter to
reconcile it with more conventional views. Rose is rather dismissive of works which
try to see greater unity in the book, characterizing them in terms of modern fashions
(pp. 21–28), and rooting his own study firmly in the scholarship of the nineteenth
and early twentieth centuries. He does not apparently entertain the possibility that a
literary-critical approach might result in an affirmation of the book's essential unity.

    9.   See Vincenz Zapletal, *Die Metrik des Buches Kohelet* (Freiburg: Universitats
Buchhandlung, 1904), and his *Das Buch Kohelet kritisch und metrisch untersucht*
(2d ed.; Freiburg: Herder, 1911). Also Paul Haupt, *Koheleth oder Weltschmerz in
der Bible: Ein Lieblingsbuch Friedrichs des Grossen* (Leipzig: Hinrichs, 1905), and
*The Book of Ecclesiastes: A New Metrical Translation with an Introduction and
Explanatory Notes* (Baltimore: The Johns Hopkins University Press, 1905). Oswald
Loretz, "Poetry and Prose in the Book of Qohelet (1:1–3:22; 7:23–8:1; 9:6–10; 12:8–
14)," in *Verse in Ancient Near Eastern Prose* (ed. Johannes C. de Moor and Wilfred
G. E. Watson; Alter Orient und Altes Testament 42; Kevelaer: Butzon & Bercker;
Neukirchen–Vluyn: Neukirchener Verlag, 1993), 155–89, gives a new twist to the
theory by attempting to distinguish verse additions to the book.

    10.   Paul Haupt, not an admirer of the many interpolators he believed to have
ruined the book, suggested that, "If the book in its present shape should have been
written by one author, he must have been a duplex personality of the HYDE–JEKYLL
type. But the book we have is not intact. It reminds me of the remains of a daring
explorer who has met with some terrible accident, leaving his shattered form
exposed to the encroachments of all sorts of foul vermin." See "The Book of Ecclesiastes," in *Oriental Studies: A Selection of the Papers Read Before the Oriental*

addressed the same problem by supposing not that the book has been supplemented, but that it included different viewpoints from the outset, either because it was quoting the views of others,[11] or because its very character was dialogic.[12]

Club of Philadelphia 1888–1894 (Boston: Ginn & Co., 1894), 242–78, esp. 254. Haupt was later to offer a more specific outline of the book's development, linking interpretations to distinct philosophical movements: "...there are a great many Pharisaic interpolations directly opposing the Epicurean teaching set forth in the poem. The genuine portions of Ecclesiastes are Sadducean and Epicurean; Stoic doctrines are found almost exclusively in the Pharisaic interpolations." See "Ecclesiastes," *The American Journal of Philology* 26 (1905): 125–71, esp. 126.

11. The best-known exponent of the theory that Qohelet uses quotations is Robert Gordis, who argued the case in "Quotations in Wisdom Literature," *JQR* 30 (1939–40): 123–47, and "Quotations as a Literary Usage in Biblical, Oriental, and Rabbinic Literature," *HUCA* 22 (1949): 157–219, then employed it in his commentary, *Koheleth: The Man and His World: A Study of Ecclesiastes* (3d aug. ed.; New York: Schocken, 1968). See also R. N. Whybray, "The Identification and Use of Quotations in Ecclesiastes," in *Congress Volume: Vienna, 1980* (ed. J. A. Emerton; VTSup 32; Leiden: Brill, 1981), 435–51, and I. J. J. Spangenberg, "Quotations in Ecclesiastes: An Appraisal," *OTE* 4 (1991): 19–35. This should be distinguished from the view, sometimes expressed by much earlier scholars, that the book is simply a collection of sayings by various authors; see, for example, Moses Heinemann, *Uebersetzung des Koheleth, nebst grammatisch exegetischem Commentar* (Berlin, 1831), 3: "Der Inhalt dieses Buches aber ist eine Mittheilung von Betrachtungen, die der Verfasser des erstern durch Veranlassung vieler Erfahrungen angestellt und gesammelt hat." Some, however, came much closer, and Ginsburg cites the opinion of Hugo Grotius from 1644, who believed the book to contain different opinions on the subject of happiness, "Quare mirari non debemus, si quædam hic legimus non probanda; omnes enim sententias cum suis argumentis recitanti...necesse erat id accidere; sed cum et initium et finis satis monstrent quod sit scriptoris propositum," which we can translate (with less of an implication of randomness than does Ginsburg himself), "For which reason we should not be surprised if we read things in it which are not to be approved, as all opinions had to be covered along with his own arguments—but both the beginning and the end show well enough what the author's opinion was." See Christian D. Ginsburg, *Coheleth, Commonly Called the Book of Ecclesiastes: Translated from the Original Hebrew, with a Commentary, Historical and Critical* (London: Longman, Green, Longman & Roberts, 1861), 145 n. 1.

12. Ginsburg, *Coheleth*, p. 164, also cites the opinion of Yeard, published in 1701 (the book, *A Paraphrase upon Ecclesiastes*, is rare, and has not been available to me) that "the preacher introduces a refined sensualist, or a sensual worldling, who interrupts him, in order to attack and ridicule his doctrine." Similar opinions were offered later in the eighteenth century by Johann Herder, who saw a dialogue, filled with interruptions, and by Johann Eichhorn, in his introduction to the Old Testament, who read the book as a discourse between a fiery young student and a calm teacher.

Those latter theories, of course, have to explain why quotations or different voices should stand unmarked in the text,[13] just as theories of supplementation should provide some rationale for supposing that redactors did not simply alter what they did not like, in a text which can hardly have been canonical at the time they made their changes.[14] There is a much more important methodological issue at stake here, however: without any external evidence or objective criteria to control them, attempts to establish coherence in the text can very rapidly become attempts to make the text say whatever each commentator believes it should say. Indeed, the very belief that the current text is incoherent in some particular respect may depend largely on presuppositions about coherence, or on interpretations of its content. When the text is then "restored" to suit those ideas, in a triumph of circular reasoning, each commentator walks away with their own, customized Qohelet.[15]

This is a dilemma of which most scholars are aware, and there is no very easy way around it. As will become clear, I do not myself believe that our text of Ecclesiastes is entirely unchanged from the original, although I do think that the principal alteration has been to its attribution,

---

See Ginsburg, *Coheleth*, 184–86. Among modern commentators, Perry holds the slightly different view that the book is a dialogic essay in which we hear two voices, that of the pessimistic Qohelet ("K"), and that of a presenter ("P"), who responds to him; see T. A. Perry, *Dialogues with Kohelet: The Book of Ecclesiastes* (University Park: Pennsylvania State University Press, 1993). As will be clear later, although I doubt that Qohelet cites the opinions of others to attack them, or that his monologue is in any sense a dialogue, I do consider it probable that the book draws quite heavily on existing ideas, and possibly also on existing literature. To the extent that any such citations or allusions are re-worked or woven into Qohelet's speech as his own words, they do not influence the meaning, but it may help to explain some of the apparent unevenness or disconnectedness of the monologue if they have exercised some constraint on the expression of its ideas.

13. See especially the very sensible remarks about method in Michael V. Fox, "The Identification of Quotations in Biblical Literature," *ZAW* 92 (1980): 416–31.

14. Rose, *Rien de nouveau*, 554, asserts that "une telle élimination était, à son époque, impensable selon les principes de la transmission. Elle garde le texte du maître; le Disciple affirmerait certainement que celui-ci, s'il avait vécu en son temps. aurait donné le même enseignement." No evidence is offered for this understanding, and, indeed, Rose's theory that the first redaction was undertaken by a disciple of Qohelet seems to be posited on this redactor's treatment of the text (cf. especially pp. 162–63), making his argument, in essence, circular.

15. So Vittoria D'Alario, *Il Libro del Qohelet. Struttura letteraria e retorica* (Supplementi all Rivista Biblica 27; Bologna: Dehoniane, 1992), 23: "la ricostruzione che ne resulta è esposta al rischio di un' estrema e incontrollabile soggettività, basandosi su ciò che l'esegeta considera logico e indica come illogico."

not its main content.[16] My interpretation has been guided in general, however, by a much stronger disbelief in the criterion of coherence as a justification for making changes to a text. It is sometimes the case that writers deliberately juxtapose contradictions in order to make a point, and we shall look much later at the example of the Egyptian text on Papyrus Insinger, which does just that, to considerable effect. Proverbs famously does this in a much smaller way at Prov 26:4–5, and I think that Qohelet does it too, for example in 4:4–5. Writers may also create less immediately visible tensions and contradictions simply because they have failed to think an issue through sufficiently, and I shall argue later that this is the case in Qohelet's ideas about free will and determinism.[17] More generally, there is a danger that we may perceive such problems where the ancient writers saw none, just because of the presuppositions and categories with which we are used to working.

Ecclesiastes presents a special problem in respect of these issues, furthermore, because it seems clear that Qohelet is concerned to address the very fact, as he sees it, of contradictions between reality and human perceptions or expectations. Given such subject matter, it would be surprising if we did not find contradictions in his speech, and Michael Fox quite rightly suggests, therefore, that, "We should listen to the uneasy dissonances that ring in his attitudes and worldview. The contradictions may reside in the world itself."[18] Although I am less persuaded than Fox that contradiction is central to the discourse of the book, it clearly has an important role, and to strip the monologue of its contradictions is to strip from it much of its meaning.

Of course, if there are significant additions in Qohelet's monologue, then it is possible that any refusal to emend the text for the sake of consistency will actually introduce to his message inconsistencies which were not originally present, or distort the interpretation in an effort to incorporate them. Such a possibility, however, hardly outweighs the certainty that such emendation is methodologically indefensible, and itself far more likely to impose a distortion. In what follows, therefore, I have refrained from emendation on those grounds (although I should say, before I sound too much like a martyr to methodological purity, that I have not found this a very troublesome constraint). My interpretation is not, however, intended to be a final-form reading of the text, and does not exclude minor emendations on other grounds.

16. See Chapter 1, below.
17. See Chapter 5, below.
18. Michael V. Fox, *A Time to Tear Down and a Time to Build Up: A Rereading of Ecclesiastes* (Grand Rapids: Eerdmans 1999), 26.

Chapter 1

QOHELET

Ecclesiastes has a title (1:1) and an epilogue (12:9–14) which frame the
main part of the work: this is a monologue, marked by virtually match-
ing declarations (or "mottoes") at the beginning (1:2) and end (12:8).
The monologue itself is presented to us as the words of an individual,
Qohelet, and is apparently intended to be understood as a single speech:
although its structure is difficult to discern, there is a strong thematic
coherence, and the words are not explicitly, at least, divided into separate
addresses. If we are not dealing with a carefully argued exercise in logic,
we are at least not dealing with a random assortment of sayings,[1] and it is
reasonable to suppose that Qohelet's many assertions and conclusions
are supposed to be read in the light of his speech as a whole.

General questions about structure in the monologue are outside the
scope of this study, but it is impossible to ignore the fact that Qohelet
begins with accounts of the world (in 1:4–11) and of his own past (in
1:12–2:26), and that these seem situated in such a way as to summarize
or to explain the positions that he is subsequently going to adopt. We
shall examine those accounts in the next chapter, but the second of them
draws attention to an important feature of Qohelet's speech more generally: it is shot through with personal claims and recollections. Qohelet is
not presented to us as a disembodied voice, but as a man with experiences. These experiences, typically observations of general or specific
situations, are variously used to ground or validate Qohelet's ideas, but
they turn the speech as a whole into something more like a personal
testimony than an abstract discussion.

As we shall see, there are other aspects of the presentation that draw
attention to Qohelet himself, and it would clearly be wrong to ignore the

---

1. Of course, there are many positions between those two extremes, although
form-critical discussions, in particular, have tended to present them as a choice. See
W. Zimmerli, "Das Buch Kohelet: Traktat oder Sentenzensammlung?," *VT* 24
(1974): 221–30.

ways in which his personality seems to shape and to contextualize his ideas: there is a narrative aspect to Ecclesiastes that we should not neglect, and that may prove illuminating when we turn to other aspects of the book. There are also, though, a number of problems which surround the identity and presentation of Qohelet. Before turning more directly to his thought, therefore, I want to try to resolve these so far as possible in this first chapter, and to draw out those aspects of Qohelet's character that will be important for our later discussion.

1. *Qohelet and Ecclesiastes*

The most basic issue is also, perhaps, the most intractable: the relationship between Qohelet and the book that now bears his name. The monologue that makes up most of Ecclesiastes is not presented as a written composition by Qohelet, but as spoken words of Qohelet which have reached written form in some unspecified way; the book itself claims to contain a report of those words in the monologue, but does not consist entirely of speech by Qohelet. This format is widely attested elsewhere, and it is not difficult to find biblical analogies: the book of Amos, for example, or the book of Deuteronomy, each report their contents as the words of Amos and Moses respectively, but they also contain third-person remarks about those characters, and it is doubtful that either of them is trying to claim that its principal speaker actually sat down and wrote the book about themselves.

We can call the speakers in such works the protagonists of the books without prejudice to the question of whether they actually spoke the words that they are reported to have spoken, but it is important to distinguish them from the creators of the books. Were a modern writer, say, to collect the speeches of an eminent politician and to supply them with a brief introduction, we would not say that the politician was the author of the book, even if it consisted almost entirely of their words. The situation might be more complicated, though, if the politician did in fact collect their own speeches, and that collection was later re-issued with an introduction and notes by another writer: such a two-stage process would arguably result in the book having two authors, although we might be inclined to call the politician the author, and to view the writer merely as an editor.

Until recently, most modern commentators have been inclined to see the composition of Ecclesiastes in these latter terms, as a work which originally comprised just Qohelet's monologue, to which an introduction and epilogue have subsequently been added by one or more editors.[2] Such an approach has seemed justified not merely by the fact that the epilogue (in 12:9–14) seems to adopt a different perspective from the monologue, but also by the very self-presentation of the book as Qohelet's words. If it seems over-complicated to posit multiple stages of creation and redaction, then scholars can point straightforwardly to comparable phenomena in the transmission of biblical texts: few these days would deny that the book of Isaiah, for example, has reached its present form through quite complicated processes of re-working and supplementation.

Some of the recent work on Ecclesiastes, however, has adopted a very different approach, one which takes its cue from a 1977 article by Michael Fox.[3] Fox pointed out that we have a number of other ancient compositions in which the speech of a protagonist is framed by other, seemingly "editorial" material, but which appear to have been created originally in that form.[4] The self-presentation of Ecclesiastes as a speech, in other words, offers in itself no argument for rejecting as secondary those parts of the book that are not contained in Qohelet's speech: they are part of an original "frame-narrative," in which the author adopts the voice of a narrator.

It is important to be clear that this approach is not just an attempt to simplify readings of Ecclesiastes by discarding questions of redaction: it is not a final-form reading, and it does not exclude the possibility that the book has, in fact, been subject to redaction or supplementation after its creation. There is no shortage of ancient analogies to the type of composition that Fox proposes, and so it is also important to be clear that his approach does not involve some anachronistic importation of modern understandings. At the same time, however, it is difficult to exclude more traditional readings of the book, even if the burden of proof has shifted, arguably, to those who would propose a more complicated redactional history. Interpreters currently seem divided, therefore, between those who see the "frame-narrative" as secondary, and those who view it as an integral part of the book. That question is much less significant for the

---

2. The existence of an editorial framework, potentially composed by others, was recognized as early as Rashbam's commentary; he included the mottoes in the work of the editors. See Sarah Japhet and R. B. Salters, *The Commentary of R. Samuel Ben Meir* Rashbam *on Qoheleth* (Jerusalem: Magnes; Leiden: Brill, 1985), 34–35.

3. Michael V. Fox, "Frame-Narrative and Composition in the Book of Qohelet," *HUCA* 48 (1977): 83–106.

4. Ibid., 92–93; Fox cites the Egyptian texts *Kagemni, Neferti, Ipuwer* and *'Onchsheshonqy*, along with the Jewish books of Deuteronomy and Tobit. A number of other texts could be added to the list.

interpretation of Ecclesiastes, however, than the more basic question of the relationship between Qohelet and the author.

The sort of authorial relationships that I touched on above, by analogy to a writer and a politician's speeches, might be expressed as follows with respect to Ecclesiastes:

1. The creator of the book of Ecclesiastes compiled from some source existing words of an earlier or contemporary individual, Qohelet, and presented them as a book.
2. Qohelet himself wrote a book, which an editor or series of editors subsequently supplemented, and perhaps changed in other ways.

In neither case can Qohelet be understood as sole author of the work that is attributed to him, at least in the form which we possess, and the information offered about him outside the monologue must be understood as the testimony of a third party, and treated with appropriate caution. On the other hand, in both cases the words of the monologue itself essentially go back to Qohelet, and we can say something about him on the basis of the assertions that he makes about himself. These are by no means the only options, however.

Fox takes the modern analogy of the Brer Rabbit stories to show how an author can employ a narrator alongside a fictional speaker (Uncle Remus) to create an interplay of voices, all of which are products of the author himself, but none of which are strictly the author's voice.[5] What we discover about Uncle Remus tells us nothing directly about his creator, and even the voice which tells us about Remus is no less a fictional creation. Fox accordingly posits a rather different relationship between Qohelet and the author of Ecclesiastes:

3. Qohelet is a character created by the real author of Ecclesiastes, who also adopted the persona of a narrator or editor in the framework of the book, in order to comment on Qohelet's words.

If that is the case, the information offered about himself by Qohelet, and about Qohelet by the narrator are part of the characterization of Qohelet by the author, and tell us nothing directly about the author. Qohelet's role in Ecclesiastes is then rather like that, say, of Job in the book of Job (except, of course, that his speech is not presented in engagement with the speeches of others). Because he discusses it in conjunction with questions about the framework and epilogue, Fox arguably undersells

---

5. Ibid., 94–96.

this important aspect of his argument, and its significance has not been picked up by all subsequent commentators. It is in essence a point, of course, that could stand even if we were to reject Fox's understanding of the epilogue, and correspondingly of the narrator's voice, and we could put the possibility more simply without reference to a narrator: Qohelet may be neither the author of the book nor the real speaker of sayings collected by the author, but entirely a fictional creation by the author.

This sounds more radical than it is: authorial attribution in the modern sense is not a general feature of ancient Near Eastern literature. Rather, texts commonly present their content as the words of some individual who may or may not be real, and who may or may not have genuinely been involved in the composition.[6] Sometimes we can tell from the content: since its story is clearly fictional, for example, the Egyptian *Story of the Shipwrecked Sailor* is certainly not based on the recollections of a real sailor (and the sailor who tells the story may, in fact, have been portrayed rather unflatteringly).[7] Sometimes, likewise, we can tell from the nature of the character: in the Mesopotamian *Instructions of Šuruppak*, for example, Šuruppak (or "the man from Šuruppak") is said to be speaking to his son Ziusudra, who was to become the legendary flood hero.[8] It is often difficult to judge the matter, however: an earlier generation of Egyptologists was inclined to accept the *Tale of Sinuhe*, for instance, as a genuine autobiography, but it is now usually perceived as a work of fiction, posing as autobiography.[9] In the case of some

6. J. P. Weinberg, "Authorship and Author in the Ancient Near East and in the Hebrew Bible," *Hebrew Studies* 44 (2003): 157–69, explores the question of authorship in ancient texts, with particular reference to Job and Qohelet, although his quest for "hidden" authors leads him to a speculative, and, I think, wholly implausible suggestion that Ecclesiastes is the work of Zerubbabel.

7. For introductions and translations, see conveniently, Miriam Lichtheim, *Ancient Egyptian Literature: A Book of Readings.* Vol. 1, *The Old and Middle Kingdoms* (Berkeley: University of California Press, 1973), 211–15, and Richard B. Parkinson, *The Tale of Sinuhe and Other Ancient Egyptian Poems 1940–1640 BC* (Oxford: Clarendon, 1997), 89–101. This is a highly sophisticated and structured composition, involving speeches tucked away inside each other like Russian dolls, but the sailor has to learn to conquer his own fear, and begins his tale as a less than admirably courageous character.

8. See Bendt Alster, *The Instructions of Suruppak: A Sumerian Proverb Collection* (Mesopotamia 2; Copenhagen: Akademisk, 1974), and now his *Wisdom of Ancient Sumer* (Bethesda: CDL, 2005), 31–220, which provides an extensively revised edition.

9. See Lichtheim, *Ancient Egyptian Literature*, 1:222–35; Parkinson, *The Tale of Sinuhe*, 21–53. The historicity of Sinuhe himself is still defended in some quarters, but that is now very much a minority opinion.

instructions, like the Egyptian *Amenemope* or the Mesopotamian *Šūpê-amēlī*, we have no specific reason to suppose that the attributions are fictional, but no proof, equally, that they are not.[10] Probably the best we can say, at the risk of some generalization across periods and places, is that the attribution of words to an individual in ancient Near Eastern literature was not solely or primarily motivated by the desire to identify the actual author of a book containing those words. When Fox views Qohelet as a character or persona of the author, therefore, he is not portraying Ecclesiastes as exceptional: such distinctions between author and protagonist have to be made in much ancient literature.

Of course, many of the most familiar instances come from later Jewish literature. Fox himself notes the case of the book of Tobit, which portrays itself initially as the words of a pious, though apparently fictional, Jew; as the narrative develops, it incorporates events of which Tobit himself had no knowledge, and switches to the third person. We also possess a wide range of pseudepigrapha attributed to famous individuals from Israel's past, or from the period before there was an Israel—Enoch is the most famous example—and these again have counterparts in much earlier literature. The *Instructions of Šuruppak* is not the only instruction to borrow the identity of some individual who was probably already known, and a number of Egyptian works are now commonly recognized to involve an attribution of their content to some individual from the more or less distant past. That sort of attribution is sufficiently common that we ought, perhaps, to consider another possible description for Qohelet:

---

10. For *Amenemope*, see Miriam Lichtheim, *Ancient Egyptian Literature: A Book of Readings*. Vol. 2, *The New Kingdom* (Berkeley: University of California Press, 1976), 146–63. For *Šūpê-amēlī*, see now especially Victor Avigdor Hurowitz, "The Wisdom of Šūpê-amēlī: A Deathbed Debate Between a Father and Son," in *Wisdom Literature in Mesopotamia and Israel* (ed. Richard J. Clifford; SBL Symposium Series 36; Atlanta: SBL, 2007), 37–51, but also M. Dietrich, "Der Dialog zwischen Šupe-ameli und seinem 'Vater'. Die Tradition babylonischer Weisheitssprüche im Westen. Anhang von G. Keydana: Die hethitische Version," *UF* 23 (1991): 33–74; Jean Nougayrol, "Textes Suméro-Accadiens des archives et bibliothèques privées d'Ugarit," in *Ugaritica V: nouveaux textes accadiens, hourrites et ugaritiques des archives et bibliothèques privées d'Ugarit: commentaires des textes historiques (première partie)* (ed. Jean Nougayrol et al.; Mission de Ras Shamra 16; Institut français d'archéologie de Beyrouth bibliothèque archéologique et historique 80; Paris: Geuthner, 1968), 1–446, esp. 273–90; D. Arnaud, *Recherches au Pays d'Aštata. Emar VI.4 Textes de la Bibliothèque: Transcriptions et traductions* (Synthèse 28; Paris: Editions Recherche sur les Civilisations, 1987), 377–83. On the attributions in these works, see my comments in *Instruction and Imagery in Proverbs 1–9* (Oxford: Oxford University Press, 2007), 22–24.

4.   Qohelet was, or was considered to be, a historical character, and
his identity has been borrowed by the author of Ecclesiastes for
his protagonist.

Such borrowings are often characterized as "pseudonymity," but this is
not an entirely appropriate term: ancient authors borrowed identities not
in the way that a modern author might use a pen-name, but as a way of
establishing the credentials of their protagonists, or as a way of providing
a particular context in which their words were to be understood.[11] In the
case of Qohelet, this possibility has to be considered not just because this
sort of attribution is common, or because we know of some historical
character by that name, but because the book as it stands seems to identify Qohelet with King Solomon, and Ecclesiastes has traditionally been
understood as a Solomonic composition. Many commentators, indeed,
suppose that this identification has a strong influence on the way Qohelet
talks about himself in the first two chapters, which would make the
identification more than merely cosmetic.

These various ways of understanding the author's relationship with
Qohelet seem, on the face of it, to imply radically different ways of
reading and understanding the book, and they do indeed have significant
consequences for the ways in which we might understand the history and
purpose of Ecclesiastes. If Qohelet is to any extent a creation of the
author, after all, then the background he claims may not be the background of the author, and the views that he expresses may not be views
that the author intends us to adopt. In practice, however, they do not
greatly influence the way in which we understand those views themselves. To take another analogy from Mesopotamia, when the famous
Akkadian poem *Ludlul Bêl Nêmeqi* describes the travails of its protagonist, it is hard to see that our understanding of the text itself would be
much changed by the knowledge either that the author was presenting a
poetic account of his own experience, or that he had entirely invented
that protagonist and his problems.[12] Ecclesiastes presents a similar case:

11.   Indeed, rather than thinking in terms of pseudonymity or authorial attribution
at all, we might do much better to compare the modern first-person novel.

12.   Conveniently, see W. G. Lambert, *Babylonian Wisdom Literature* (Oxford:
Clarendon, 1960), 21–62, and his "Some New Babylonian Wisdom Literature," in
Wisdom in Ancient Israel: Essays in Honour of J. A. Emerton (ed. John Day, Robert
Gordon and H. G. M. Williamson; Cambridge: Cambridge University Press, 1995),
32–34. A new edition and translation of the text has recently become available, how-
ever, with much fuller coverage: Amar Annus and Alan Lenzi, *Ludlul bēl nēmeqi:
The Standard Babylonian Poem of the Righteous Sufferer: Introduction, Cuneiform
Text, and Transliteration with a Translation and Glossary* (Publications of the

when we read what Qohelet says, it does not really matter whether we are hearing a presentation by an author of his own views and experiences or the voice of a character whom he has created. In both cases, we experience a character talking to us in the same way, and the distinction becomes important only when we look beyond the text to ask questions about authorial motive or historical context. Similarly, when we look at Qohelet as a person in the text, we might expect to see the same things whether they are real characteristics of the author, deliberately displayed or accidentally betrayed in his self-presentation, or whether they are traits of a fictional protagonist, artfully sketched.[13]

We cannot ignore questions about the relationships between Qohelet and the author of Ecclesiastes, or between the monologue and the epilogue. To some extent, though, we can set them aside for the time being without undermining our examination of the book's ideas. Indeed, it might be better to do so, when it is clear that such questions cannot be resolved without consideration of those ideas and of the book more generally.

2. *Qohelet, Son of David, King over Israel*

It is less easy to avoid the questions that surround Qohelet's association with Solomon. As has often been observed, Ecclesiastes seems both to proclaim and to withhold the royal identity of its protagonist, and although early commentators were in no doubt that they were dealing with the words of King Solomon, this name is never mentioned explicitly in the text. In the superscription at 1:1, we are told first of all only that the book records the words of Qohelet, a "son of David, King in Jerusalem"—which implies that Qohelet was a Judahite king, or at least a descendant of David (since "King in Jerusalem" could be read as a description of David himself here).[14] After Qohelet himself has begun to

Foundation for Finnish Assyriological Research 2; State Archives of Assyria Cuneiform Texts 7; Helsinki: The Neo-Assyrian Text Corpus Project, 2010).

13. Gary Salyer, *Vain Rhetoric: Private Insight and Public Debate in Ecclesiastes* (JSOTSup 327; Sheffield: Sheffield Academic, 2001), observes, however, that the use of a first-person speaker in the book has significant consequences in itself for the way in which the book is read, and explores these consequences to considerable effect.

14. James L. Crenshaw, *Ecclesiastes: A Commentary* (Old Testament Library; Philadelphia: Westminster, 1987; London: SCM, 1988), 56, asserts that since "the word *ben* also denotes close relationships of mind and spirit without implying actual physical kinship...*ben-dāwid* does not require the identification of Qohelet with Solomon"; it is difficult, however, to think of an occasion when בן in a construct

speak, though, he offers the further information in 1:12 that he was "King over Israel in Jerusalem." If we take "Israel" literally, then this limits the reference: only Saul, David and Solomon qualify; Rehoboam might also have claimed the position briefly (cf. 1 Kgs 11:43), but the kingdoms were, according to the biblical account, divided when he inherited his father's throne. The first two of these kings were not "sons of David," so if 1:1 and 1:12 are taken together, they point towards Solomon specifically, if rather coyly.[15] If "Israel" is taken in a broader sense, then there is no specific reference, and Qohelet could be any Judahite king—but since no king is called "Qohelet" in the biblical accounts of Judah, the book still invites its readers to make an identification, and the wise Solomon is an obvious candidate.

When it comes to the affirmation of the Solomonic identity elsewhere in the book, scholarly opinions vary quite considerably. Some of the other material is at least compatible with this identification of the protagonist as Solomon, and, as we shall see, sections of ch. 2 are often read with reference to the king. There is little or nothing outside 1:1 and 1:12, however, which actively demands such an identification, even if those verses do, and some things—not least the description of Qohelet in the epilogue—seem to sit uncomfortably with the idea that he is Solomon. Although some commentators push for a "Solomonic" reading of the book throughout,[16] then, it is common to view Qohelet's claim as a sort of temporary disguise: after a couple of chapters, he takes it off—not with any great flourish, but like a man at a costume party, putting down his mask as he picks up his glass. When he has finished with his "royal

relationship with a proper name would most naturally be read as meaning something other than, literally, "son," or at least "descendant of *N*." A quite different spin is put on the phrase by Nicholas Perrin, "Messianism in the Narrative Frame of Ecclesiastes?," *RB* 108 (2001): 37–60, who claims that "Eccl 1:1 is not a pseudepigraphical appeal, as if the writer hoped to pass off Ecclesiastes as being of Solomonic origin. What the final editor of Ecclesiastes is claiming is that the words of Qoheleth are spoken in the spirit of Solomon, as an extension of the Solomonic wisdom tradition. The incipit then would serve to equate the wisdom contained within Ecclesiastes with the very words of Wisdom, who in the frame-writer's mind is also identified with the messianic Son of David." The latter equation is questionable anyway, but this whole claim would only be anything more than fanciful if there were any reason to suppose that readers found the expression "Son of David" awkward here in any way.

15. G does, in fact, provide all the information in 1:1: υἱοῦ Δαυιδ βασιλέως Ισραηλ ἐν Ιερουσαλημ. It was generally recognized even by ancient commentators, though, that Ισραηλ is a secondary addition; Jerome notes in his commentary, "superfluum quippe est hic Israel quod male in Graecis et Latinis codicibus inuenitur."

16. For example, Y. V. Koh, *Royal Autobiography in the Book of Qoheleth* (BZAW 369; Berlin: de Gruyter, 2006).

fiction," on this reading, Qohelet does not really trouble even to pretend that he is a king, let alone Solomon.[17]

If that really is the case, then there is an unusual level either of sophistication or of confusion in the characterization of the book's protagonist. As we have noted already, ancient authors regularly put their words into the mouth of some historical character, real or imagined, and that character might lend authority to what was said, or at least supply a context for interpretation. Here, though, we seem to have a character who creates his own character: whether Qohelet is the author or, in some sense, a persona of the author, he is presented as the principal speaker. He then, however, seems to adopt, only subsequently to drop, the persona of Solomon—unless, of course, as the text may be suggesting initially, we are supposed to be seeing Qohelet as a persona of Solomon. Furthermore, the information is offered piecemeal: Qohelet at first acquires only a rather general royal association in 1:1, which becomes more specifically (though never explicitly) an identification as Solomon when the reader acquires additional information in 1:12. The book then allows that identification to fall into disuse. Eric Christianson puts it more positively: "Qohelet does not lose his identity in Solomon's. He enjoys the unique opportunity of being 'Solomon the Qohelet', or simply the more elusive 'Qohelet'—at times a wholly separate identity."[18] This is categorically not, however, the usual way in which characters were identified or employed by ancient writers, and the identification of Qohelet with Solomon is odd in itself, even if we set aside questions about the maintenance of that identification.

a. *Qohelet as Solomon*
The difficulties of the presentation are compounded in 1:12 by the way Qohelet introduces himself: "I, Qohelet, have been king," or perhaps, "I am Qohelet; I have been king." The use of the perfect tense *hāyîtî* has been discussed by many scholars, and it is now generally acknowledged that it need not imply that Qohelet has ceased to be king.[19] Clearly,

17. Discussing the issues raised by fiction in scripture, Rüdiger Lux, "'Ich, Kohelet, bin Konig...': Die Fiktion als Schlüssel zur Wirklichkeit in Kohelet 1,12–2,26," *Evangelische Theologie* 50 (1990): 331–42, remarks of this text that, "...gilt dieser Text in der alttestamentlichen Exegese seit langem als Paradigma fiktiver Literatur in der Bibel," and himself uses the metaphor of Qohelet holding a mask to his face when he introduces himself in 1:12 (p. 335).

18. Eric S. Christianson, *A Time to Tell: Narrative Strategies in Ecclesiastes* (JSOTSup 280; Sheffield: Sheffield Academic, 1998), 158–59.

19. See especially Bo Isaksson, *Studies in the Language of Qoheleth: With Special Emphasis on the Verbal System* (Studi Semitica Uppsaliensia 10; Uppsala:

though, it could be read in just such a way, and commonly was by early readers. The Targum here, for instance, tells how Solomon was deposed by the demon Asmodeus, so that he now wanders Israel crying "I am Qohelet, who was formerly known by the name Solomon; I was king over Israel in Jerusalem."[20] Such a reading, of course, also furnishes an explanation for the double identity Qohelet/Solomon, and for the limited reference to Qohelet's kingship. It is unlikely that such legends were already in existence when Ecclesiastes was written, and the book itself probably helped to shape them, so they tend to emphasize that the difficulties of Qohelet's presentation arise from more than mere pedantry.[21]

In fact, the tense of the verb probably suggests that 1:12 must be read not as a free-standing self-introduction, but as part of a narrative sequence which continues into the following verses: "I, Qohelet, became

Uppsala University Press, 1987), 50–51. Discussions of the tense of the verb are reviewed in Anton Schoors, *The Preacher Sought to Find Pleasing Words: A Study of the Language of Qoheleth*. Part I, *Grammar* (OLA 41; Leuven: Peeters and Department Oriëntalistiek, Leuven, 1992), 172–73. Hans-Peter Müller, "Theonome Skepsis und Lebensfreude. Zu Koh 1,12–3,15," *BZ* 30 (1986): 1–19, suggests that far from indicating the past, this is an announcement of the royal fiction (p. 3), which would mean "I, Qohelet, am now being a king," and he compares the use in, for example, Gen 17:8. His examples are characterized, however, by the use of forms with *waw*-consecutive, and we certainly would not expect the perfect here for what would be, in effect, a future tense—as he puts it, "bin jetzt / hiermit ein König."

20. For the text of the Targum, see especially Peter Stephan Knobel, "Targum Qoheleth: A Linguistic and Exegetical Inquiry" (Ph.D. diss., Yale University, 1976); Luis Díez Merino, *Targum de Qohelet. Edición Príncipe del Ms. Villa-Amil no. 5 de Alfonso de Zamora* (Bibliotheca Hispana Bíblica 13; Madrid: Consejo Superior de Investigaciones Científicas, 1987); and Madeleine Taradach and Joan Ferrer, *Un Targum de Qohélet. Ms. M–2 de Salamanca, Editio Princeps. Texte araméen, traduction et commentaire critique* (Le Monde de la Bible 37; Geneva: Labor et Fides, 1998). See also Etan Levine, *The Aramaic Version of Qohelet* (New York: Genesis/Sepher-Hermon, 1978); Charles Mopsik, *L'Ecclésiaste et son Double Araméen* (Les Dix Paroles; Rieux-en-Val: Verdier, 1990); and Frédéric Manns, "Le Targum de Qohelet—Manuscrit Urbinati 1. Traduction et commentaire," *Liber Annuus* 42 (1992): 145–98. The textual history is complicated, and Sperber's edition convenient but far from ideal; cf. Alexander Sperber, *The Bible in Aramaic: Based on Old Manuscripts and Printed Texts*. Vol. IVA, *The Hagiographa: Transition from Translation to Midrash* (Second Impression; Leiden: Brill, 1992), 150–67.

21. A much more complicated version of Solomon's dealings with Asmodeus is told in the Babylonian Talmud (*b. Giṭ*. 68 a–b), and it is noteworthy there that the story not only arises in the context of interpreting a phrase from Ecclesiastes, but is several times linked explicitly back to other phrases from the book. On the Talmudic versions generally, see, for example, Peter Stephan Knobel, "The Targum of Qohelet," in *The Aramaic Bible*, vol. 15 (ed. K. Cathcart, M. Maher, and M. McNamara; Edinburgh: T. & T. Clark; Collegeville: Liturgical, 1991), 23 n. 14.

king over Israel in Jerusalem, and I set my heart to enquiring…"[22] The strange position of this "introduction," which is discussed as a problem in the midrash, may also be explained by its connection to what follows: this is not the beginning of Qohelet's speech, and its purpose is not to tell us who is speaking.[23] That has been accomplished already in 1:1, and 1:12 is instead the starting-point of an account in the first person, which will reach its conclusion in ch. 2.

Qohelet's account is initially of a quest:

> And I set my heart to inquiring and exploring through[24] wisdom concerning everything which is done beneath the heavens: is it a bad job which God has given humans to work at? (1:13)[25]

22. With the interpretation adopted here, cf. G ἐγενόμην, and, for example, Thomas Krüger, *Kohelet (Prediger)* (Biblischer Kommentar Altes Testament 19; Neukirchen–Vluyn: Neukirchener Verlag, 2000), 124–26; ET *Qoheleth: A Commentary* (Hermeneia; Minneapolis: Fortress, 2004), 56. The Mesha inscription and other texts are cited in C. L. Seow, *Ecclesiastes: A New Translation with Introduction and Commentary* (Anchor Bible 18C; New York: Doubleday, 1997), 119, as evidence for the sense "I have been a king," but in these texts the use is similarly a narrative one; so Mesha says, … אבי מלך על מאב שלשן שת ואנך מלכתי אחר אבי ואעש, "My father (was) king over Moab for thirty years; and I reigned after my father, and I built…" (*KAI* 181:2–3).

23. On the basis of other self-introductions in Semitic inscriptions, Oswald Loretz, *Qohelet und der alte Orient: Untersuchungen zu Stil und theologischer Thematik des Buches Qohelet* (Freiburg im Breisgau: Herder, 1964), 144, suggests that we must regard 1:12 as the original beginning of the book, to which an editor has prefaced what is now the prologue. There would be more weight in this argument if the book actually was a Semitic royal inscription, and if forms were as rigidly fixed in ancient literature as scholars sometimes assume, but it hardly, in any case, justifies a re-arrangement of the book as it stands. Fox, "Frame Narrative," 87–88, explores the more general question of using "logical order" as a criterion for emendation of the material here. I believe myself that, because it looks like a beginning, this self-introduction serves not only to begin the subsequent narrative, but to mark the introductory character of the preceding material.

24. I take the ב- on בחכמה to be instrumental, although the preposition can mark the object of either verb (cf. 1 Sam 28:7; Judg 1:23); this has led some scholars to see wisdom as the object here of one or both; for example, Aarre Lauha, *Kohelet* (Biblischer Kommentar Altes Testament 19; Neukirchen–Vluyn: Neukirchener Verlag, 1978), 38, states, "nach Weisheit zu suchen und zu forschen in Hinsicht auf alles." Schoors, *Pleasing Words*, 1:198, is sympathetic to this approach, but note his change of mind in *The Preacher Sought to Find Pleasing Words: A Study of the Language of Qoheleth*. Part 2, *Vocabulary* (OLA 143; Leuven: Dept Oosterse Studies and Peeters, 2004), 10–11.

25. The expression עניַן רע occurs also in 4:8 and 5:13: in the latter, the reference seems to be to a set of circumstances in which money is lost, probably because of

We shall look in more detail later at this quest, or series of quests: our main concern here is with the information offered about Qohelet himself. At first, there is little of this, although he does tell us in 1:16 that, "I have amplified and increased wisdom to a point beyond anyone who was in Jerusalem before me, and my heart has seen much wisdom and knowledge." Then, apparently as part of his quest to experience pleasure, he pours out a great deal more about his activities:

> I accomplished great things: I constructed buildings for myself, planted vineyards for myself; I made for myself nurseries[26] and groves,[27] and I planted in them a tree for every kind of fruit; I made for myself pools[28] of water, from which to irrigate a forest sprouting timber;[29] I acquired servants and maidservants, and home-born slaves.[30] I also had livestock for myself—cattle and herds: I had more for myself than all who were

an unsuccessful business venture. The expression may mean something. like a "bad deal."

26. Not "gardens": גנות is used elsewhere of places where crops of various types may be grown, and it is really just a plot of cultivated land (see, e.g., Amos 4:9).

27. פרדסים is a loanword from Persian, and ultimately the source of the English "paradise." Its original sense is rather different, however, and the Hebrew term does not connote a pleasure park: in Neh 2:8 it refers to a royal timber plantation, in Cant 4:13 to a pomegranate orchard. J. A. L. Lee, *A Lexical Study of the Septuagint Version of the Pentateuch* (SBL Septuagint and Cognate Studies Series 14; Chico: Scholars Press, 1983), 53–56, discusses the uses of παράδεισος in Greek, where it was also borrowed. In Xenophon, it is used of the Persian royal parks filled with trees and animals for hunting, but by the third century B.C.E. it appears in papyri as a common agricultural term: "It is clear first of all that a παράδεισος was composed chiefly of fruit-trees of various kinds...παράδεισοι are mentioned frequently in the papyri and were clearly a common feature of agriculture in Ptolemaic Egypt... A παράδεισος, then, may be defined as 'an area of cultivated ground containing chiefly fruit-trees, at times also other types of tree, vines, and possibly other plants, and perhaps protected by a wall.' There is no exact equivalent to this term in English. 'Orchard' is probably the nearest to it. 'Garden' is unsatisfactory..." (pp. 54–55). This suits the usage in Ecclesiastes very well, and reminds us that Qohelet's understanding of the term may have been shaped more by local agricultural usage than by a recollection of Achaemenid splendour.

28. The term ברכה is used of reservoirs or cisterns which channel or contain water for practical purposes (see, e.g., 2 Kgs 20:20; Isa 22:11; Nah 2:9); again, there is no connotation of luxury involved.

29. The reference is not to the orchards mentioned before: יער is used of wild forests where timber can be cut (e.g. Deut 19:5; 2 Kgs 19:23; Isa 10:34); in Cant 2:3, the beloved stands out like an apple tree in a forest—an image which could hardly work if יער meant "orchard."

30. Literally "children of the house(hold)"; the meaning of the similar יליד בית is clear from Gen 17:12–13.

before me in Jerusalem. I accumulated for myself also silver and gold, along with kingly possessions and provinces.[31] I put together for myself singers, men and women, and those human luxuries, a fine wine-table and settings.[32] And I made myself rich, going beyond anyone who was before

31. The relationship between the words here, וסגלת מלכים והמדינות, is unclear. Most modern translations and commentaries have followed G in reading סגלת as being in a construct relationship with both מלכים and המדינות, hence RSV "the treasure of kings and provinces." Such a series would be unusual anyway, but the fact that one noun in the absolute is determined, while the other is not, makes this very awkward. A similar expression in Gen 40:1 means "the butler of the king of Egypt and the baker," not "the butler of the king of Egypt and of the baker," so we might understand literally "the possessions of kings and (their) provinces." Although it is almost universally translated "treasure" or somesuch, סגלה is not something of particular value, but something that is owned personally by somebody. So, in 1 Chr 29:3 it refers to what is offered to the Temple by David out of his personal wealth, and in later rabbinic usage it indicates property which is to be kept distinct within a larger estate for a minor to claim later (*b. Bat.* 52a); the cognate verb is used often of setting money aside for oneself. I think the expression here refers to the personal property and public provinces of a king, the two constituting the totality of a king's wealth—possibly in terms of his land rather than his riches. What Qohelet probably means, then, is that he accumulated an estate comparable to everything that a king owns.

32. שדה ושדות is a notorious crux which has attracted a great deal of scholarly attention, but which remains mysterious. In particular, there have been many unconvincing attempts to show that there is a reference to women or concubines, a fact which reflects the desire of commentators to see here a link with the story of Solomon (or possibly just their own idea of what should constitute a luxurious lifestyle). The use of בני האדם, rather than אנשים, would not be impossible in the preceding clause were the reference here sexual, but it is still odd, and תענוגת in that clause has no specifically erotic implication, despite its use also in Cant 7:7: it probably indicates no more than a certain level of luxury or comfort, perhaps with some nuance of gentility (cf. Mic 1:16; 2:9, where the reference is perhaps to the genteel lifestyle at home, from which women and children are to be torn, and the use of the cognate adjective ענג in Deut 28:54, 56; Isa 47:1). Offered with no great confidence, my translation is based on a very early understanding. Jerome reports in his commentary that "Symmachus licet uerbum non potuerit exprimere de uerbo... dicens: mensarum species et appositiones," "Symmachus was apparently unable to render the word literally, ...saying 'a type of tables and fittings'." That might just suggest that Symmachus had enough information to be thinking in terms of something very specific. Jerome himself compares Aquila's κυλίκιον καὶ κυλίκια, which should probably be understood not as "a goblet and goblets," but as κυλικ(ε)ιον και κυλίκια, "a stand for drinking-vessels (or a sideboard) and little cups." I am reminded of my parents' friends showing off their cocktail cabinets in the 1970s, and if something similarly fashionable is in mind here, it may explain why the expression slipped so quickly into obscurity.

me in Jerusalem. My wisdom remained with me, moreover, and nothing which my eyes demanded did I keep out of their reach—I did not hold my heart back from any pleasure, for my heart was pleased in[33] all my business, and this was what was mine from all my business. (2:4–10)

It is this account which is widely perceived to lie at the heart of the book's "Solomonic fiction." Seow, for instance, claims that, "These verses paint a picture of legendary success. In particular, they call to mind the activities and fabulous wealth of Solomon in 1 Kgs 3–11. Indeed, it is difficult not to think of Solomon when the author concludes in 2:9 that he 'became great and surpassed' all who preceded him in Jerusalem."[34] That sort of interpretation influenced the Targum, which adds details from the biblical accounts of Solomon to achieve a better match: in doing so, though, it draws attention to the distinct lack of specific correspondences between those accounts and this passage. Even the point which Seow makes about 2:9 is a little forced: Solomon in 1 Kgs 10:23 "became greater than all the kings of the earth in wealth and wisdom," while Qohelet, more modestly, outdoes only his predecessors in Jerusalem (as he had already in wisdom, according to 1:16—Solomon surpasses "all the sons of the East and all the wisdom of Egypt," according to 1 Kgs 5:10 [ET 4:30]). Correspondingly, many commentators have been more circumspect, and claimed only that Qohelet is drawing on a broader tradition of royal inscriptions listing achievements, or on ideas about contemporary royalty.

Qohelet's account, though, is very distinctive. He notably does not boast about great public works or achievements—the meat and drink of royal inscriptions: the things which he creates are repeatedly and specifically "for me" (that expression [*lî*] occurs eight times in 2:4–8) and they include nothing which serves any obvious public function. His works, furthermore, are not monumental, but geared to the generation

---

33. Only Symmachus supports the מכל of MT, and other versions have apparently read בכל. A few commentators have tried to make much of the -מ, and to disassociate Qohelet's pleasure from his business; see, for example, Lauha, *Kohelet*, 39, 52, who renders, "die Freude meines Herzens war größer als all mein Mühen"; differently, Krüger, *Kohelet*, 125, 127 (ET 57–58), prefers "Mein Herz freute sich über all meinen Besitz" (ET "My heart rejoiced over all my possessions"). I think MT has probably assimilated an original בכל to the subsequent מכל, but we should anyway understand "in" (cf. Prov 5:18).

34. Seow, *Ecclesiastes*, 150. See also his "Qohelet's Autobiography," in *Fortunate the Eyes that See: Essays in Honor of David Noel Freedman in Celebration of His Seventieth Birthday* (ed. Astrid B. Beck et al.; Grand Rapids: Eerdmans, 1995), 275–87.

and spending of wealth. The "gardens and paradises" of 2:5 are explicitly planted with fruit-trees, and the "pools" of 2:6 are dug to irrigate a timber-forest, so these are agricultural projects, not primarily designed for leisure. Furthermore, 2:7 depicts a workforce of slaves, listed alongside Qohelet's cattle, rather than a genteel household, and it is only in the next verse, after Qohelet has described his accumulation of wealth, that we turn to a brief, and rather modest, listing of luxuries. There is a general resemblance to royal inscriptions in all of this, but the theme and point are very different. As part of his quest to explore pleasure, begun in 2:1 and continued through to 2:10, Qohelet's accomplishments are simply a means to an end, and they relate to his pursuit of that quest, not to his success or grandeur as a king.

Indeed, only in 2:8 do we find any specific reference to kingship, when Qohelet talks of his "kingly possessions and provinces," using a somewhat awkward Hebrew expression which has caused commentators a lot of trouble. These are not things paid as tribute to Qohelet (as the Targum takes them to be), but more likely things "fit for a king": in any case, the reference is not to Qohelet himself as king.[35] There is nothing in the account which obliges us to consider Qohelet a king, and certainly nothing which points to him as Solomon. With the existing biblical descriptions of Solomon's building works and possessions, these verses present a very obvious opportunity for an affirmation of Qohelet's identity as Solomon, but it is an opportunity which the author does not appear to grasp.

Furthermore, if we are supposed to read the Solomonic identity into this account, rather than draw it from there, then certain discrepancies start to pose a serious problem. To be sure, it is difficult to know what other traditions about Solomon might have been known already to the author and original readers, but the biblical account of Solomon's reign makes no association between Solomon's wealth and the sort of activities described by Qohelet. In 1 Kgs 3:10–13, Solomon is promised wisdom, wealth and honour by God, and his wisdom is delivered instantly (cf. 1 Kgs 3:28; 5:9–10 [ET 4:29–30]), not accumulated progressively like Qohelet's (Eccl 1:16). He goes on to enjoy tributes from countries under his rule (1 Kgs 5:1 [ET 4:21]), but by the time he has finished his major building works he is having to sell cities in the Galilee to Hiram in return for gold (1 Kgs 9:10–14). It is through a trading partnership by sea with Hiram that he begins to generate a substantial income once more (1 Kgs 9:26–28; 10:11, 14, 22), supplementing this with tax income (1 Kgs 10:15)

---

35. See the note to the translation, above.

and gifts (1 Kgs 10:25). Although he earns and spends a great deal of money, he does nothing so rustic as growing fruit or breeding cattle,[36] and there are no points of contact between the ways in which Solomon and Qohelet become wealthy.

There is also a significant gap in quantity, or at least quality: the silver of which Qohelet boasts (Eccl 2:8) was disdained as worthless in the days of Solomon, according to 1 Kgs 10:21, and when Qohelet talks of his male and female singers, we might reflect that even the exiles returning from Babylon were able to muster a couple of hundred of these, according to Ezra 2:65 and Neh 7:67. We do not know what the final items in Qohelet's list were (I have translated "a fine wine-table and settings" in accordance with the understanding of early interpreters, but the Hebrew words are obscure and unattested elsewhere—see the notes to the translation above); despite many attempts to find a reference in them to Solomon's concubines, though, there is no clear correspondence to anything in the Solomon narratives. In short, the extraordinary wealth and luxury of Solomon's court finds little echo in Qohelet's story, and the sources of Solomon's wealth are quite different from Qohelet's.

There are also some more minor obstacles to a Solomonic identification here. As the midrash observes at 2:9, only David preceded Solomon as king in Jerusalem, so even if claims to have outdone "all who were before me" might be regarded as formulaic in royal inscriptions, it seems hard to attribute to Solomon Qohelet's more specific claim, that he has surpassed "anyone who was before me in Jerusalem" (1:16; 2:9). If we read further forward, to 2:18–19, moreover, we find Qohelet expressing ignorance about his successor: this becomes richly ironic when read in the light of Rehoboam's failure to retain his inheritance, but there is no reason to suppose that it was originally intended as anything more than an expression of actual ignorance. Solomon, of course, knew his heir and, according to 1 Kgs 11:11–13, precisely what was going to happen. These observations may carry little weight in themselves as objections: they reinforce, though, a much broader impression that any correspondence between Solomon and Qohelet in this section arises more from the imaginative expectations of interpreters than from any deliberate cross-references in the text.

---

36. Koh, *Royal Autobiography*, 33, understands 1 Kgs 5:3 (ET 4:23) to be referring to Solomon's possession of flocks: it does not. Cattle and sheep are merely listed among the daily provisions for Solomon which are provided by his officers, apparently through provincial taxation.

Once we pass beyond Qohelet's account of his quest, moreover, the details offered about Qohelet in the rest of the monologue become too few and too vague to make any further comparison productive. Christianson, who believes that the Solomonic guise is maintained elsewhere, points to the repetition of motifs from the quest in later chapters—an argument which would have little force even if the correspondences were stronger in the account of the quest itself. Otherwise he finds only two specifically Solomonic passages—the notoriously difficult 7:25–29, which he seeks to understand in the context of Solomon's no less notorious womanizing, and the description of Qohelet in the epilogue (12:9–11), with its references to proverb-composition[37] and to shepherds (supposedly compared with kings in 1 Sam 25:7, although that interpretation seems a bit of a stretch).[38] If we presuppose that Qohelet is supposed to be Solomon throughout, then it is possible that we might be able to read these passages as references to Solomon, but they do not demand such a reading in themselves.

Despite the discrepancies, it would be hard to prove that Qohelet's account in the first two chapters actually rules out any identification of Qohelet with Solomon. On the other hand, if we were not being impelled to make such an identification by tradition and by the implications of 1:1 and 1:12, it seems far from certain that so many modern commentators would make a connection between the two simply on the basis of the text itself. Important though it may have been for the subsequent reception of Ecclesiastes, the link between Qohelet and Solomon is very sketchy in the book itself. It arises from no single explicit statement, but only from a combination of the statements in 1:1 and 1:12, while the detailed account of Qohelet's quest offers more by way of contradiction than confirmation. Even if that account has been coloured in a general way by the biblical stories of Solomon's wisdom and wealth, which is by no means unlikely, it has not obviously been fashioned to evoke some more specific association of Qohelet with Solomon.

b. *Qohelet as King*
The presentation of Qohelet as a king is explicit in 1:1 and 1:12, and does not rest on mere implication. Again, though, it is hard to find specific references to Qohelet's kingship elsewhere in the text, and it is not mentioned in the epilogue. In 2:12, Qohelet possibly refers to himself as

---

37. 1 Kgs 5:12–13 (ET 4:32–33) attributes three thousand sayings to Solomon, although none of them is said to be on a topic ever found in Ecclesiastes.

38. Christianson, *A Time to Tell*, 143–47.

king, but the passage is difficult, and that understanding seems to have been rejected by the Septuagint (LXX) and by Symmachus.[39] Many commentators, though, have observed a resemblance between Qohelet's account of his quest and a range of "royal" texts or inscriptions—that is, texts composed in the first person and attributed to kings. Tremper Longman, indeed, has gone so far as to link Ecclesiastes with a group of Akkadian texts that can be described as fictional royal autobiography, and has perceived a common (if rather loosely defined) structure.[40]

It is difficult to know how much weight to place on such resemblances, or what exactly they imply. In the contexts of Mesopotamian and North-West Semitic inscriptions, first-person "autobiographical" accounts are almost invariably royal, and this is a product both of cultural factors and of the circumstances which gave rise to preservation of the texts: even if commoners were to have found any right or reason to create such compositions on their own behalf, it seems unlikely that others would have found any reason to copy or to keep them. In Egypt, on the other hand, tomb autobiographies by commoners are found from an early period, and we have other non-royal, first-person compositions

---

39.　In the context, "Then I looked round to observe wisdom, and confusion, and wrongheadedness… And I saw that there was an advantage for the wisdom over the wrongheadedness like the advantage of light over darkness" (2:12a, 13), we expect 2:12b to specify the reason for or nature of Qohelet's turning to observe wisdom. However, it reads, כי מה האדם שיבוא אחרי המלך את אשר־כבר עשוהו, which would seem to mean, literally, something like "for what the person who will come after the king, what already he has done." The text, however, is barely coherent as it stands, and really needs a verb, at least to govern the object-clause at the end. In rendering it with forms from βουλή, G and σ′ have probably been swayed by the context to associate המלך with the Aramaic term מְלַךְ, "counsel"; many other readings and emendations have been suggested for the verse, and a full discussion would be impractical here. One strong possibility, however, is that אחרי was supposed originally to be read with a first-person suffix, as in 2:18 (לאדם שיהיה אחרי), and that המלך is a corruption of some original verb (possibly with interrogative ה), arising from a misunderstanding of its function in the sentence. That verb is unlikely to have been מלך, since that does not take a direct object, *contra*, for example, Ginsberg, *Studies*, 9, and see also his קֹהֶלֶת (*Qoheleth*) (A New Commentary on the Torah, the Prophets and the Holy Writings; Tel-Aviv: Newman, 1961 [Hebrew]), 70; Fox, *A Time to Tear Down*, 182; and Seow, *Ecclesiastes*, 134. Those scholars would all repoint the consonantal text as a verbal form. Daniel Lys, *L'Ecclésiaste ou que vaut la vie? Traduction, introduction générale, commentaire de 1/1 à 4/3* (Paris: Letouzey et Ané, 1977), 236, would instead emend to המלך מֹלֵךְ. Rose, *Rien de nouveau*, 183, emends to וְיָמְלִךְ, but takes the following את to mark an accusative of specification.

40.　Tremper Longman III, *Fictional Akkadian Autobiography: A Generic and Comparative Study* (Winona Lake: Eisenbrauns, 1991), esp. 120–23.

(some of which are probably fictional, literary creations).[41] There are also extensive first-person accounts in the Hebrew Bible, such as Nehemiah's "memoir" or long sections in Hosea, Jeremiah, and Ezekiel which are clearly not "royal," and though there are legitimate questions about whether they constitute autobiography, these demonstrate clearly that first-person speech has no such implication just in itself. Elsewhere in Jewish literature, the first few chapters of Tobit are an autobiographical account on almost any reckoning, complete with some strong assertions of the speaker's good deeds and virtue, but Tobit is certainly not a king. We cannot say that autobiography *per se* must be royal, and if we are to claim that Qohelet's account would have connoted a royal setting, then a more detailed assessment of content and genre is surely required.[42]

Such an assessment is probably beyond our competence, especially when it comes to judging what connotations a genre might have had outside its own environment. If, say, the author of Ecclesiastes was indeed consciously imitating the style of fictional Akkadian autobiographies, then it does not necessarily follow that he was also conscious of the way such biographies were understood in Mesopotamia, or that he would have expected his own readership to pick up particular generic implications from a type of text they might well not have known. More broadly, it is famously difficult to assess just what it is that marks genres for readers, and what it is that markers of any particular genre convey to readers.

---

41. The term "biography" is commonly preferred by scholars, since it is unlikely that many of the Egyptian accounts, although composed in the first person, were actually written by the individuals they commemorate. On the genre as a whole, see especially Miriam Lichtheim, *Ancient Egyptian Autobiographies Chiefly of the Middle Kingdom: A Study and an Anthology* (OBO 84; Freiburg: Universitätsverlag; Göttingen: Vandenhoeck & Ruprecht, 1988). Also Shannon Burkes, *Death in Qoheleth and Egyptian Biographies of the Late Period* (SBL Dissertation Series 170; Atlanta: SBL, 1999), 171–208. *Sinuhe* has been noted above as most probably a fictional autobiography; from a later period, the *Tale of Wenamun* and the *Tale of Woe* (Papyrus Pushkin 127) are apparently fictional first-person memoirs of a different sort—the former a report (see Lichtheim, *Ancient Egyptian Literature*, 2:224–30, for translation), the latter, found alongside it in the same pot, a literary letter: see Ricardo A. Caminos, *A Tale of Woe: From a Hieratic Papyrus in the A. S. Pushkin Museum of Fine Arts in Moscow* (Oxford: Griffith Institute, 1977), who discusses other ancient literary letters on p. 79.

42. Craig Bartholomew, *Ecclesiastes* (Baker Commentary on the Old Testament Wisdom and Psalms; Grand Rapids: Baker Academic, 2009), 65–74, offers an interesting discussion of the attempt to link Ecclesiastes with royal autobiographies.

Without going into that thorny problem here, we can say with some confidence, at least, that simple verbal resemblances are a poor basis for comparison. A number of commentators, for instance, draw attention to the formulation "I (am) Qohelet" in 1:12, which resembles the self-introductions in many royal inscriptions as well as in fictional auto-biographies. This is clearly not, however, a formulation confined to royal inscriptions—Tobit, again, introduces himself in the same way (Tob 1:1), personified wisdom uses it in Prov 8:12, and it is a common feature of ancient aretalogies. We can hardly go further than to say that this is a type of formal self-presentation. Noting a subsequent list of actions is even less helpful if no attention is paid to the nature of those actions. Kings in royal inscriptions do not just do things, they do particular sorts of things which make them appear good kings, such as protecting or reclaiming territory, restoring temples or engaging in other public works. When Qohelet does things, but not these things, he is not acting as a king; when his actions are not kingly actions, his talking about them does not make him seem kingly: we cannot legitimately use the simple fact of Qohelet's account to suggest that he was a king.

3. *"Qohelet"*

It seems apparent that Qohelet's identity as Solomon, although implied by 1:1 in combination with 1:12, is essentially confined to those verses: there is nothing else in the text that would push us towards such an identification, and Qohelet's description of his own background shows little correspondence with biblical accounts of Solomon's life. Qohelet's royal status may have marginally more substance to it, and it is certainly asserted more explicitly. If the text presumes it, however, it seems to make little actual use of it.

There is one further aspect of this problem to be considered, though, and that is the term "Qohelet" itself, which was understood by early commentators to be a name or epithet of Solomon, and which is still associated with the Solomonic attribution by many modern scholars. We need to consider whether this term might indeed have been intended to imply that the monologue was really the words of Solomon—and this proves much more difficult than it might sound, because the form and usage of "Qohelet" are profoundly problematic. Rather than go into a lengthy technical excursus here, I have discussed the problems in Appendix 1. To summarize, though, it appears very difficult to take the epithet as "meaningful," in the sense of being an explicit title or description: its form does not lend itself readily to such an interpretation, and the term appears inconsistently both as a name "Qohelet" and as a title "the Qohelet" in the earliest versions of the text which we can recon-struct. If we do try to find such a meaning, the most natural link is with words connoting "assembly" or "assembling," and early commentators tried to connect this sense with ideas of Solomon assembling people or proverbs. It seems clear, however, that this connection was based on an existing supposition of Solomonic authorship, and that the term Qohelet did not itself give rise to that supposition.

In the absence of any evidence that the word was already somehow associated with Solomon when Ecclesiastes was composed, it would seem difficult to argue that the protagonist's identification as Qohelet might have been intended to imply that he was actually Solomon. In fact, the textual problems and later interpretative gymnastics would seem to suggest the opposite—that readers who presupposed Solomonic author-ship were left trying to explain the attribution to Qohelet. We may never find a satisfactory explanation for "Qohelet," if the word was indeed invented by the book's author, and invested with some deliberate signi-ficance. I am inclined to suspect that it was supposed originally to have been read as a proper name "Qohelet," and that "the Qohelet" entered some texts as an attempted reconciliation of the name with the Solo-monic attribution. If it was a proper name (possibly supposed to be vocalized in some quite different way), then it may have had connota-tions of status or ethnicity for the original readership, which are entirely lost on us now. This is speculative, however, and the key point for our present purpose is not what the word "Qohelet" might have meant, but that it almost certainly was not some direct reference to King Solomon.

4. *Qohelet Uncrowned*

As it stands, then, the book of Ecclesiastes presents the bulk of its content as the speech of this individual called "Qohelet" or "the Qohelet." In the superscription to this speech at 1:1, and then again in 1:12, it identifies the speaker as a king, and uses expressions which point to him being King Solomon. When Qohelet talks about his own past, however, there is no correspondence to anything specific in the biblical accounts of Solomon, and very little which relates to his own purported kingship. It is hard not to sympathize with those scholars who suspect that the presentation we have now has arisen more through secondary attempts to associate the book with Solomon than from any original intention.[43] If

---

43. It has been almost conventional until quite recently for scholars to assign the description of Qohelet as son of David and king in Jerusalem in 1:1 to the work of a secondary editor, although they have usually tended to retain the less specific

we are reluctant to start cutting words from 1:1 and 1:12, then it may be easier to think in terms of an authorial afterthought, or to emphasize that the book never actually mentions Solomon. Either way, though, the implicit attribution to Solomon has effectively made the explicit attribution to Qohelet redundant, and left readers with the problem of explaining it as a designation of the king. Remove the Solomonic complication, and one is left with an attribution to some unknown Qohelet, who may or may not have been a king, but who is at least no more mysterious than the Agur of Prov 30:1, or the Lemuel of Prov 31:1.

If "Qohelet" had some meaning or implication, then it is probably lost to us now, and if Qohelet was not originally Solomon, then all of the information offered in the first chapter about his kingship in Jerusalem is suspect. He is not altogether a blank, however, and plenty of clues about Qohelet's character are offered, along with some explicit information, in his speech itself.

a. *Qohelet as a Businessman*
Even if the account of his business empire in ch. 2 is not some evocation of Solomon, Qohelet is still apparently portrayed as a very wealthy man, and as one who has created a successful enterprise spanning several different markets. He attributes this success, in 2:18–23, to his own abilities and hard work, and, although his retrospective view of that work suggests that he is no longer engaged in it, there are other indications in the monologue that Qohelet's outlook is still very much that of a businessman.

When he asks in 1:3 what it is that humans gain from their work, a question which sets much of the agenda for his speech as a whole, Qohelet uses a term *yitrôn*, which will recur frequently in the monologue, although it is used by no other biblical writers.[44] From context, it is obvious that this word must indicate some sort of advantage or benefit, but Hebrew words from the same root commonly refer more specifically

description of him as king in 1:12 (so, e.g., Lauha, *Kohelet*, 29; Kurt Galling, "Der Prediger," in Ernst Würthwein, Kurt Galling, and Otto Plöger, *Die fünf Megilloth* [2d ed.; Handbuch zum alten Testament 1/18; Tübingen: J. C. B. Mohr (Paul Siebeck), 1969], 73–125, esp. 84). In large part, this retention stems from a perception that the memoir in ch. 2 is explicitly royal, even if it is not explicitly Solomonic. J. A. Loader, *Ecclesiastes: A Practical Commentary* (Text and Interpretation; Grand Rapids: Eerdmans, 1986), 19, puts the position succinctly: "The superscription, in all probability, is the work of an editor. By this heading he has extended the royal fiction, which really applies only to the long passage 1:12–2:26, to the entire book." Of course, if the memoir is not royal, then there is no compelling reason to regard the attribution of kingship in 1:12 as any more original.

44. See also 2:11, 13; 3:9; 5:8, 15; 7:12; 10:10, 11.

to things which are left over, or are in excess. It is not surprising, there-fore, to find the cognate term *ytrwn* in two Aramaic texts from Saqqara, one of which seems to suggest that it indicates money remaining at the end of a year.[45] The Greek term περισσεία used by the LXX here can have the same sense, and it is widely recognized that *yitrôn* is likely to have been a commercial term, indicating profit: it is what one carries away from a deal, or what one has left when accounts are settled and the books are closed.[46]

A little later, in 1:15, Qohelet describes all the deeds or achievements which he sees under the sun using another term, *ḥesrôn*, which probably comes from the same sphere, but which implies the opposite—a loss.[47] Although many scholars would emend it, the verb used of *ḥesrôn* there is found in 2 Kgs 12:11 (ET 12:10) with reference to counting money: Qohelet is speaking of "loss which is beyond counting," and may again be using recognizably commercial language. Later still, Qohelet uses the similar term *ḥesbôn* (7:25, 27; 9:10; and possibly 7:29), which is again not used by other biblical writers, but is quite widely documented as a term in business or accountancy—it seems to refer to a reckoning or calculation.[48] It is more difficult to say whether other terms reflect such a background, especially where they have some general usage also, but we might suspect, for example, that Qohelet sometimes uses *ḥēleq*, "share, portion," in a fairly technical way: as I shall argue later, it seems to

---

45. One of these reads just]ויתרנ ת[, so offers little context, but in the other there is a reference to]||| |||בשנת, יתרנ כספא זי קימ זי כספא, "the balance of money remaining in year 6," apparently referring to a profit or surplus. There is a related term יתרא in another text, which reads ויתרא מנ אב, perhaps "…and the surplus from Ab…" See J. B. Segal, *Aramaic Texts from North Saqqâra: With Some Fragments in Phoenician* (London: Egypt Exploration Society, 1983), 34, 38, 124; the texts cited are his nos. 149 (line 2), 19 (line 2) and 23 (rev. line 3).

46. So E. H. Plumptre, *Ecclesiastes: Or, the Preacher, with Notes and Introduction* (The Cambridge Bible for Schools and Colleges; Cambridge: Cambridge University Press, 1881), 104, understands it in Ecclesiastes as, "the surplus, if any, of the balance-sheet of life."

47. חסרון itself is *hapax* in Biblical Hebrew, but it is probably related to a number of other words, most notably the verb חָסֵר, which means not only to "want" or "lack," but "to be absent," or "be deficient" (cf. 9:8; 10:3). The most likely connotation in this context, then, is of absence or shortage, and Jastrow offers numerous examples from later Hebrew of חֶסְרוֹן/חִסָּרוֹן being used to indicate a deficiency or deficit. In general, the usage points to the term meaning a shortage of something, rather than specifically an absence, which would make it quite an exact counterpart to יתרון. Seow, *Ecclesiastes*, p. 123, notes a financial use of the Aramaic חסר to indicate the loss made on a deal or activity.

48. The evidence is collected in ibid., 260–61.

indicate a benefit that humans can achieve which is distinct from profit, and we might think of it, perhaps, as the salary or dividend which one takes from a continuing business, where *yitrôn* is the final profit from a business wound up or sold.[49]

Qohelet's usage can also be interesting where the commercial background of a term is not in doubt. When *śākār*, "wage," is used in 4:9, for example, it is in the normal context of receiving a return for labour; when the word recurs in 9:5, however, it is used of the dead, who receive nothing because no-one remembers them. Nobody expects to be paid when they are dead, so it is a curious point to make, but it is wholly in line with Qohelet's perspective on death: when we die, we take nothing away with us from our work (4:15), and receive no wage or dividend (9:5–6). Some might suggest that this would seem to be the least of our problems, but it is an indication that Qohelet's perspective is itself distinctive: this is a man, after all, who begins his speech by demanding to know what profit we can achieve in life, and who comes to hate all that he has achieved when he realizes that he cannot keep it (2:18–23).

Of course, we shall look at Qohelet's thought in more detail below, and it will become clear then both that his attitude to wealth is rather complicated, and that money itself is only one issue among many in the book. Here our concern is not so much with what Qohelet says as with how he says it—and the commercial terms which he employs do seem to affirm that Qohelet is supposed to be seen as a businessman, who looks at the world in ways shaped by that perspective.[50] The presentation of his

---

49. חלק is the portion assigned to someone from the whole, their "share" of it, so the term is often associated with the assignment and distribution of land, booty or inheritances, but it can also be used of having a "stake" in something (e.g. 1 Kgs 12:16), or throwing in one's lot with others (Ps 50:18; Isa 57:6). At Eccl 11:2 it is used of the fractions into which something is to be divided, and in 9:6 of the stake which the dead no longer have in the world.

50. His business vocabulary has often been noted. See, for example, the list on p. 221 of Mitchell Dahood, "Canaanite–Phoenician Influence in Qoheleth," *Biblica* 33 (1952): 30–52, 191–221; recently, Stephen Garfinkel, "Qoheleth: The Philosopher Means Business," in *Bringing the Hidden to Light: The Process of Interpretation. Studies in Honor of Stephen A. Geller* (ed. Kathryn F. Kravitz and Dianne M. Sharon; Winona Lake: Eisenbrauns/Jewish Theological Seminary, 2007), 51–62. James Kugel, "Qohelet and Money," *CBQ* 51 (1989): 32–49, goes beyond the vocabulary to look at other aspects of Qohelet's attitude to money, concluding that Qohelet "inhabits a world, or more precisely a class, of financial high-rollers" (p. 46). J. L. Crenshaw, "Qoheleth's Quantitative Language," in *The Language of Qohelet in Its Context: Essays in Honour of Prof. A. Schoors on the Occasion of His Seventieth Birthday* (ed. A. Berlejung and P. van Hecke; OLA 164; Leuven: Peeters and Department of Ooesterse Studies, Leuven, 2007), 1–22, looks less specifically at

past in ch. 2, therefore, is not just an isolated passage, but a key part of the way in which Qohelet is characterized, and, as we shall see, it is also crucial to the way his thought is depicted as developing in the book.

b. *Qohelet as an Old Man*

Other aspects of Qohelet's character seem less clearly defined. If we take seriously Qohelet's own accounts, both of his commercial success and of his extensive experience, then it seems unlikely that we are supposed to see him as a young man. Indeed, when he calls on the young to enjoy youth (11:9), or worries about the passing of his estate to an heir (2:18–23), we seem to be hearing the perspective and pre-occupations of a man late in life. That suspicion is lent further weight by the climax of the monologue in 12:1–7, which is usually read either as an allegorical description of old age, or as a more literal account of dying: the final verse is unambiguously about death. Since some types of ancient advice literature conventionally attribute their advice to fathers addressing sons, and may link it to death and the passing of generations, it is possible that the very fact of Qohelet looking back over his life and offering advice would have conjured up for early readers a picture of Qohelet as an old man.

It would be wrong to press that last point too far, given the distinctiveness of the book, or to make too much of the fact that autobiographies are commonly associated with the dead.[51] It is also important to note that the epilogue, although it speaks rather obscurely about Qohelet in 12:9, might be read as suggesting that he continued to work after saying what is said in the monologue:[52]

financial terms, but notes the quantitative aspect of some key terms in the book, along with its various references to numbers, and speculates that this may reflect immersion in the documentation of business transactions.

51. Leo Perdue, in fact, argues from the form of the book that Qohelet must already be dead. See, for example, his *Wisdom Literature: A Theological History* (Louisville: Westminster John Knox, 2007), 190: "Royal Testaments and grave autobiographies present the fiction of a dead person who, speaking from the tomb, undertakes to instruct the living in the wisdom of life." To be sure, instructions more generally are associated with death and the passing of generations, but Qohelet's view of Sheol, especially as expressed in 9:10, would seem to sit uneasily with the idea that he could be speaking from beyond the grave.

52. If this is an original part of the book, then it suggests that the author probably envisaged Qohelet's survival beyond his delivery of the monologue, but if it is the work of a very early redactor, as often supposed, then it is an argument against any suggestion that readers would have been impelled to view Qohelet as dead by the genre of the work.

> And the rest of what happened: Qohelet was wise still. He taught the people knowledge, and he listened, and he examined. He set in order a great many sayings.[53]

In fact, even if we set aside the epilogue, it is not at all clear that Qohelet's account of his activities in ch. 2, the only explicit presentation of his life, is supposed to bring us virtually to the point of his death. The position of this account potentially gives it an introductory quality, and, as we shall see, it seems to serve as an explanation for the views that Qohelet will go on to present. Qohelet is old enough, then, to look back on his past and to face his own mortality, but there is nothing that points directly to his monologue being a deathbed speech.

c. *Qohelet as a Wise Man*

The observation in 12:9, that Qohelet "set in order a great many sayings," is elaborated in the next verse, where we are told that he "sought to find words that give pleasure, and a proper writing of words that convey truth" (12:10). This is then picked up in the following discussion of books by wise men, and the dangers of reading too many (12:11–12), so we are left in no doubt that the epilogue views Qohelet as a writer. When he is talking about his own past life, however, Qohelet talks of his wisdom in more general terms, both as an intellectual quality which he has cultivated to an unprecedented degree (1:16), and as a tool which he uses in his work (2:19; cf. 2:21) or in his analysis of what is around him (1:13; 7:23). We are told little that is specific about it, and Qohelet himself is curious about wisdom as a more abstract concept (1:17; 7:25). If "wise" conveyed some particular social or professional implication, there is no sign of that, and we should be wary of importing such implications into the characterization from theories about "wise men" rooted in other texts.

The book's comments about wisdom are unusual, though, and without going into Qohelet's own ideas on the subject just yet, we can see how some of the things that he says tend to convey aspects of his own personality. So, for instance, the sayings of 7:4–6 depict the wise as rather a

---

53. There are several significant problems in this verse, most of which need not concern us here. The first word, ויתר, elsewhere indicates superfluity in Ecclesiastes (2:15; 7:16; 12:12), or the edge which one person might have over another (6:8, 11; 7:11), but it is construed here with a following relative clause rather than a preposition, so is unlikely to mean "besides the fact that Qohelet was wise," and we probably have to take it as a noun (cf. 1 Sam 15:15). The subsequent עוד, "still" can be read either with the statement that Qohelet was wise, or with the statement that he taught: the former avoids a statement of the blindingly obvious, but both indicate a continuation of his activity.

miserable crowd: their heart is in "a house of mourning," while the heart of fools is in "a house of joy," and the wise offer rebukes while fools sing songs. Qohelet himself reaches the conclusion that wisdom brings pain (1:18), and so long as he continues to affirm his own wisdom, such generalizations correspondingly affirm his own misery. When he is exercising his wisdom in 2:2, indeed, Qohelet initially reacts to laughter and pleasure as "mindless" and "useless": although his views are apparently to change in the light of subsequent experience (contrast 8:15, for example), this first, utilitarian reaction is as telling in its own way as Scrooge's "Bah! Humbug!" Qohelet also talks about himself in a way that separates him from his own heart, which is in some sense his accomplice in wisdom (e.g. 1:13, 16–17; 2:3; 7:25; 8:9, 16) but also perhaps a more receptive and impulsive part of himself (2:1, 10; compare the uses with respect to other people in 2:23; 5:1 [ET 5:2]; 8:11; 11:9). There is a sort of detachment here that seems indicated also by his status as observer: Seow notes that Qohelet speaks of himself or his heart "seeing" things some 26 times in the book;[54] unless we count his conversations with his heart, however, Qohelet does not actually engage with others anywhere.

Of course, this may be driven by Qohelet's project and his subject-matter—but those are themselves driven by the questions which he is seeking to answer. Wisdom is not an end in itself for Qohelet, and his attitudes toward it are shaped by his more general search for an edge or a profit—so when he regrets his wisdom in 2:15, it is not because of the pain it induces, but because it ultimately fails to give him what he wants. To that extent, wisdom remains no more than a tool, and Qohelet's portrayal as a wise man is subsidiary to other aspects of the characterization.

d. *Qohelet's Language*
On a rather different note, it seems important to say a few words here about the language of the book, even though that is a topic more commonly considered in the context of questions about date and background. In that context, indeed, the language of Ecclesiastes may well have been subjected to closer scrutiny than the language of any other biblical text.[55]

---

54. Seow, *Ecclesiastes*, 21.
55. There is a considerable literature, much of which is surveyed by Antoon Schoors in the introduction to his own his own magisterial study (*Pleasing Words*, 1:1–16), and almost all of which seems to be mentioned in the course of that work. Note also the review in Francesco Bianchi, "The Language of Qohelet: A Bibliographical Survey," *ZAW* 105 (1993): 210–23.

The principal reason for this is its peculiarity in a variety of respects, and a recent, wide-ranging study of linguistic dating points out that "Qohelet and the Song of Songs must be treated as special cases. There is no historical period of which we have knowledge when their variety of Hebrew was the normal language of literature."[56] The oddities of the Hebrew in Ecclesiastes have been explained in many ways, and they may represent no single phenomenon: it has certainly become clear in recent studies that date is not the only factor involved. The distinctiveness is significant in itself, though, and it is important to realize that the language of the book would probably have struck contemporary readers as unusual: for all its literary polish in certain other respects, Ecclesiastes is not written in a standard literary form of Hebrew. Whether readers would have interpreted its characteristics as colloquial or dialectal is much harder to say, and it is doubtful that we possess enough data to judge that issue definitively, although a strong vernacular element seems likely.[57] Whether or not it is compatible

---

56. Ian Young and Robert Rezetko, with the assistance of Martin Ehrensvärd, *Linguistic Dating of Biblical Texts* (2 vols.; London: Equinox, 2008), 2:77.

57. Colloquial language is attributed to Qohelet by Joseph Carlebach, in *Das Buch Koheleth. Ein Deutungsversuch* (Frankfurt am Main: Hermon, 1936), 64, although he links it to a sort of "plain speaking," which is an inappropriate description for Qohelet and for other wisdom literature: "Wir sehen vielmehr im Stil des Buches die echte, zu allen Zeiten im jüdischen Volke gängige Volkssprache. Das Buch lehnt mit Bewußtsein den klassischen Stil der Poesie und das Pathos der Propheten ab. Es ist nicht in edelgewählter Fassung gehalten, sondern in der 'Sprache der Weisen', die immer das volkstümliche Idiom bevorzugten. Dieses aber klang seit altersher viel stärker an das Aramäische an." Much more recently, Seow, "Linguistic Dating," 64, has noted, rightly I think, that "not all the linguistic features in the book may be explained merely as reflexes of Late Biblical Hebrew. There are some traits in Qohelet that are attested only exceptionally…and others that do not appear at all in other late biblical texts… It is frequently assumed that those differences between the Hebrew of Qohelet and other Late Biblical Hebrew texts are evidence that Qohelet is linguistically more advanced than other postexilic texts… Yet, as has been demonstrated in a number of recent studies, the Hebrew of Qohelet cannot be identified with what we find in the Hebrew of Ben Sira, Qumran, Wadi Murabba'at, Nahal Ḥever and the Bar Kochba letters. The truth is that a number of the linguistic features probably have no chronological significance. They are, rather, evidence of the extensive use of colloquialisms in the book." Michael Wise, "A Calque from Aramaic in Qoheleth 6:12; 7:12; and 8:13," *JBL* 109 (1990): 249–57, remarks similarly that, "Qoheleth, it seems, wrote Hebrew of a type much closer to the spoken language than that of any other postexilic book of the Bible—and, in fact, than that of most Hebrew works of the entire Second Temple period. In linguistic terms, he chose to write in a code that approaches that of the spoken

with an early date for the book, furthermore, it is improbable that this idiosyncratic Hebrew would have been identified as archaic, and there are some reasons to suppose that it might have been considered northern.[58] In any case, it seems unlikely that Qohelet would have sounded to his Jewish readers like an educated Jew, let alone an early Judahite king.

Hebrew of Jerusalem in the third century BCE" (p. 250). See also Hans-Peter Müller, "Kolloquialsprache und Volksreligion in den Inschriften von Kuntillet ʿAḡrūd und Ḥirbet el-Qōm," *ZAH* 5 (1992): 15–51, esp. 17.

58. Building on a suggestion by C. H. Gordon, James Davila, "Qoheleth and Northern Hebrew," *MAARAV* 5–6 (1990): 69–87, argues that previously observed affinities with Phoenician and Aramaic, as well as with later Mishnaic Hebrew, may be explained by the influence of northern Hebrew on Qohelet's language. His case is very plausible, but we have few extended texts which certainly represent that dialect, and so any discussion necessarily rests on evidence that is open to challenge. A series of articles by Mitchell Dahood draws attention to supposed influences on Qohelet from Phoenician language and orthography: as well as his "Canaanite–Phoenician Influence in Qoheleth," see "The Language of Qoheleth," *CBQ* 14 (1952): 227–32; "Qoheleth and Recent Discoveries," *Biblica* 39 (1958): 302–18; "Qoheleth and Northwest Semitic Philology," *Biblica* 43 (1962): 349–65; "Canaanite Words in Qoheleth 10,20," *Biblica* 46 (1965): 210–12; "The Phoenician Background of Qoheleth," *Biblica* 47 (1966): 264–82; "Scriptio Defectiva in Qoheleth 4,10a," *Biblica* 49 (1968): 243; "The Phoenician Contribution to Biblical Wisdom Literature," in *The Role of the Phoenicians in the Interaction of Mediterranean Civilizations: Papers Presented to the Archaeological Symposium at the American University of Beirut; March 1967* (ed. William A. Ward; Beirut: The American University of Beirut, 1968), 123–52; "Three Parallel Pairs in Eccl. 10:18: A Reply to Prof. Gordis," *JQR* 62 (1971): 84–87; "Northwest Semitic Philology and Three Biblical Texts," *JNSL* 2 (1972): 17–22 (which appears to be an extended version of the preceding). William Albright broadly accepted these suggestions by his student, and himself claimed that the author of Ecclesiastes "was an influential Jew who lived...probably in southern Phoenicia"; his writings were intended to be Hebrew, but "their written form betrays Phoenician influence in spelling, morphology, syntax, vocabulary, and content"; see "Some Canaanite–Phoenician Sources of Hebrew Wisdom," in *Wisdom in Israel and in the Ancient Near East* (ed. M. Noth and W. Winton Thomas; VTSup 3; Leiden: Brill, 1955), 1–15, esp. 15. Most other scholars have been less sympathetic; see, for example, Robert Gordis, "Was Koheleth a Phoenician? Some Observations on Methods in Research," *JBL* 74 (1955): 103–14, and Whitley, *Koheleth*, esp. 111–18, who notes that Dahood's observations often help to throw light on particular usages, but do not add up to evidence for his theory. Seow, "Linguistic Dating," 654–57, concludes that "The possibility that some idioms in Qohelet are a result of Phoenician influences cannot be ruled out even though that possibility cannot be demonstrated beyond question," and he goes on later to suggest (p. 665) that "the possibility that the Hebrew of Qohelet reflects a non-Judean dialect cannot be ruled out, although it is difficult to identify the dialect specifically."

Of course, it is not clear to what extent this unusual feature of the book arose from the circumstances of its composition, and it would be inappropriate to assume that we are dealing with a deliberate aspect of Qohelet's characterization or self-presentation. Indeed, since at least one peculiarity of the language extends into the epilogue (the relative pronoun *š-* in 12:9), it is doubtful that we can separate out the protagonist's voice—although this is, of course, an argument for the authenticity of the epilogue. On the other hand, if it is reasonable to suggest that the author was conscious of dialectal or colloquial characteristics in his composition, then we should not exclude the possibility that he viewed them as appropriate for his protagonist, and that they would have evoked particular ideas about Qohelet's background for the original readership.

5. *Conclusions*

The relationship between Qohelet and the book of Ecclesiastes is approached in different ways by recent commentators: some deal with Qohelet as a character or persona of the book's author, others continue to see him as, in fact, the author. Neither of these approaches can be rejected in principle, and it is not necessary to choose between them before we investigate Qohelet's ideas—although we shall have to return to the topic when we look later at the purpose of the book.

The identification of Qohelet as Solomon is a more pressing problem. It has exercised a profound influence on the interpretation of Ecclesiastes, but it fits badly with the information offered about Qohelet outside 1:1 and 1:12, and, if we set Solomon aside, then the Qohelet of the monologue emerges as a rather different sort of character—a successful businessman, who uses the vocabulary of commerce to describe the world, and whose priorities seem to have been shaped by ideas of profit and loss. He is probably old enough to confront the prospect of death, and his wisdom is not a source of happiness for him; he also retains, though, a certain detachment from the world. Less certainly, and depending on how we judge the way he speaks, it is possible that he is supposed to be a common man, or perhaps a foreigner: at the very least, he does not speak the standard Hebrew of the classic biblical literature, or even that of later literary works.

Situated so far from the original context of the book, we are probably not good readers of such things. That does not excuse us, however, from the need to engage with them. Ecclesiastes is offered to us as an intensely personal account, punctuated throughout by first-person observations and recollections, and in the first two chapters Qohelet takes the trouble to tell us a great deal about himself. Correspondingly, we must not lose sight of the fact that his monologue is a speech, grounded in experiences which he recounts, and shaped by his own, idiosyncratic outlook. This will have important consequences when we turn later to ask how the book was supposed to be read, but more immediately it reminds us that Qohelet's character and experience, as they are presented to us, must be the starting-point for any assessment of what he believes.

Chapter 2

QOHELET'S WORLD

The idiosyncratic nature of Qohelet's speech becomes evident almost as soon as it has started. When 1:3 asks, "What profit (*yitrôn*) is there for a person in any of their business, at which they work beneath the sun?," the question is less straightforward than it seems. People generally do work, after all, in the expectation of some return for their labour, whether in the form of a salary, produce or even just good will, and they do generally receive it. Qohelet himself gets plenty of financial return on his own business in the next chapter (cf. 2:8), and so it is apparent that it is not this sort of profit which interests him here. In 1:15, again in the context of human activity beneath the sun, he speaks of an "incalculable loss (*ḥesrôn*)," using, as we saw earlier, a second commercial term. Even before we look at the specific meaning of these terms in his usage, it seems clear that Qohelet is somehow applying the standards of business or accountancy to human life, and perhaps also asking a question which would not occur to most people.

In seeking to explain what he is asking, and perhaps also why he is asking it, Qohelet offers first a particular understanding of the relationship between humans and the world, and then subsequently an account of his own investigations. Much of what will follow in the monologue seems to proceed from these, and in this chapter we shall try to draw from them the underlying concerns and assumptions that inform or motivate Qohelet, though it will again become clear that his reactions to what he sees are intimately tied up with his own, sometimes very individual, attitudes and expectations. As I shall argue below, the first part of ch. 3 has to be understood in terms of these initial accounts, and in some sense forms a conclusion to them, so we shall review that material also before trying to summarize the key themes and ideas.

1. The Prologue: Ecclesiastes 1:4–11

Between the superscription in 1:1 and Qohelet's introduction of himself in 1:12, the book contains a series of statements and observations, and these appear to serve as a sort of prologue to the monologue, foreshadowing some of the major themes that it is going to address. Although their tone and subject-matter are rather different from what follows, there are no good grounds either to reject 1:2–11 as secondary, or to regard them just as some sort of overture. It is here, after all, that Qohelet first offers his opinion that "all is vanity" (to use the traditional translation), and this characterization will not only conclude his monologue in 12:8, but will be used of more specific actions and situations throughout the book. It is also here that Qohelet first asks what profit can be achieved from human endeavours "beneath the sun," initiating what will again be a recurrent theme. These important pronouncements are set beside each other, and then followed by observations and assertions about more specific phenomena, which are read most naturally as an attempt to explain or validate the initial claims. Accordingly, if we can understand the way in which he illustrates his case in vv. 4–11, then we can better understand just what it is that Qohelet means in vv. 2–3, and perhaps what he is trying to say in the book as a whole.

Of course, if it were that easy, then Ecclesiastes might not still be subject to the huge variety of interpretations current in modern scholarship, and this section of the book is no less elusive and perplexing than many others. The content of vv. 4–11 can, nevertheless, be outlined quite straightforwardly. Qohelet first sets the going and coming of human generations alongside the constancy of the world:[1]

> One generation goes, another generation comes,
> while the world stays forever constant.[2]

1. D. N. Freedman and J. Lundbom, "דּוֹר, *dôr*," *TDOT* 3:169–81, esp. 174, makes it very clear that any reference to eras in the term דור is grounded firmly in the idea of human generations, but commentators persist in the idea that there is an ambiguity between "eras" and "generations" here, often citing that article as their authority. See, for example, Doug Ingram, *Ambiguity in Ecclesiastes* (LHBOTS 431; New York: T&T Clark International, 2006), 59, who develops at length the suggestion made in Crenshaw, *Ecclesiastes*, 62, that "*dôr*...suggests both nature and people. The primary sense here is probably the former: the generations of natural phenomena. But the other nuance must also be present, lending immense irony to the observation that the stage on which the human drama is played outlasts the actors themselves." Cf. also Lindsay Wilson, "Artful Ambiguity in Ecclesiastes 1,1–11: A Wisdom Technique?," in Schoors, ed., *Qohelet in the Context of Wisdom*, 357–65, esp. 360. Although there may be a somewhat extended poetical sense in a few passages, such as Isa 51:9, there are not two meanings, and correspondingly there can be no ambiguity.

2. עמדת, literally, "is standing." The verb עמד can connote endurance, but can also mean "stand still" (e.g. Josh 10:13), and it seems likely that that sense is in play here, in opposition to the preceding verbs of motion.

He then draws attention to the motion of the sun and wind, and of rivers which flow into the sea without ever filling it. After the slightly obscure v. 8, often regarded as a parenthetical exclamation, he finally, in vv. 9–11, asserts that everything that will happen is already happening, so that nothing is new, merely forgotten, just as everything will ultimately be forgotten.

Although it is these questions of novelty and forgetfulness which conclude the section, most commentators have been inclined to emphasize the distinctive depiction of natural phenomena as Qohelet's primary concern, with human activity set against or implicated within the constant, endless motion in nature. This is typically perceived either as weary and meaningless, or as something so impressive that it almost defies human comprehension, but in either case it is taken to act as a type or model for the actions of humans themselves. Whether or not the emphasis is justified, however, it is questionable whether the book really intends such an analogy between nature and humanity.

a. *Natural Phenomena (1:5–8)*
Especially in modern times, v. 5 has been taken as a key to understanding the rest of vv. 5–7, and its general sense is clear: the sun completes its daily course through the sky, only to return each day, in order to do it again:

> and the sun rises, and the sun goes down
> and panting[3] towards its place, it rises there.

The movement of the sun is cyclical, and since we should expect some consistency across all the illustrations, many commentators have assumed that they must all be understood as similarly cyclical.[4] On this understanding, the wind blows in endless circles, streams flow into the sea but

---

3. The verb שואף implies effort or longing (like "gasping" and "gasping for" in English), but has no necessary connotation either of exhaustion and "struggling" (as Seow, *Ecclesiastes*, 107, asserts), or of desire. Most Hebrew manuscripts place a disjunctive accent on מקומו, to give the sense "panting it rises there," and Lohfink thinks that the Masoretes had in mind the snorting of Helios' horses, but this seems fanciful. See Norbert Lohfink, "Die Wiederkehr des immer Gleichen. Eine frühe Synthese zwischen griechischem und jüdischem Weltgefühl in Kohelet 1,4–11," *Archivo di Filosofia* 53 (1985): 125–49, esp. 135.

4. Among recent studies, see, for example, Michael Carasik, "Qohelet's Twists and Turns," *JSOT* 28 (2003): 192–209; Katherine J. Dell, "The Cycle of Life in Ecclesiastes," *VT* 59 (2009): 181–89. Perhaps the strongest modern exposition of a cyclical view, though, is in Graham Ogden, *Qoheleth* (2d ed.; Readings: A New Biblical Commentary; Sheffield: Sheffield Phoenix, 2007).

then back to their sources, and perhaps even the "generations" of v. 4 are not merely human generations, but the cycles of nature, standing in contrast to the immovable earth.[5] The idea has proved attractive to ancient and modern interpreters alike, not least because it lends a certain purpose to the motions described: they are not continuous in the sense of being never-ending, but each achieve an end repeatedly. It is difficult, however, to interpret all these phenomena as cyclical, and that may not be the point which Qohelet is trying to make even about the sun.

Here matters are made more difficult by the relationship between vv. 5 and 6, and more specifically the place of v. 6a, "going southward, and turning northward." The two clauses in this half-verse have no explicit subject, which would usually lead us to take as implicit the preceding subject—the sun. In that case we would read:

> and the sun rises, and the sun goes down
> and panting towards its place, it rises there,
> going southward, and turning northward.

The Masoretic punctuation, however, groups v. 6a with v. 6b, so that the verbs may instead anticipate a new subject, the wind. Noting that the sun does not actually appear in the north, almost all modern critical commentators have adopted this latter reading,[6] and some have seen a

---

5.   On this interpretation of 1:4, see especially Graham S. Ogden, "The Interpretation of *Dôr* in Ecclesiastes 1.4," *JSOT* 34 (1986): 91–92, and the response by Michael Fox, "Qohelet 1.4," *JSOT* 40 (1988): 109, who points out that "דור, whatever its etymology, never means 'cycle' in Hebrew (or in any other Northwest Semitic language); and it is not cycles that 'go and come', but rather things within cycles." Peter R. Ackroyd, "The Meaning of Hebrew דור Considered," *JSS* 13 (1968): 3–10, esp. 9–10, expresses serious reservations about connecting the term to cyclic concepts of time.

6.   Whitley, *Koheleth*, 9, is a notable exception, although he believes that v. 5b is a secondary intrusion, concealing and confusing the original sentence, which incorporated all four points of the compass. See also Heinrich Graetz, *Kohélet* קהלת *oder der Salomonische Prediger. Übersetzt und kritisch erläutert. Nebst Anhang über Kohélet's Stellung im Kanon, über die griechische Uebersetzung desselben und über Graecismen darin und einem Glossar* (Leipzig: Winter, 1871), 55–56, who translates: "Die Sonne…geht dort (wieder) auf, geht gen Süden und wendet sich gen Norden," and approves the reading of those versions which take the sun to be the subject, but offers no specific justification. Rarely noted (and arguably not the most critical of commentators) is Adam Clarke, *The Holy Bible, Containing the Old and New Testaments: The text carefully printed from the most correct copies of the present authorised translation, including the marginal readings and parallel texts: with a commentary and critical notes; designed as a help to a better understanding of the sacred writings.* Vol. 3, *Job to Solomon's Songs* (2d ed.; London: William

deliberate device in the accumulation of five verbs before the subject is specified, or thought that Qohelet is deliberately leading the reader into an initial misunderstanding of the subject (although why he should do so here seems unclear).[7] The certainty surrounding this reading in modern scholarship is matched, however, by an equal but opposite certainty among ancient commentators, who mostly take the sun to be the subject not only of v. 6a, but of v. 6b as well (with "the wind," *hārûaḥ*, being then the "spirit" of the sun, or perhaps meaning "side").[8] These older readers saw no problem with northward movement of the sun, noting either that it moves seasonally along a north–south axis (and hence only rises or sets due east and west at the equinoxes),[9] or that it moves through the north daily after setting, even if we cannot see it. Although it is sometimes suggested that the author of Ecclesiastes believed the sun to travel directly back to the east underground,[10] that is a view rejected as non-Jewish in some sources, and we really cannot say for sure what he believed, except that it is unlikely to have excluded north–south

Tegg & Co., 1854), ad loc. (the pages are unnumbered), "These verses are confused by being falsely divided. The first clause of the *sixth* should be joined to the *fifth* verse."

7. See, for example, Edwin M. Good, "The Unfilled Sea: Style and Meaning in Ecclesiastes 1:2–11," in *Israelite Wisdom: Theological and Literary Essays in Honor of Samuel Terrien* (ed. John G. Gammie et al.; New York: Scholars Press, 1978), 59–73, esp. 66–67: "In the northern hemisphere, one never looks north for the sun, except in Arctic latitudes... Notice how the poet fends us off, forces us to hold our breath in suspense... To delay certainty of meaning as shrewdly and as long as these lines do is remarkably effective... The delay is of the essence. And it is affective. The technique at once makes clear a continuity of image, that of circling, and shrewdly masks a discontinuity of subject, from sun to wind. It thus first fulfills the expectation that vs. 6 has a place in the series of repetitions begun with the generations, then frustrates a hypothetical meaning that the sun continues to be the subject, and finally delays identification of the subject to remarkable lengths." Perhaps I am just not such a good reader, but I do not find myself holding my breath in suspense, so much as scratching my head in confusion.

8. See Sara Japhet, "'Goes to the South and Turns to the North' (Ecclesiastes 1:6): The Sources and History of the Exegetical Traditions," *Jewish Studies Quarterly* 1 (1993–94): 289–322.

9. Cf. Clarke, *Holy Bible*, ad loc., "the author refers to the approximations of the sun to the *northern* and *southern tropics*, viz., of *Cancer* and *Capricorn*." (The italics are original—Clarke shows a great fondness for them.)

10. For example, Krüger, *Kohelet*, 113 (ET 50); Tremper Longman III, *The Book of Ecclesiastes* (NICOT; Grand Rapids: Eerdmans, 1998), 69; R. N. Whybray, "Ecclesiastes 1:5–7 and the Wonders of Nature," *JSOT* 13 (1988): 105–12, esp. 107–8.

movement of the sun either daily or seasonally.[11] Furthermore, since the wind in Palestine typically shifts between east and west, with some more complicated cyclonic movements during the winter months, v. 6a can hardly be regarded as more self-evidently a reference to wind than to sun.[12]

For purposes of translation, it is better, perhaps, to recognize an ambiguity, deliberate or otherwise, than to force one subject or the other on v. 6a. If it is Qohelet's intention, however, to depict the east–west cycle of the sun, followed by a north–south cycle of the wind, then the deferral of the subject only undermines this intention, and obscures his purpose. If, on the other hand, the sun is supposed to be the subject of v. 6a, then the account becomes one of various movements, and hardly establishes a cyclical pattern at all. Although this pattern, furthermore, can be read into the subsequent descriptions—and often is—it does not really arise out of them. For all that *sĕbîbōt* is commonly given the unique sense "circuits" or "circles" in v. 6b, so that the wind travels "on its circuits," or "in its circles," this seems to defy common human experience: the wind does not generally blow in circles, let alone fixed circuits (and if it did, then people would hardly have to observe its movements, as at 11:4); indeed, the wind does not always blow at all. Here it is better to take the normal, widely attested meaning of that word: the wind turns and turns, but always returns to blow on its surroundings.[13] For all its movement, in other words, the wind never achieves completion.

11. *B. Bat.* 25b records the view of R. Eliezer that the sun simply reverses direction after setting, and returns "above the firmament," while R. Joshua (citing Ecclesiastes) argues that the world is like a tent, on which all sides except the north are open, and the sun moves round to the north, behind the tent and so out of sight. At *b. Pesaḥ.* 94b, the idea of an underground route is attributed to non-Jewish scientists, while the traditional Jewish understanding is taken to be that the sun returns "above the sky." Rashbam interprets 1:5–6 as saying that the sun "travels during the day from the east towards the south, and goes via south and west until it turns and travels towards the north, and arrives at its place in the east"; cf. Japhet and Salters, *Rashbam*, 92.

12. See Efraim Orni and Elisha Efrat, *Geography of Israel* (3d ed.; Jerusalem: Israel Universities Press, 1971), 139–42. Hertzberg, "Palästinische Bezüge," 113–14, suggests that the wind may pass through the north or south as it shifts between the west and east, so that the verse refers to those transitions, rather than to sustained north–south winds. Yet the summer breezes do not involve the wind veering: they are a simple reversal. The winter conditions in the area are more complicated, but do not usually involve winds blowing from, or moving through, the south.

13. סביבות is most commonly used adverbially to mean "around" or "about," but can be used as a substantive. In Jer 17:26, for instance, it means "the environs (of Jerusalem)," and in Ezek 16:57; 28:26; 34:26; Dan 9:16 it similarly refers to

In v. 7, similarly, a number of commentators have seen an account of the rivers returning to their sources after reaching the sea, so that they too travel in circles. This is an interpretation found also in the ancient versions, and some pre-modern commentators explain the verse in terms of the evaporation, or the return of the water through subterranean channels. It is difficult to achieve that sense without emendation of the text, however, or a problematic equation of "there" with "from there,"[14]

"neighbouring" areas or people; in both usages, it commonly takes a suffix pronoun, as here, referring to whatever is being surrounded. So, for example, Ps 44:14 (ET 44:13): תשימנו חרפה לשכנינו לעג וקלס לסביבותינו: "You have made us a reproach for our neighbours, into objects of mockery and derision for those around us." It is important to note also here the use of the preposition על with the noun. There are no grounds for emending this to אל, and although it can come close to the same sense when used with שוב, many commentators have found it unexpected here; the use of both in 12:7 seems to suggest that the book distinguishes the uses—although Ludger Schwienhorst-Schönberger, *Kohelet* (Herders theologischer Kommentar zum Alten Testament; Freiburg im Breisgau: Herder, 2004), 156, in fact takes this as evidence that they are interchangeable. If סביבות refers to surroundings, על is quite natural, and we need not resort to understanding it as a reference to cause, as, for example, Seow, *Ecclesiastes*, 108, "on account of its rounds." Seow cites Friedrich Ellermeier, *Qohelet. Teil 1 Abschnitt 1. Untersuchungen zum Buche Qohelet* (Herzberg am Harz: Erwin Jungfer, 1967), 201, but Ellermeier suggests that the preposition "gibt…weniger den Grund an als den Zweck."

14.   The text reads אל מקום שהנחלים הלכים שם שבים ללכת, literally, "to (the) place which the streams (are) going there they (are) continuing/returning to go." The sense, correspondingly, hinges largely on the meaning of the relative particle ש in מקום שהנחלים הלכים, and whether it indicates their point of departure or arrival. Norman Whybray, *Ecclesiastes* (New Century Bible Commentary; Grand Rapids: Eerdmans; London: Marshall, Morgan & Scott, 1989), 42 (cf. his "Ecclesiastes 1:5–7," 108), continues to defend the ambiguity of the expression, and supports the understanding that the streams are returning to the place where they started by arguing that this image must be cyclical to suit the rest. Such an understanding of the context underpins other attempts to extract this meaning, but most commentators recognize that it is not the natural sense of the text as it stands, especially since שם is probably to be read with the first clause and not the second (cf., e.g., Gen 13:3). Emendation of the text, however, to restore either משם or משם שם, finds little support among the ancient versions: the Vulgate's *ad locum unde exeunt flumina revertuntur*, like *ad locum de quo torrentes exeunt illuc ipsi reuertuntur* in Jerome's commentary, are probably derived from Symmachus' εἰς τὸν τόπον ἀφ' οὗ οἱ ποταμοὶ πορεύονται καὶ ἐκεῖ αὐτοὶ ἀναστρέφουσιν. That does not read משם, but takes שם with the second clause and imputes the sense "from" to ש: modern commentators are not the only readers influenced by a desire to find cycles here. Other scholars have sought other routes. For example, Allgeier, *Das Buch des Predigers oder Koheleth. Übersetzt und erklärt* (Die Heilige Schrift des Alten Testamentes 6/2; Bonn: Hanstein, 1925), 21–22, gives הלכים the sense "entstehen," and Young-Jin Min,

while ancient explanations for the constant level of the sea do not always involve removal or re-cycling of its water.[15] If we are to suppose that Qohelet is deliberately promulgating a view of natural processes as cyclical, it seems curious that we should have to gloss his words here in order to discover a cycle. When we look back also to the ambiguity which confused his account of undoubtedly cyclical solar movements, and to his choice of the wind as an example, despite its apparently non-cyclical nature, it does seem clear either that Qohelet is putting across his point about cycles rather badly, or that that is not his point at all.

It would be wrong to judge the meaning of vv. 5–7 without consideration also of v. 8, which starts in precisely the same way as v. 7 ("all" + plural noun + participle), suggesting that we are being offered a further illustration, not a new section, and which seems to pick up the idea of the sea remaining unfilled in its own references to the eye and ear. These are largely unproblematic: the text states, literally, that "an eye will not be too sated for seeing, and an ear will not be filled by listening." An alternative understanding of the first part, taking it to mean "an eye will not be sated by seeing" seems less likely, but anyway makes no significant difference to the sense. Most discussion has focused on the first two clauses, where Qohelet apparently declares first that "all words/ things (*dĕbārîm*) are weary," then that "a man will be unable to speak"; there is no conjunction or other particle indicating the relationship between these statements, but the first presumably furnishes the circumstances for the second. The juxtaposition of the two would also seem to suggest that the *dĕbārîm* are "words," rather than "things," and are

"How Do the Rivers Flow? (Ecclesiastes 1:7)," *Bible Translator* 42 (1991): 226–30, esp. 228, insists that שוב can only "be used for completed actions repeated after an interval," although his argument then requires him to stretch this definition far enough to encompass a continuous flow which passes through its own starting-point. It seems clear, at the very least, that the text does not positively illustrate a cycle, and that a cyclical reference can only be found in it with some effort.

15. *Midrash Qoheleth* offers an interesting discussion of the distillation and return of water to the earth through evaporation and condensation, which is the way in which Ibn Ezra understands it to return, over against the underground passages envisaged by the Targum (which speaks of the rivers flowing into Oceanus, and thence to the "Deep"). It goes on, however, to note an alternative interpretation of the passage in terms of the ocean's ability to take up water without being filled (and incidentally to describe a supposed demonstration of sea-water's ability to absorb fresh water without changing its volume). Interestingly, much the same idea is found in Ephrem the Syrian's commentary on Genesis, cited in ACCS, 197: "Rivers flow down into seas lest the heat of the sun dry them up. The saltiness [of the seas] then swallows up [the rivers] lest they increase, rise up and cover the earth. Thus the rivers turn into nothing, as it were, because the saltiness of the sea swallows them up."

connected with the reference to speaking. Many commentators, however, have seen this as a summary: Qohelet is declaring that everything is so weary (or wearisome) that it leaves a human observer dumbstruck, unable to express what they see, or even to take it all in. To divorce *děbārîm* from the subsequent cognate verb seems awkward, however, and it is also difficult to associate the rest of the verse with this understanding: if the eye and ear are simply not filled with seeing and hearing, just as the sea is not filled by the rivers, then they are continuing the thought of v. 7, and the supposed exclamation is intrusive. If, on the other hand, they belong with the exclamation, then their claims seem odd: even allowing for ellipsis of an indirect object, they more naturally state that the eye and ear can never get enough of perceiving the phenomena, than that they are overwhelmed by them—and that would set them in contrast to the statement about speech, not in parallel with it.

Since the last two clauses of v. 8 are fairly clear and unambiguous, it seems better to understand the verse in terms of what they say. If their theme is that sensory input never reaches a point of completion, so that eyes and ears just keep seeing and hearing, then it is reasonable to suspect that the first two clauses are saying something similar about speech: that the mouth, in effect, never runs out of words. It is straightforward, in fact, to read those clauses as saying precisely the opposite: "when all words are weary, a man cannot speak," which would be an assertion that speech stops when all the words are used up or worn out. Since that is clearly untrue, however, and since it so precisely contradicts what follows, it seems likely that we are dealing with a rhetorical question, and I would venture to translate the verse as argumentative:

> When all words are worn out, can one no longer speak?
> An eye will not be too sated for seeing, nor an ear filled with listening.

If this is the true sense, and the second part, at least, is quite often translated this way, then Qohelet is not concluding his illustrations from nature with a somewhat laboured gasp of appreciation, but is extending his discussion to include human actions alongside natural phenomena. These human actions—speaking, seeing, and hearing—similarly reach no conclusion, but they are quite definitely not cyclical. Taken altogether, then, vv. 5 to 8 offer a list of activities characterized not by circularity or repetition, but by their common lack of completion and consummation:

> One generation goes, another generation comes,
> while the world stays forever constant:
> and the sun rises, and the sun goes down
> and panting towards its place, it rises there,
> going southward, and turning northward.

Turning, turning, goes the wind,
and upon its surroundings, the wind blows again.
All streams go to the sea, and the sea is never filled:
to the place where the streams go, they keep going.
When all words are worn out, can one no longer speak?
An eye will not be too sated for seeing, nor an ear filled with listening.

This list offers no support for attempts to emphasize some cyclical motif, or to treat any items in the list as implicitly cyclical when they are not explicitly so, and it is important to bear that in mind as we turn to the second part of the prologue.

b. *Past, Present and Future (1:9–11)*
In v. 9, Qohelet seems to take the discussion in a new direction, and if we are not constrained by the idea that the preceding verses are all about cycles, we need not try to impose a cyclical interpretation here. Indeed, this verse is far from being a simple statement that what goes around, comes around:

What will be, will be whatever is,
and what will be done, whatever is done[16]—
and with nothing new[17] beneath the sun.

It is difficult to take this simply as a logical consequence of what is asserted in vv. 5–8, and it may be better to see its antecedent in the claim of v. 4, that the world is constant. If vv. 5–8 have spelled out one consequence of that constancy—that there are no endings—vv. 9–11 now spell out another, that there are, equally, no beginnings.[18] If this understanding

---

16. The two parallel clauses are each structured as tripartite nominal clauses (*x* הוא *y*, meaning *x*=*y*; cf. J-M §154j), with relative clauses acting as the nominal elements (*that which... = that which...*). The usual word-order in tripartite clauses like this is predicate–pronoun–subject, so the statements are probably to be read as statements about the nature of the future, not about the past/present (cf. Ellermeier, *Qohelet I.I*, 208). The tense is a more difficult question, and the issues are discussed in detail by Isaksson, *Studies*, 69–76, who argues persuasively that נעשה should be read as perfect but rendered here as present tense. From that point of view, the vocalization as perfect *qatal* or as a participle, discussed by Fox, *A Time to Tear Down*, 169, 285, and Schoors, *Pleasing Words*, 1:96–97, makes little difference. It is important to note, though, that the text imposes no actual distinction between past and present, and the declaration can embrace both.

17. Literally, "there is not/will not be anything new"; expressions with אין are nominal clauses, and so derive their tense from context. Although I think this is most naturally read as a further statement about the future, it may be more general.

18. Krüger, *Kohelet*, 110 (ET 47–48), suggests that Qohelet's claim, אין כל חדש, means not "there is (absolutely) nothing new," but, less radically, "there is nothing

is correct, then Qohelet is elaborating upon, and extrapolating from a conclusion which he has asserted at the outset. Accordingly, the endless efforts of nature are presented not as his *evidence* that nothing can be resolved or that there can be nothing new, but merely as a corollary of his belief that the world is constant. The idea seems to be lent weight, moreover, by Qohelet's approach to human experience in the closing vv. 10 and 11. There is more here than simply an attempt to forestall objections, as he uses the imagined claim that something is new to describe the limits of human understanding. Just as v. 4 set the passing of generations beside the lasting constancy of the world, so these verses now assert the inadequacy of human memory, perhaps even cumulative human memory, when confronted by the vast spans of the world's existence:

> Should someone say, "Look! this is new!"[19],
> it has already been, in the aeons which have existed out of our sight:[20]
> there is no memory of the earlier times,
> and likewise of the later, which will be—

absolutely new." The suggestion is attractive but would require us to suppose a highly unusual use of כל (perhaps as in the difficult Ps 39:6, כל הבל?). Other uses of אין כל (cf. Num 11:6; 2 Sam 12:3; Prov 13:7) do not furnish precise parallels, but point to the conventional understanding.

19. Probably not "Look at this! It's new," despite the accents: זה...הוא is a common expression in the monologue (Barton, *Ecclesiastes*, 75, notes 2:23; 4:8; 6:2; cf. also 5:18, with היא), and the writer commonly uses it to form a tripartite nominal clause (like those preceding here), with the predicate between the two pronouns.

20. מלפני is not used in any other passage to express time (although cf. Isa 41:26 מלפנים), and usually appears in the context either of separation from the presence or sight of someone, or of, for example, fear, humility when confronted by someone. These normal senses are found elsewhere in Ecclesiastes (3:14; 8:12, 13; 10:5), but G and most modern commentators have seen a basic equivalence with לפנינו here; see, for example, Gordis, *Koheleth*, 208; Schoors, *Pleasing Words*, 2:308. I think, however, that it is difficult both to assign an abnormal temporal sense, and to overlook the word's usual connotation of separation, so that I take the clause to foreshadow the next verse: the ages are, as it were, out of our sight and presence, and so we can know nothing of them. See also M. Cohen, "'aššūrênû 'attâ sᵉbābûnî (Q. sᵉbābûnû) (Psaume XVII 11A)," *VT* 41 (1991): 137–44, esp. 141: "il n'y a plus de place pour aucune équivoque dès que l'on a affaire aux formes diversement composées de *lipnê* et telles que *millipnê*… Toutes ces formes dénotent *exclusivement* l'adverbe de lieu 'devant'. Jamais un adverbe de temps. Il nous paraît donc arbitraire de donner en Qoh. i 10b une valeur temporelle à la forme de *millepānênû*." He concludes that if the context for the word in Ecclesiastes demands a temporal sense, then it must be considered an instance of מלפנים "mal résolu."

there will be no memory of them, along with[21] those which are going to be (still) later.

The initial claim here has to be understood in terms of process, not instantiation. Even if Qohelet were to believe that history repeats itself, or that everything will be duplicated in the infinite permutations of an infinite world, it is clearly not the case that a particular object or event can never be new: if I build a table, it is a new table, even if there have been a thousand just like it before. The claim might be sustainable were we to take it as a reference to originality rather than strictly to newness, although it is not clear that the Hebrew *ḥādāš* can bear the sense "unprecedented." If we were to take it that way, then Qohelet would be saying that no new pattern or template can be introduced, and that everything possesses a form or character which has already come into existence. I think it is more probable, in the light of his previous emphasis on continuity, both of the world and of the processes within it, that Qohelet's point here is a little different: nothing comes into being out of nothing, and everything traces its origin into the distant past; correspondingly, all actions and objects are simply manifestations of much longer-term processes.

This idea, in fact, will be picked up later in the book using similar terms. Ecclesiastes 3:14–15, although it presents certain difficulties and adds the dimension of divine action, clearly relates the fact that, literally, "It already is, whatever is, and what is to be already is," to Qohelet's supposition that "all which God has achieved will exist forever: there is no adding to it and there is no subtracting from it." In that place again, though, Qohelet's focus is upon the human inability to perceive the

---

21.   The preposition עִם here is commonly taken to mean "among," and the clause construed as a statement that the memory will not persist among those coming still later. However, in 2:16 we find a very similar statement: אֵין זִכְרוֹן לֶחָכָם עִם הַכְּסִיל לְעוֹלָם. There, the same preposition has its common meaning "along with," and it recurs later in the verse: both uses establish the parity of the wise man and the fool, while the verse itself makes a clear reference back to this verse. Cf. Gerrit Wildeboer, "Der Prediger," in Karl Budde, Alfred Bertholet, and G. Wildeboer, *Die fünf Megillot (Das Hohelied, Das Buch Ruth, Die Klagelieder, Der Prediger, Das Buch Esther)* (Kurzer Hand-Commentar zum Alten Testament 17; Freiburg im Breisgau: J. C. B. Mohr [Paul Siebeck], 1898), 109–68, esp. 125, who translates "*ebensowenig* wird ein Andenken sein *an diejenigen, die darnach leben werden*" (his italics). So, despite the affirmation of the conventional reading in Schoors, *Pleasing Words*, 1:201, this verse probably does not say that there is no memory of the first period, and will be no memory of the second period among those in a third; rather, it says that there is no memory of the first period, and will be no memory of the second period, along with any subsequent period(s?).

bigger picture: the divine achievement referred to in 3:14 has already been described in 3:11: "that which no human can discover—the achievement which God has achieved from start right through to finish." The key point which he wishes to make in ch. 3, as here, seems to be that the continuity of the world and its processes can never properly be understood by humans, whose brief lives and short memories are inadequate to comprehend actions that stretch across aeons. We see only snapshots of the endless processes which characterize the world, and so, for Qohelet, the human is like a mayfly, which sees the sun rise once: the limits of our perception cause us to proclaim the commonplace unique, and the infinitely old as new.

c. *Conclusions*

Such a reading suggests that Qohelet is concerned in this section not with the character of the world *per se*, so much as with the difference between humans and that world, and that we should not be reading the accounts of natural phenomena in 1:5–7 as models of human existence or activity. Despite the efforts of some scholars to link cyclical ideas about nature with the passing generations of 1:4, these phenomena belong to the other part of that verse, the constant world (as the conjunction starting v. 5 might be taken to suggest). On that reckoning, however, the same must surely be true of the speaking, seeing, and hearing in 1:8, which are human activities, and which therefore present a challenge to any notion of a simple dichotomy between humans and the world. Qohelet is apparently concerned not to distinguish humanity from nature, but to distinguish individual human lives from a continuing world, which itself incorporates the human race as an entity. Without going so far as Michael Fox, and describing Qohelet's world as "'le monde' rather than 'la terre,'"[22] we can at least say that it includes the human and biological, alongside the cosmic and geological.

There is a contrast implicit in 1:4, then, but not a strict separation. The succession of human generations is itself a constant, natural activity within the world as a whole, and the issues which it raises concern the individual, not the species. Equally, the individual is not wholly disconnected from the endless processes of the world. When Qohelet presents speaking, seeing and hearing as analogous to the natural phenomena of the previous verses, then, the point of similarity is their essential endlessness, not some cosmic or inanimate quality that they possess, and these are only some of the innumerable ways in which individual humans

22. Fox, *A Time to Tear Down*, 166.

can engage in endless processes. Just as Qohelet is not distinguishing between the human and the natural, then, he is also not characterizing all human activity as finite in nature, except insofar as it is presumably limited by the lifespan of the individual. Indeed, it may be the crucial point here that each human reaches completion, as it were, but their work in the world does not—and that is a theme that Qohelet is to pick up in his next account.

2. *The Memoir: 1:12–2:26*

We have already looked briefly in the last chapter at Qohelet's account of his business activities, but only in the context of his identity. Having observed there that this account does not seem principally concerned with assertions of his Solomonic persona or royalty, if those are concerns at all, we may reasonably ask what other purpose, in fact, it might serve. To answer that question, though, it is important first to say something about the context in which the account is presented.

a. *Qohelet's Quests*

After introducing himself in 1:12, Qohelet tells us in 1:13–15 that he embarked on an investigation:

> And I set my heart to inquiring and exploring through wisdom concerning everything which is done beneath the heavens: is it a bad job which God has given humans to work at?[23] I looked at all the achievements which are achieved beneath the sun, and behold, it was all *hebel*, and wishing for the wind: crooked,[24] it is beyond straightening out; and as a loss, it is beyond counting.

I have left the word *hebel* untranslated here: as we shall see below, it is a key metaphor in the book, but we do not need to address its implications at this point. It is one of several features, however, which forge a link between these verses and the preceding 1:2–3, which stated that everything is *hebel*, and then asked what profit there is for humans in their work beneath the sun. Qohelet asks a new question about human work,

---

23. For notes on the translation of 1:13, see Chapter 1, above.

24. The verb עָוַת (which appears also in 7:13; 12:3) is generally found in the Piel or Pual (12:3 Hithpael), and it refers to bending, or being bent. It is far more commonly used in a figurative way, however, with the sense of perverting or subverting justice (so, e.g., Job 8:3; Lam 3:36), and Amos 8:5 uses it of falsifying measures. There is probably, then, a strong implication in the term that everything is in a state where it functions incorrectly, giving, as it were, the wrong results.

phrased in terms of divine appointment to tasks (cf. 3:9–10), but concludes again that what humans achieve beneath the sun is *hebel*, and that it constitutes not a profit, but an incalculable loss. The way in which the earlier verses are picked up may alert us to a degree of continuity here, and Qohelet has clearly not finished with the issues that he addressed in the earlier part of the chapter, but there is also a sort of progression: he seems to be dismissing human achievements definitively at this point, and turning his attention to other matters.

In 1:16–18, Qohelet examines not what humans do, but the tool which he had previously used in 1:13 to examine those achievements:

> I conversed with my heart, saying, "Behold, I have amplified and increased wisdom to a point beyond anyone who was in Jerusalem[25] before me, and my heart has seen much wisdom and knowledge—so let me set my heart to knowing wisdom and knowledge, confusion and wrongheadedness."[26] I realized of this too, that it is worrying about the wind, for in much wisdom is much exasperation, and whoever gains in knowledge gains in pain.

This appears to mark a shift to the investigation of something more intellectual: wisdom and its various counterparts. This new investigation, however, would seem to be governed broadly by the rubric of the previous one: Qohelet is looking for purpose, and still perhaps profit, in a different area of human development. He does not now dismiss what he finds simply as *hebel*, but he does find the gains provided by wisdom and knowledge undesirable.

Finally, in 2:1–2, he begins yet another investigation, this time of the senses. The Hebrew is very difficult, although the general sense is plain:

> I said in my heart, "Come on then, I shall stuff you with[27] pleasure, and you must see what good it does!" And behold, it too was *hebel*. Of fun, I said "Mindless!," and of pleasure "What does it do?"

25. The major Masoretic manuscripts have עַל, "over" Jerusalem, but בּ appears as a variant, and seems to underpin the versions. Goldman in *BHQ*, 68*, has raised the possibility that עַל reflects adaptation toward Solomonic authorship, specifying Qohelet's royal status, but it may just be assimilation to the preceding occurrence in the verse.

26. A full discussion is not needed here, but these concepts of הוללות and סכלות in the book are probably not quite synonymous, and the usage of related terms might suggest that הוללות is acting badly without thought, סכלות the unwillingness or incapacity to do the right thing.

27. The verb אנסכה is most naturally read, perhaps, as a cohortative form of נסך, "pour." The subsequent בשמחה, however, cannot be a direct object, and an absolute use of the verb would probably imply the pouring of libations. That does not seem to suit the context, unless the text is changed to link the verb with the wine mentioned in v. 3—which is why N. H. Tur-Sinai (= Harry Torczyner), "Dunkle Bibelstellen,"

Here Qohelet seems to dismiss enjoyment almost instantly as pointless, so that he has found nothing that he seems to want in human work, in human wisdom, or in human pleasure. Two of these three things are going to be considered again shortly, however, in 2:11 ("Then I looked round among all my achievements, which my hands had achieved, and at the business which I had worked to achieve..."), and in 2:12 ("Then I looked round to observe wisdom, and confusion, and wrongheadedness..."). Enjoyment, furthermore, is then going to be the subject-matter of 2:24–26, where, as we shall see, Qohelet will regard it in a very different light. It seems as though Qohelet is undertaking the same investigations twice, or at least undertaking them once and then talking about them twice, and there has been considerable discussion about what is going on here, and how the various parts of the account are supposed to fit together.

The problem is compounded by the deep obscurity of 2:3. A mention of wine in this verse often leads commentators to see it as a continuation of Qohelet's quest to study pleasure, which would then embrace the

in *Vom alten Testament Karl Marti zum Siebzigsten Geburtstage gewidmet von Freunden, Fachgenossen und Schülern* (ed. K. Budde; BZAW 41: Giessen: Töpelmann, 1925), 274–80, esp. 279–80, proposes to move ביין את בשרי ולבי נהג from there; see also his "דברי קהלת" ("The Words of Qohelet"), in הלשון והספר: בעיות יסוד במדע הלשון ובמקורותיה בספרות (*The Language and the Book: Fundamental Issues in the Study of the Language and in its Literary Sources*) (Jerusalem: Bialik Institute, 1950 [Hebrew]), 2:389–408, esp. 402. Ginsberg, *Studies*, 7–8, accepts the suggestion, but implausibly emends אנסכה to איט(י)בה, rendering 'I will gladden my flesh with wine'. Many more commentators have preferred to follow G πειράσω σε, taking אנסכה to be a Piel imperfect/cohortative from נסה, "test," with a second person object suffix written plene: "I shall/let me test you." If, however, Qohelet is testing something here, the context shows that it is not himself but forms of pleasure. Moshe Greenberg, "נסה in Exodus 20:20 and the Purpose of the Sinaitic Theophany," *JBL* 79 (1960): 273–76, has argued that to "test" X with (ב) Y means to give X experience of Y. Some commentators correspondingly take the sense here to be "let me make you experience pleasure." Greenberg's examples, however, point to something less experiential than formative, and with this sense of the verb, therefore, the preposition is simply instrumental (cf. 7:23): our clause would mean "I shall use pleasure to make you experienced," which will hardly do. A final possibility, not considered elsewhere so far as I know, is that we are dealing with the verb אנס, which can be used of compulsion or constraint more generally, but is used in Esth 1:8 specifically of forcing people to drink, and in Sir 31:21 (*sub* 31:22 in ms B) of filling oneself or being filled (Niphal) with (ב) too much food. This at least gives a good sense, and, for want of a better solution, I take the original reading to have been אאנסכ(ה), an imperfect Qal from that verb, with a second-person suffix. The omission of an aleph in the present text would then be more probably an error, arising from the sequence of three alephs in נאאנסכ, than an orthographic variant.

account of his works in 2:4–8, and culminate in his note at 2:10, that, "nothing which my eyes demanded did I keep out of their reach—I did not hold my heart back from any pleasure..." It does seem clear, however, that 2:3 includes a restatement of Qohelet's initial undertaking, to "...see where there is any good for humans, which they might do beneath the heavens for the limited duration of their lives." Combined with the fact that he has already pronounced on the uselessness of pleasure, this would seem to suggest that 2:3 marks a new start, not a continuation.

Accordingly, I take this verse to suggest that Qohelet is trying something different. The examinations in 1:13–2:2 are undertaken, essentially, in Qohelet's head: "I set my heart to inquiring and exploring through wisdom... let me set my heart to knowing... I said in my heart, 'Come on then...'" There is an experiential component to these examinations, insofar as Qohelet claims to have looked at all the achievements under the sun (1:14), to have acquired the wisdom which he studies (1:16), and probably to have sampled pleasure deliberately (2:1). The image we are given, however, is of a man in conversation with himself (cf. 1:16; 2:1), not in dialogue with the world around him. In 2:9–26, on the other hand, Qohelet's comments on work, wisdom and pleasure are all grounded firmly in the circumstances surrounding the work which he does in 2:4–8. He moves, in other words, from what is effectively an intellectual, armchair critique, through to a study of his own life experience. Indeed, he may well be undertaking this experience for the sake of his quest, and 2:3 is probably to be understood in terms of him taking the plunge: "With my heart I researched how to sustain[28] my body with wine and my guiding heart with wisdom, and how to keep a hold on wrongheadedness

---

28. משׁך is used principally of pulling or stretching, sometimes literally, of animals drawing a plough or cart, for example, or of humans pulling on a rope, fishing-line, or bow, but often also in the figurative senses of luring someone, or especially of prolonging some activity or situation (e.g. Exod 19:13; Jer 31:3). Although *HALOT* includes the sense "refresh," which Delitzsch, *Koheleth*, 241, understands here, this is now usually recognized to result from a misreading of *b. Ḥag.* 14a. Various emendations have been proposed, none of them very convincing, and among efforts to extend the sense of משׁך itself, Alan Corré's is surely the most memorable: he thinks Qohelet is referring to the drawing down of flesh over the penis to conceal circumcision; see "A Reference to Epispasm in Koheleth," *VT* 4 (1954): 416–18. I take the use of משׁך to be similar to that found in Job 24:22, Pss 36:11; 85:6; Prov 13:12; Isa 13:22; Jer 31:3; Ezek 12:25, 28: Qohelet is seeking to sustain ("prolong") his body, in the sense of keeping it going until he has achieved his aim. This retains the verb in a common meaning, but imputes a different function to the wine. G. R. Driver, "Problems and Solutions," *VT* 4 (1954): 225–45, esp. 225, reaches the same conclusion by a different route. For wine as a source of sustenance, see 2 Sam 16:2.

until I might see where there is any good for humans, which they might do beneath the heavens for the limited duration of their lives."

This new approach leads to conclusions about work and wisdom which are similar to those that Qohelet has already reached; indeed, 2:11 offers no significant advance on 1:14 in its dismissal of work, and 2:12–16 merely elaborates or explains the idea of wisdom as a source of pain. Arguably, Qohelet's views on pleasure remain consistent also: although he comes to commend it in 2:24, for reasons which we shall examine below, he does not actively contradict the conclusion of 2:2, that it is useless. This commendation perhaps reflects, rather, an acceptance that usefulness is not the only measure of value. Qohelet's shift in perspective, however, and the new application of his questions to his own life, rather than to the world at large, tend to affirm that the initial conclusions are not mere summaries of the more detailed account. Whether or not we are supposed to think literally in terms of two series of investigations, there do seem to be two stages involved in Qohelet's thinking, and the distinction is made clearest, perhaps, in the echo of 1:16 by 2:9: Qohelet starts out with all-surpassing wisdom, and then asks his questions again when he has achieved all-surpassing wealth (while explicitly retaining that wisdom).

b. *Qohelet's Business*

As we have seen, Qohelet does not seem to recount the establishment of his business in terms which are deliberately evocative of Solomon, and 2:4–8 is, at best, muted in its references to kingship more generally. From the outset, of course, the passage does seek to emphasize the greatness of the achievements involved, echoing the vocabulary of 1:14: if Qohelet is to pronounce on human achievements (* maʿăśîm*) generally, then it is to be from a position where he has accomplished great achievements (*maʿăśîm*) himself, just as his former pronouncements on wisdom in 1:16 were grounded in great personal wisdom. The statement about pleasure in 2:10 is probably to be understood in similar terms. To that extent, the story offers a basis for Qohelet to pronounce authoritatively on such matters, although there is no indication that he is exercising power to experiment freely with different sorts of achievements or sensations. Indeed, the story says much less about what Qohelet does with his wealth than about the way he gains it, and his pleasure in 2:10 is not linked explicitly to the luxury of his lifestyle so much as to his efforts.

For all the attempts to read luxury into this story, indeed, there is not much of it there. Qohelet makes buildings (of an unspecified sort) and plants vineyards (2:4). Any suspicion that the "gardens and parks" of 2:5

are merely decorative is swept aside by the immediate observation that he fills them with fruit trees, and Qohelet's pools of water are for irrigation of a timber-forest, not boating. Of course, none of this is going to create an unpleasant environment, but when it is followed by an account of his many cattle and flocks, in 2:7, it does appear that the business aspect is uppermost in Qohelet's mind. Associated with the statement about flocks is an observation about his acquisition of slaves, including some who were born as slaves in the household, and this draws attention to another aspect of the business: it is built to last. Qohelet is not growing annual crops like salad or grains, but vines, fruit and timber; he has animals and even slaves that will reproduce themselves, and a significant investment in infrastructure.

This becomes a crucial point in 2:18. Qohelet has dismissed all his achievements as *hebel* in 2:11, as we might expect by now. In 2:12–17, furthermore, his re-consideration of wisdom has led him to regret the effort he had spent on it, because the same fate comes to both wise and foolish: like each other, they die and are forgotten. This mention of death, though, leads him back to his work, with the realization that what he has accomplished must pass to somebody else, who may not be wise:

> And I hated all my business,[29] at which I had been the one working under
> the sun, that I shall leave it behind for the person who will be after me—and

29. The term עמל is clearly important to Qohelet, and the way he uses it suggests that it means more than just his "labour"—not least because here it is something that can be conveyed to another person. Whitley, *Koheleth*, 23, argues that the term must connote "wealth" or "gain," and other scholars have tried to make a case for some such sense: see, for example, Ginsberg, *Studies*, 3 n. 2; Dahood, "Phoenician Background," 3. Here, however, the man who will acquire Qohelet's עמל will not simply acquire it, but will have specific rights over it, and the עמל itself is not spoken of as something which might be dispersed, like a pile of gold, but as something which constitutes a specific entity. Rabbinic usage, furthermore, seems to link the term not to wealth *per se*, but to income, or sources of income. Rainey's idea that עמל refers to one's "trade" seems rather forced and limited, and it fits badly the use in Ps 105:44, which is often adduced as evidence for עמל meaning the product of work; see "A Second Look at Amal in Qoheleth," *Concordia Theological Monthly* 36 (1965): 805. That text, however, also seems to demonstrate that more than just wealth is meant: when God gives Israel the lands of the nations and they thereby "come into possession of the עמל of the peoples," it surely does not mean simply that they get to take whatever piles of money or crops are lying around. Rather, Israel takes over the fields, vineyards, and all the other mechanisms which have been produced by the work of the peoples, and which will now be worked to create their own produce. The key uses of עמל to indicate something other than labour do not point to it being simply the income derived from that labour after its completion: it is, rather, the continuing income, or sources of income, established by that labour. In

who knows whether he will be wise or wrong-headed, yet he will have the rights[30] over all my business, for which I have worked and for which I have been wise under the sun. This too is *hebel*. So I turned away, letting go of my concern[31] with all the business at which I had worked under the sun. For there may be a person whose work has been with wisdom and with knowledge and with determination,[32] but it is going to be to a person who

this context, the term would presumably refer to the flocks, groves, forests etc. which Qohelet had created—the infrastructure of his fortune.

30. The discussions over the technical use of the cognate Aramaic שׁלט have mostly focused upon questions of date; here we need note only that שׁלט ב- refers, at least in the Persian period and possibly beyond, to the possession of legal rights over something. See especially Douglas M. Gropp, "The Origin and Development of the Aramaic *šallīṭ* Clause," *JNES* 52 (1993): 31–36, and Dominic Rudman, "A Note on the Dating of Ecclesiastes," *CBQ* 61 (1999): 47–52.

31. יאשׁ is generally used in the Niphal, where it is used of giving up or abandoning an effort (1 Sam 27:1; Job 6:26; Isa 57:10; Jer 2:25; 18:12). In later Hebrew, the verb is found with direct objects, used of accepting that something is lost. There are no grounds for taking the verb to be causative, so that Qohelet is making his heart do something about his עמל, and the use of the Piel in this verse, although unparalleled, is unlikely to affect the sense significantly. The rabbinic usage, of accepting that something is lost, embraces the related Hithpael form, and the noun יאושׁ, used of accepting loss (see Jastrow), seems to be derived from the Piel itself. I take the object of the verb to be the expression לבי על כל־העמל, where לב על connotes the interest or attachment which Qohelet feels toward his עמל. There are similar uses at 2 Sam 14:1; Ezra 6:22; Jer 22:17; Mal 3:24 (*bis*).

32. כשׁרון is only found in Ecclesiastes, and it is not clear precisely what it means. Words from the root כשׁר are used in mishnaic Hebrew principally to indicate suitability or fitness, although the sense of "being pleasing," found at Esth 8:5, also persists, especially in the Targums. Some usage suggests, however, that there could be a connotation of vigour (as sometimes in Syriac ܟܫܪ, ܟܘܫܪܐ etc.), and in Sir 13:4 תשׁכר is used in contrast with תכרע. This may well be the sense of the verb when it is used by Qohelet at 11:6, and an understanding in those terms probably explains why G uses ἀνδρεία, literally "manliness," for כשׁרון here and on its other occurrences in 4:4 and 5:10, and for the verb at 10:10. The connotation of "success" or "prosperity" is often suggested but less firmly established. The usage in Ecclesiastes itself points in the direction of כשׁרון being something required for achievement, not something achieved as a result of work: here it is set alongside the mental qualities of wisdom and knowledge, applied to work, and in 4:4 it is aligned with an emotion; in 5:10, "looking on" is the only כשׁרון left to the owner as he sees his goods consumed. These suggest that כשׁרון is something in the mind, not the pocket. "Skill" is often suggested also, but it is not clear what sort of skill might be meant here which is not covered by חכמה or דעת, and the sense seems inappropriate for the other occurrences. It is possible that כשׁרון is the act of succeeding, but I think the reference is more probably to attitude and motivation, or perhaps aptitude, than to ability or achievement: such a meaning seems appropriate to 4:4, in particular, but also makes good sense in 5:10 and fits comfortably here.

has not worked on it that he will give it, (to be) what is his.[33] This too is *hebel*, and utterly bad. For what is there for a person in any of his business, and in the worrying of his heart about that at which he is doing the work under the sun? For through each of his days, pains and exasperation have been his job;[34] at night, too, his heart has not relaxed. This too, it is *hebel*. (2:18–23)

There seem to be several related issues here, although they all stem from the same situation, and each is characterized as *hebel*. In the first place, Qohelet comes to hate his business when he realizes that, although it was built up through his own industry and wisdom, it is ultimately going to be inherited by someone whose personal qualities are unknown and irrelevant: they will own what was his whether they are wise or foolish. Secondly, he seems to move from hating the business to disowning it, and ceasing to care about it, when he generalizes from his own resentment to the more universal problem that anyone who has worked hard and well for something is going to have to give it to somebody else who has done nothing for it. The third point is more or less an elaboration of this second, but shifts the emphasis: if it is a fact that the business will go to somebody else, then it is reasonable to ask what the creator of the business has gained for themselves in return for all the stress and trouble it has caused them.

The nature of the inheritance is important here: Qohelet is not talking about the distribution of cash from an estate, or the passing down of personal possessions. In his own case, from which he goes on to extrapolate a universal problem, he has created what should be, with minimal further work, a permanent and self-perpetuating business, from which the fruit, timber and animals merely need to be cropped or culled at an appropriate rate. He has made a fortune from this, and if somebody else takes it on, they will presumably make a fortune too. We may recall that Qohelet's account of his achievements is peppered with the expression "for me": he made what he made, and acquired what he acquired, explicitly for himself. Now, however, he has become aware that what he made is not really his, since ownership of it will pass to someone else, and that he has not really been working for himself. His further observation that the new owner may not be wise should not be understood, in

---

33. Literally, "(as) his portion," חלקו.
34. The sentence could also be construed "all his days were pains, and exasperation was his job," which is how G and Jerome have taken it; that reading is also indicated by the disjunctive accent on מכאבים in the Masoretic pointing. On the other hand, the sentence is followed by one in which those days clearly correspond to the expression בלילה, which means, unambiguously, "at night," and it seems likely that the statements are supposed to be in parallel.

this context, as a concern that they may mismanage the estate: the problem is that it will pass to them regardless of their personal qualities.

This is related to his second point. The fact that one person's accomplishments may pass to another implies that the possession of a successful business, with the accompanying lifestyle, is not necessarily a reward for wisdom or hard work: anyone can possess one if they are lucky enough, say, to inherit it. Correspondingly, a business may be handed over to somebody who has contributed nothing to it up to that point, and so has in no sense been making it theirs. Implicit in this, and in the question that begins Qohelet's third point, is a sort of disconnection between work and merit, on the one hand, and possession on the other: the effort and worry involved in work do not result in an actual gain for the worker, since what they make is not really theirs.

Of course, these concerns imply in themselves that Qohelet has a very particular idea of what constitutes gain and possession, and it seems likely that this idea is tied up with his concern for "profit." Indeed, 2:22 is broadly a restatement of the question asked back in 1:3: "What profit is there for a person in any of their business, at which they work beneath the sun?" It also incorporates, however, an idea that was stated at the beginning of Qohelet's quests, that human activity may constitute an actual loss, rather than just a failure to gain, and it seems likely that the "incalculable loss" mentioned in 1:15 resides in the effort that is expended by humans without a return. Indeed, the suspicion that God has assigned humans a "bad job," which apparently motivates Qohelet's quests, probably encompasses some similar understanding. As I noted earlier, if the expression used in 1:13 ('*inyan rā'*) has the same implication as in 5:13 (ET 5:14), and perhaps 4:8, referring to a deal or venture in which money has been lost, then in his characteristically commercial way, Qohelet is really asking whether, or suggesting that, what humans have been given to do is "bad business," or a losing deal. On his understanding, therefore, the profit and loss accounts for every human must include their expenditure of effort, but must exclude their lasting achievements, since these do not really belong to them.

c. *Pleasure and Providence*

This curious aspect of Qohelet's accounting is affirmed by the way he talks about pleasure in 2:10:

> My wisdom remained with me, moreover, and nothing which my eyes demanded did I keep out of their reach—I did not hold my heart back from any pleasure, for my heart was pleased in all my business, and this was my *ḥēleq* from all my business.

With his use of *ḥēleq*, "portion," Qohelet seems to be suggesting that there is something which humans can actually possess, and he uses the term similarly elsewhere with reference to pleasure or pleasurable experiences (see especially 2:10; 3:22; 5:17–18 [ET 5:18–19]; 9:9). Since he is going to dismiss his work as *hebel* in the very next verse, it seems that a *ḥēleq* is not the sort of gain which Qohelet is seeking from it, but the idea that humans may have a "share" or "portion" from what they do during their lifetimes would seem not to be incompatible with his idea that they cannot gain a profit.[35] It is apparently not something available to them after death (9:6), and this sort of "portion" seems not to be material, but emotional or experiential, so it appears that Qohelet is not talking about the "lifetime interest" which an individual may have in what they (temporarily) own, but rather in the benefit that they may feel as a consequence. As I suggested earlier, it may not be inappropriate to think in terms of a dividend, and this may be more of Qohelet's commercial language.

Be that as it may, the fact that the experience of pleasure from work and ownership does not seem to constitute "profit" for Qohelet reinforces a sense that his idea of proper gain involves both permanent, exclusive possession, and possession of something material. He wants, in effect, to be able to take his business with him when he departs the world. The impossibility of such profit will lead him later to characterize pleasure, and one's "portion," as the best that can be achieved, and the ability to enjoy one's work will play, as we shall see, an important role in his thought. When he returns to enjoyment at the end of ch. 2, however, it is not clear that these ideas have yet crystallized, and the point may be rather different:

---

35. A number of studies have emphasized this distinction between "profit" and "portion" in Qohelet's thought. For example, Diethelm Michel, *Untersuchungen zur Eigenart des Buches Qohelet* (BZAW 183; Berlin: de Gruyter, 1989), 19–20, rejects the understanding of חלק as a partial gain, and observes that it is something passing and transitory, while יתרון, which Qohelet asks about, is something permanent—he puts that distinction nicely in terms of 3:1–15: "*ḥēlœq* korrespondiert *'et, jitrôn* dagegen *'olām!*" (p. 20). Ludger Schwienhorst-Schönberger, *Nicht im Menschen Gründet das Glück (Koh 2,24): Kohelet im Spannungsfeld jüdischer Weisheit und hellenistischer Philosophie* (Herders Biblische Studien 2; Freiburg im Breisgau: Herder, 1994), 68, remarks that "Kohelet hat Freude erfahren. Dies ist sein Anteil (חֵלֶק), aber kein Gewinn." See also Marie Maussion, *Le mal, le bien et le jugement de Dieu dans le livre de Qohélet* (OBO 190; Fribourg: Editions Universitaires; Göttingen: Vandenhoeck & Ruprecht, 2003), 177–78.

There is no good in the person who eats[36] and drinks and lets himself take pleasure in his business. This too have I observed, that it is from the hand of God, who eats and who worries apart from me.[37] For to a person who seems right to him[38] he has given wisdom and knowledge and pleasure; while to one who is wrong he has given the job of piling and accumulating to give to one who seems right—this too is *hebel*, and wishing for the wind. (2:24–26)

Of course, there are various facets of the text and translation which are open to debate here, not least because the passage has often been understood in terms of Qohelet's later statements about pleasure. Following directly on from his rejection of his business, though, and his despair at the wastefulness of human effort, it seems more likely that this concluding section marks a return to the question that began the quests in 1:13, and to the issue of divine dispensation.

Since possession is disconnected from personal qualities, anyone like him, who can feed themselves from their work and even enjoy it, is doing so not because of any inherent virtues: food and worry are

36. In 8:15, when Qohelet suggests that there is nothing good except eating, drinking, and taking pleasure, the expression used is ... אין־טוב לאדם ... כי אם־לאכול, while 3:22 declares that אין טוב מאשר ישמח האדם. We must be wary of attempting to harmonize the various statements, and it is probably a reminiscence of 8:15 (and perhaps of 6:12) which has led some Hebrew mss to read לאדם in place of the more difficult באדם here; this may also have happened in the source-text of G. Most commentators seek to emend the next word from שיאכל to משיאכל, but of the similar texts commonly cited in support of emendation, only 3:22 uses the comparative מ, while 3:12 and 8:15 both use כי אם, and the original reading of G here was probably ὃ φάγεται, which supports the Masoretic reading. There are no solid grounds, then, for emendation.

37. M here reads חוץ ממני, and is supported by T בר־מיני and V *ut ego*, but it seems apparent that G πάρεξ αὐτοῦ, S ܠܒܪ ܡܢܗ, and Jerome's *sine illo* in his commentary all reflect חוץ ממנו, with a third-person suffix (which is also found in a handful of Hebrew mss); these are not necessarily theological interpretations seeking to imply reliance on God, and it is difficult to choose between "חוץ me" and "חוץ him" on purely text-critical grounds. The normal meaning of חוץ, however, is "except" or "besides" rather than "without," and the most obvious sense with a third-person suffix would have been "Who eats…except God?"—hardly what can have been intended. The implication here is probably "It is up to God who gets to eat and drink and worry when I am gone," referring to the previous problem of his estate passing to another.

38. Literally who is "good before his face"; the expression avoids a simplistic contrast between inherent goodness and badness, but places the emphasis on God's attitude toward the individuals; see K. Galling, "Kohelet-Studien," *ZAW* 50 (1932): 276–99, esp. 289.

parcelled out by God.[39] This, of course, meets the point that an heir, deserving or undeserving, may be prospering from a business they did not build. Correspondingly, "right" and "wrong" are probably not to be taken as moral judgments in 2:26, but as statements of suitability: God assigns abilities and tasks to the appropriate individuals, and those who are inappropriate for one role may be set to another, serving those who are appropriate.[40]

Qohelet began his search with a perception that individuals do not retain what they gain, and a corresponding suspicion that God has set humans to work at activities which can never generate a profit for them, to set against all their efforts. In the course of ch. 2, though, he not only affirms this idea (while conceding that they may receive some modest return in the form of pleasure), but comes to the more radical conclusion that there is a problem not only in the loss of their achievements at death, but in the subsequent ownership of those achievements by others, which implies that ownership and prosperity need have no direct connection with personal ability or virtue. This in turn, of course, informs his ideas about the divine assignment of tasks: individual human roles are assigned not on the basis of individual virtues, but in response to divine requirements.

3. *Times and Time (3:1–15)*

In 3:9 Qohelet asks again a question similar to that which he posed in 1:3, and in 3:10 he once again picks up the theme of 1:13, declaring that, "I have seen the work which God has given to humans to work at." These verses are both very close to the language of the earlier verses. Shortly afterwards, in 3:12, he seems similarly to evoke the conclusion of 2:24—"I know that there is no good in [humans]…"—while 3:15 is a clear echo of 1:9–10: "It already is, whatever is, and what is to be already is…" It seems undeniable, therefore, that in 3:9–15 Qohelet is still dealing with the issues raised by the first two chapters, and, as we shall see, it seems that these verses serve directly as a response to some of the problems which they have raised. Since 3:16, furthermore, moves on both to a different topic and to the more disconnected style that characterizes the rest of the monologue, there are clearly good reasons to see that verse as marking a break.

39. So, for example, W. E. Staples, "'Profit' in Ecclesiastes," *JNES* 4 (1945): 87–96, esp. 90.
40. Similar language is used in 7:26, the context of which is very obscure. Here the deadly woman "whose heart is snares and whose hands are fetters" will catch whoever is wrong, while whoever seems right to God will escape her.

Qohelet, of course, frequently harks back to points that he has already made, so the fact of him doing so in 3:9–15 is not remarkable in itself. The concentration of such recollections, though, and the general continuity with what has preceded, suggest that it would not be inappropriate to link these verses to the material in chs. 1–2, and that all the material before 3:16 can be understood in terms of a single, coherent discussion. This raises some important questions, however, about the place of 3:1–8—Qohelet's famous list of times, which is often treated as the start of a new topic.

a. *A Time for Every Matter (3:1–8)*
Whether or not it is a poem, as such, Qohelet's list is a memorable and evocative set-piece, and it has lent itself to many interpretations over the years:

> For everything an occasion, and a time for every matter beneath heaven:
> A time for birth[41] and a time for dying;
>   a time for planting and a time for pulling out what is planted;
> A time for killing and a time for curing;
>   a time for wrecking and a time for building;
> A time for weeping and a time for laughing;
>   a time of mourning and a time of dancing;[42]
> A time for throwing stones down and a time of gathering stones up;
>   a time for embracing and a time for avoiding an embrace;
> A time for seeking out and a time for letting slip;
>   a time for keeping and a time for throwing out;
> A time for ripping and a time for stitching;
>   a time for being silent and a time for talking;
> A time for loving and a time for hating;
>   a time of war and a time of peace.

It should not be considered wholly out of its context, however, and the next verses pick up the theme of time:

> What is the lasting gain from the worker[43] in that at which he toils? I have seen the work which God has given to humans to work at: he has made everything fine[44] in its time; he has also put "forever" into their

---

41. Either "being born" or "giving birth": the Hebrew does not express a distinction, although it was open to the author to indicate one or the other.
42. The absence of ־ל is probably euphonic, although it emphasizes that these are not purpose clauses. See below.
43. The analogous use without ־ל at 5:8 (ET 5:9) suggests that this should be the יתרון derived from the worker, rather than that which accrues to them; contrast 1:3; 2:22; 5:15 (ET 5:16); 6:11.
44. Even in quite late biblical usage, יפה refers to beauty (e.g. Esth 2:7), and when God makes something יפה in Ezek 31:9, it is its physical perfection which

heart,[45] for lack of that which no human can discover: the achievement
which God has achieved from start right through to finish. (3:9–11)

This subsequent discussion presents notorious difficulties of interpretation, but the clearest section in a difficult passage is Qohelet's claim that
"[God] has made everything fine in its time," which seems to summarize
the point of the preceding list, and offers an important key to its interpretation.

The list itself is a little less consistent and symmetrical than it appears
at first glance. The different activities are usually described using a verb
in the infinitive with a prefixed preposition *l-*. This construction can have
a variety of senses, including the expression of purpose, so that we could
understand the list to be saying that "(there is) a time to do *x* and a time
to do *y*." Correspondingly, we might suppose the point to be about acting
at the right time (compare, e.g., Hos 10:12): Qohelet would then be
evoking some traditional understanding that there are correct times for
every action, which the wise man must learn to recognize.[46] The obvious
problem with that interpretation, of course, is that the very first actions
expressed are actions over which humans generally have little or no
control—birth and death—so they would seem to be a curious way of
establishing that message.[47] Furthermore, the same construction is not
used throughout: the preposition is missing before a number of the

provokes envy. In later usage, it can connote goodness or value more generally, and
it seems to be used this way in 5:17, where it stands in parallel with טוב. There is no
reason to suppose, however, that it ever took on the specific sense "appropriate" or
"fitting." The statement here is clearly not simply aesthetic, but it is equally not
explicitly moral or functional: Qohelet is saying no more than that all things have an
appreciable, even admirable, value in their time.

45. I shall not even attempt to go into the many debates which surround this
expression. See below for my own understanding.

46. Several commentators have seen behind the list an ancient "science of times";
as Crenshaw, *Ecclesiastes*, 92, puts it succinctly: "Ancient sages believed that there
was a right time and a wrong time for everything, and they devoted considerable
energy to discerning proper times. Qohelet concurs in the view that everything has
its own moment (3:1–9), but he insists that humans cannot know those times (3:10–
15), for God withholds that information." Von Rad, among others, sees this as the
essential meaning of the list, even though it has been given a different sense in
context by Qohelet; see his *Weisheit in Israel* (Neukirchen–Vluyn: Neukirchener
Verlag, 1970), 182–88; ET *Wisdom in Israel* (London: SCM, 1972), 138–43. Such an
interest in times is manifest, of course, in ancient astrological and divinatory
practices; it is not, however, a distinct or prominent topic in advice literature.

47. Although Joseph Blenkinsopp, "Ecclesiastes 3:1–15: Another Interpretation,"
JSOT 20 (1995): 55–64, suggests that the reference to death may in fact be to
suicide, and that Qohelet is quoting a poem inspired by Stoicism.

infinitives, and the list ends with nouns, placed in a simple construct relationship with the word for "time." These difficulties suggest that we should not read expressions of purpose here, but expressions of possession: each of the activities has its own time. This is apparently the point also of 3:11: God has made each thing fine in its own time, not made times which are fine to do each thing. His emphasis here is not on there being a time which is appropriate or pre-ordained, then, but on the essential right-ness of every activity when it happens, because it happens as part of something larger, under divine control. This may well presume some sort of determinism, but it is not itself a statement about the pre-ordination of events.

That may prompt us, indeed, to recall that Qohelet has been discussing divine determination in the verses which immediately precede his list, 2:24–26, where he reached the conclusion that human activities are assigned by God according to his own criteria, so that this list of human actions is sandwiched between statements about divine activity. The subsequent statement that God has made things fine in their time, furthermore, is linked in 2:10–11 to Qohelet's claim that he has "seen the work which God has given to humans to work at." The context of the list suggests, therefore, that Qohelet is using it in some way to talk about the activities which humans are given by God to undertake, and on that reading he appears to be saying that whatever humans do is in some sense right when they do it, or at least accords with the divine will.

This point is emphasized by pairing together actions which are opposites, and if there is some tendency for each pair to set a more positive or creative action in contrast to one which is more destructive in nature, there is nothing in the list for which most readers would find it difficult to imagine a suitable context. The implications, however, are rather more radical than the actions listed might suggest, because if it is true that absolutely all actions have some place in a divine purpose, then that means that the most terrible crimes must also be fine in their time, and that God has in some sense appointed their perpetration. If everything that happens is in accordance with the divine will when it happens, then nothing can stand inherently in contradiction to that will. Correspondingly, if deeds are "good" or "bad" in any sense at all, it cannot be in the sense that they contradict God's wishes on the occasion that they happen. On the other hand, the fact that deeds have times must be considered to impose a limit as well, so that actions (considered in the abstract) are not inherently or perpetually fine.[48] Correspondingly, an *act*

---

48.   The type and degree of determinism in this passage has been much discussed, and, I think, the notion of time or occasion much over-emphasized. In *A Time to*

of theft may be "right" when it happens, in terms of its part in something greater, but that does not make *theft* right.

b. *Humans and the Divine Purpose (3:10–15)*

Qohelet's subsequent statements do not engage directly with such implications, although his later discussions may suggest that he is not unaware of them. Instead, he pursues the consequences of all this for an understanding of human activities, and when in 3:9 he picks up the earlier question of 1:3, he does so with an interesting change to the wording. Literally, 1:3 read "What profit (is there) for the human in all his work…?," but 3:9 now seems to say, "What profit (is there) *from* the doer in that at which he works?"[49] Where 1:3 asked what profit humans could gain for themselves, in other words, 3:9 asks whether any human action can produce a profit at all, with the apparent implication that it cannot. The reason for this is stated shortly afterwards, in 3:14–15, when Qohelet re-states his idea that there can be nothing new in the world: if nothing can be added to what is already in existence, then no human action can contribute anything substantial; if nothing can be taken away, of course, it also follows that humans cannot remove anything to keep for themselves:

> I know that all which God achieves is what will exist forever:[50] there is no adding to it, and there is no subtracting from it—and God has achieved

Tear Down, 197–98, Michael Fox distinguishes his current from his earlier views in terms of "a less rigid determinism" (p. 197)—he no longer adheres to the opinion, popular among commentators, that every action has a pre-ordained moment at which it will inevitably happen, but thinks rather in terms of appropriate occasions. However, "This is not to say that in Qohelet…time is identical with its content. It is not the act of sewing that makes a certain moment 'a time to sew.' The Catalogue of Times would be a tautology if a 'time to sew' were merely any moment when someone happens to be sewing" (p. 198). I think, though, to use Fox's example, Qohelet is saying that "when someone is sewing, then sewing is good, because everything that humans do is the right thing to do when they do it; when they rip something, that too is right for the same reason. Whatever the morality or otherwise of the human motives, no action can be other than good when it happens as part of a divinely-approved plan or process."

49. See the note to the translation, above.

50. Literally, "this will be for ever." Fox, *A Time to Tear Down*, 212, is right to criticize the view of Jenni, "Das Wort ʿōlām im Alten Testament," *ZAW* 64 (1952): 197–248; 65 (1953): 1–35, that עולם can mean unchanging (*ZAW* 65: 22). He himself, though, translates "is always what will be," which elides two different meanings of the English "always": עולם can mean "forever," but can most probably not mean "on every occasion," as he wants it to here.

[humans'] fear before him.⁵¹ It already is whatever is,⁵² and what is to be already is, and God will seek what is pursued.⁵³ (3:14–15)

First, though, Qohelet states the reasons for the difficulty that humans experience in comprehending their situation:

> I have seen the work which God has given to humans to work at: he has made everything fine in its time; he has also put "forever" into their heart, for lack of that which no human can discover: the achievement which God has achieved from start right through to finish.⁵⁴ I know that there is no good in them⁵⁵ except taking pleasure and doing good⁵⁶ in one's life, and also that every person who⁵⁷ eats and drinks and takes pleasure in all his business—this is a payment⁵⁸ from God. (3:10–13)

51. Probably not "God has acted *so that* they may fear": the relative -שׁ is more probably serving to substantivize the clause than to introduce an expression of purpose or consequence, although it is apparently taken that way in the versions.

52. The likely sense is that "what God has achieved is already whatever exists."

53. The Hebrew is fairly straightforward, but the meaning obscure. I think the emphasis may be on the subject: whatever things (plans, outcomes?) are to be pursued in this world, it is God who does the pursuing.

54. See above for notes on the translation of 3:9–11.

55. There are no text-critical grounds for emendation of the preposition בּ (cf. 2:24) to ל. The expression "in them" is odd, though, when the surrounding verses talk of "the human" in the singular. Some commentators have tried to make "them" the events or divine action mentioned previously, but we have a plural suffix on בלבם in the previous verse as well as on בם here, along with a plural subject for שׁיראו in 3:14, all without explicit specification, and Qohelet is most probably switching loosely between a representative "human" and the collective idea of "humans."

56. The juxtaposition with לשׂמוח has led many commentators to suppose that the sense of לעשׂות טוב here is not "doing good," but "doing well"—experiencing prosperity or enjoyment. Elsewhere, however, Qohelet apparently contrasts יעשׂה טוב with יחטא (7:20), and note in 2:3 the quest for a טוב לבני האדם אשׁר יעשׂו.

57. The construction is difficult. If we read -שׁ as a simple relative here, it is difficult to find a reference for היא at the end of the verse; if we take it to be sub-stantivizing the clause which follows (so, e.g., Seow, *Ecclesiastes*, 164—his citation of Whitley is puzzling, though, as the latter ventures no opinion), that problem is solved, but then כל האדם becomes stranded instead.

58. The conventional translation for מתת here and in 5:18 (ET 5:19) is "gift," but the Hebrew probably bears no implication that what is offered has not been earned. In Sir 42:7, where the context is trade or financial accounting, a מתת is an expenditure or disbursement, as opposed to a receipt (לקח), and the מתת promised in 1 Kgs 13:7 is a financial payment or reward; cf. also Prov 25:14; Ezek 46:5, 11. The noun appears in Phoenician for an offering made to a deity (*KAI* 29:2), but the scope of the term is clearly broader than "gift," and it commonly implies payment or compensation.

There are many difficulties in this passage, and it has been the subject of much discussion, but two points do seem to be clear. First, as Qohelet has already claimed most explicitly in 1:13, humans are in some sense employed by God: they are given things to do, and the pleasure which they may achieve is a form of compensation—this is, after all, the only benefit to himself that Qohelet could find in his own work. Secondly, humans are not able to discover the whole of the achievement of God, to which their own efforts presumably contribute. This would seem to be evoking the point made back in 1:4–11, about the inadequacy of the transient human perspective, rather than a declaration that God has deliberately or actively obscured what he is doing. Qohelet also remarks, though, that God has in some sense "put 'forever'" into human hearts. The idea of putting something into somebody's heart is not uncommon in biblical usage, and the expression is generally used of inspiring people with an ability or with a desire for something. How this relates to the human ignorance of divine activity is much debated, but the Hebrew most obviously suggests that God gave humans a desire for perpetuity either without also giving them knowledge, or as compensation for their lack of knowledge. Correspondingly, as 3:14 goes on to point out, humans like Qohelet are able to "know" that "all which God achieves is what will exist forever," even without knowing the content of that achievement, and it is in this way, perhaps, that God inspires human fear of him: they know there is something to know, but they don't know what it is.

When he responds to the question of 3:9 in the closing verses, therefore, Qohelet has already established the subordination of humanity to the divine purpose, and this goes hand-in-hand with the human inability to make any substantial change to the world. His closing words are a little obscure, but it may be the emphasis, suggested by the word order, which is important for understanding them. In a world where humans accomplish nothing for themselves, and which is ultimately unalterable, "(it is) God (who) will seek what is (to be) pursued."

4. *Summary and Conclusions*

In the course of the first three chapters, Qohelet presents three pieces for discussion, pieces which are formally separate and differ from each other in many ways, but which comprise the longest continuous discussions in the book. These passages also seem to draw on each other, and together offer an outline of the basic questions and understandings which he brings to his examinations of the world.

The first passage, in 1:4–11, portrays the world as a place of endless processes, within which recurrent achievements mark no final consummation. Humans each occupy this world only briefly, and so can be misled by what they see, and can achieve no overall understanding of it. In the second part, 1:12–2:26, Qohelet turns to his own experience, or at least a version of it, recounting his attempts to discover just what it is that humans can gain from the work that God has given them to do in this world. These attempts, based initially on the considerable wisdom which he has achieved, culminate in his establishment of a prosperous business and a wealthy lifestyle for himself, and he realizes that he can at least achieve pleasure from that work, even if it does not offer the more lasting profit which he seeks. He is shocked, however, both by the further realization that his wisdom will bring him no benefit, and by the perception that what he made was not really for himself, since it will go on to be the property of another when he dies; nothing, he realizes, actually belongs permanently to its owner, and ownership is not a mark of ability or virtue. Rather, tasks and possessions are assigned to individuals by God, according to whatever distributions suit him. In the third part, finally, Qohelet sets all human actions within the framework of these divine purposes: everything that is done is what should be done at that time, and has been in some way appointed by God. Humans themselves can contribute nothing, and can take nothing out of the world: they are aware of being temporary, but have no insight into the whole of divine action as it unfolds. So, again, the world is unchanging, and God is the only real actor within it.

If there is a single theme in all this, it is the subordination of human actions to much greater processes, which it is beyond the human capacity to comprehend. This aspect of the discussion is less evident in Qohelet's memoir than elsewhere, but it is the bigger issue which his concerns about inheritance merely epitomize. In a world where things do not simply start or stop, everything has a permanence of sorts, except human life and possession. The story of Qohelet's despair serves the important purpose, though, of highlighting and personalizing the significance of this for humans' understanding of what they are doing. Although 1:10–11 offered a general indication of the ways we might be misled, Qohelet's story exemplifies the problem: he put a lot of effort into working for himself, only to find that he was ultimately working for others and keeping nothing—contributing to the greater processes, and not permanently to his own prosperity.

It is in ch. 3, though, that the implications are drawn out most fully: human actions are individually fitted to a divine understanding of what should be happening, and humans are somehow employed by God. Qohelet has nothing here to say about predestination or about the implications of this for free will (issues which we shall turn to much later ourselves), and his point is rather that we are not acting on our own behalf—that everything we do is tied up with something much greater, about which we know only the little that we can each see. There is also no suggestion in any of this that the world is unreal: indeed, its reality is beyond question, but it is also, to a great extent, beyond our grasp. The situation of humans leads them to experience and to understand so little of what is happening that they are liable to misapprehend what they do see, and when they act in accordance with that misapprehension, thinking that they are working on their own behalf, and blind to both the future and the past, they may face significant disappointments.

Chapter 3

LIVING IN QOHELET'S WORLD

The world which Qohelet portrays in the first three chapters is one that extends far beyond human lives and comprehension, but he will have little else to say about it directly in the rest of the book. Rather, he shifts his focus more specifically to the ways in which this situation affects humans, and to the ways in which they are inclined to misapprehend it. At the same time, the book becomes much more difficult structurally: it is not always easy to discern or to inter-relate the particular discussions which follow, although it is clear that certain points are picked up and elaborated repeatedly. If we are to consider the key themes and ideas in the rest of the book, therefore, we cannot do so just by following Qohelet's own scheme—if, indeed, he has one.[1]

1. As I remarked above, broader questions of structure are outside the scope of this study, but it may be clear by this point that I am sympathetic to Michel's idea that the first part of the monologue, up to 3:15, serves as a basic presentation of Qohelet's ideas, and that this largely answers the initial questions which he has posed (*Untersuchungen*, 1–83). I am also open to the idea that there is a broader structure in the book, but not convinced that it has been identified, or, given the very many opinions expressed, that it can ever be identified beyond doubt. The ingenious studies by Addison Wright are perhaps the best-known attempt to elaborate a precise structure, and these began with "The Riddle of the Sphinx: The Structure of the Book of Qoheleth," *CBQ* 30 (1968): 313–34, which focused on the repetition of different phrases and motifs. The situation is less tidy than he suggests, but it is possible that his observations do point to a significant principle of arrangement in the latter part of the book, at least, and they have rightly been taken seriously in some subsequent work. His subsequent articles should be distinguished from that. "The Riddle of the Sphinx Revisited: Numerical Patterns in the Book of Qoheleth," *CBQ* 42 (1980): 35–51, and "Additional Numerical Patterns in Qoheleth," *CBQ* 45 (1983): 32–43, seek numerical patterns, noting such things as the fact that the number of verses in the book is 186, which is five times the number of occurrences of *hebel*, which is itself equivalent to the numerical value of *hebel* (see "Revisited," 45–46)—except that there are 38 occurrences of *hebel* (Wright thinks one should be omitted from 5:6 or 9:9, he does not care which), and that five times 37 is actually

Equally, though, it is difficult just to disentangle the various things which Qohelet has to say, as though they stood in isolation from one another. Although it is far from being a structured argument, his discussion is in part cumulative, and sometimes involves building on his previous statements about one topic in the light of what he has just said about another. Merely assembling and combining his thoughts on any single subject seems likely, then, to over-simplify, or even to misrepresent them. Accordingly, I shall attempt in this chapter to follow certain of these ideas through the book, before returning to a general discussion of their place in his thought, and of some broader points which he is apparently trying to make.

1. *The Place of Pleasure*

As we saw above, Qohelet found pleasure in his own work (2:10), and considered this pleasure the "portion" that was his from that work. At the end of the account in ch. 2, furthermore, he associated the ability to take such enjoyment from work with a sort of divine dispensation. This was picked up again in 3:10–13, in the context of Qohelet's discussion about the role of humans in the world, where the ability to "eat, drink and take pleasure in all one's business" was characterized as a payment or reward from God. Later, in 5:17–19 (ET 5:18–20), Qohelet again goes on to commend eating, drinking, and pleasure in work, once more speaking of such pleasure as a "portion," and seeing it in terms of divine reward. These references to portion and reward are absent in the otherwise similar commendations at 8:15 and in 9:7–10, but in 3:22 there is also a simpler affirmation that one should take pleasure in work, because that is one's portion. Although there are differences of emphasis and expression, therefore, this is a motif which runs throughout Qohelet's monologue, and his call to enjoy life is undoubtedly the most famous aspect of his message. To the extent that such a call is also interwoven with ideas

185 (who cares about a difference of one?), and that the figure of 186 is anyway reached only by leaving a lot of verses out from the beginning and end, and that the sytem of versification is anyway a late imposition on the text. This work has been less influential, for self-evident reasons, and has unfortunately lessened the impact of the first article. Among the many other suggestions that have been made, Backhaus' is plausible, and has been accepted by Seow in his commentary (*Ecclesiastes*, 46–47); see F. J. Backhaus, *"Den Zeit und Zufall trifft sie alle": Studien zur Komposition und zum Gottesbild im Buch Qohelet* (Bonner Biblische Beiträge 83; Frankfurt am Main: Hain, 1993). It says something for the character of the problem, however, that the very fact of agreement between two scholars should be noteworthy.

about age and death in 11:7–10, before his closing account, we might even say that the need to take pleasure in life is the principal conclusion which Qohelet draws from his discussion as a whole.[2]

a. *Pleasure and Possession*

On each occasion when he commends enjoyment, however, Qohelet sets that enjoyment over and against something more negative, and here his presentation is less consistent. In 2:10, of course, enjoyment was what he could himself gain from his business, when nothing else was ultimately his own, and this is probably the theme also in 5:17–19 (ET 5:18–20). Where ch. 2 later extrapolated from Qohelet's personal experience, here his commendation follows the anecdote of a man who has lost everything in some bad deal (5:12–16 [ET 5:13–17]), but again draws a more general conclusion. The unfortunate man will leave the world as naked as he came, carrying nothing with him—but that is, of course, what will happen to every human. Just as that man should have enjoyed his work instead

---

2.   That is not to say that I find myself inclined to support the view of Qohelet's monologue as ultimately joyful, espoused most famously in R. N. Whybray, "Qohel-eth, Preacher of Joy," *JSOT* 7 (1982): 87–98; cf. especially N. Lohfink, "Qoheleth 5:17–19—Revelation by Joy," *CBQ* 52 (1990): 625–35, and, at greater length, Maussion, *Le mal, le bien*. The view has been opposed most directly by Antoon Schoors, in an article which appeared in two different versions: "Qoheleth: The Ambiguity of Enjoyment," in *The Bright Side of Life* (ed. Ellen van Wolde; Concilium 2000/4; London: SCM, 2000), 35–41, and "L'ambiguità della gioia in Qohelet," in *Il Libro del Qohelet. Tradizione, redazione, teologia* (ed. Giuseppe Bellia and Angelo Passaro; Cammini nello Spirito. Biblica 44; Milan: Paoline, 2001), 276–92. Schoors points out, rightly I think, that Qohelet wants a profit and is obliged to settle for a portion; and he does not regard this as significant or adequate. Some interesting attempts have been made to find a *rapprochement* between the two positions. Eunny P. Lee, *The Vitality of Enjoyment in Qohelet's Theological Rhetoric* (BZAW 353; Berlin: de Gruyter, 2005), aligns the calls to enjoyment with Qohelet's emphasis on fear of God, portraying them as, in essence, a religious duty. Very differently, Bertrand Pinçon, *L'enigme du bonheur: Etude sur le sujet du bien dans le livre de Qohélet* (VTSup 119; Leiden: Brill, 2008), puts a strong case for understanding a development in Qohelet's attitude to pleasure, so that he moves from resignation to a positive affirmation of joy in the second half of the book. As he acknowledges, this conclusion is close to the position reached in a much briefer study by Gianto, "The Theme of Enjoyment in Qohelet," *Biblica* 73 (1992): 528–33, who speaks of enjoyment as "an important yet muted theme" in the first stage of Qohelet's message (p. 531), and the position reached by Niccacci, in his studies "Qohelet o la gioia come fatica e dono di Dio a chi lo teme," *Liber Annuus* 52 (2002): 29–102, and "Qohelet. Analisi sintattica, traduzione, composizione," *Liber Annuus* 54 (2004): 53–94. If these scholars are right, their conclusion tends to affirm the experiential, narrative aspect of the monologue as a whole.

of spending his days in darkness, exasperation, pain and anger, so every-body who is allotted by God both prosperity and the ability to enjoy it should accept that divine reward. In both places, then, Qohelet sets his commendation of pleasure over against the transitoriness of human possessions, and the potential pain involved in gaining them.

Chapters 2 and 5 also emphasize that the ability to take pleasure is in some way dependant on God, and that theme is pursued in ch. 6, imme-diately after the commendation of pleasure at the end of ch. 5. In 6:1–6, Qohelet pictures another man, who has in fact been granted the wealth which we have just been told God may allot (6:2; cf. 5:18 [ET 5:19]). He has not, however, been granted the corresponding ability to take advan-tage of those possessions: it is a foreigner (perhaps, that is, someone quite different)[3] who will get to "consume" them. This is a terrible thing, but Qohelet goes on to imagine worse: a man who has a hundred children and a long life, but finds no satisfaction or even a final resting place. Where his earlier example of a ruined man was left in the same position as a newborn baby, this man is actually worse off than a miscarried child, who has known nothing, but at least has rest. Ending hyperbolically, Qohelet declares that even a life of two thousand years has no value without enjoyment, as ultimately everybody is going to the same place.[4]

In these passages, then, Qohelet commends pleasure over against wealth or other things in life which might commonly be considered desirable. The fact of death renders such things meaningless, and the

---

3. Robert Salters, "Notes on the Interpretation of Qoh 6:2," *ZAW* 91 (1979): 282–89, argues that the איש נכרי should be understood as someone from another family, as opposed to an heir who was the man's own child. On the hyperbolic use of נכרי, see Weeks, *Instruction and Imagery*, 199: such use in family contexts (Gen 31:15; Ps 69:9 [ET 69:8]) could indeed imply treatment of somebody as though they were not a part of the family, but Job 19:14–15 seems to extend the sense further, and we might understand it here as in Prov 27:2, "Let it be a stranger who praises you, and not your own mouth: someone quite different (נכרי), and not your own lips."

4. Fox, *A Time to Tear Down*, 129–30, suggests that 6:2 "shows that God's 'enabling' a man to consume his wealth means simply that God does not take it away from him." That verse is ambiguous taken by itself—it is not clear whether his possessions are enjoyed by someone else and not him because they are taken away from him, or because he finds no pleasure in them while he owns them, but then somebody else enjoys them. In the following verses, however, it is clear that Qohelet's theme is the contrast between possession of good things (children, long life) and the failure to enjoy them. On the interpretation of 6:2 by modern com-mentators in this respect, see Françoise Laurent, *Les biens pour rien en Qohéleth 5,9–6,6 ou La traversée d'un contraste* (BZAW 323; Berlin: de Gruyter, 2002), 97–99, who herself emphasizes that the verse does not specify the mechanism of removal.

effort, pain and lack of rest in life make it a bad experience, whatever one may own, if the discomfort is not neutralized by pleasure—5:19 (ET 5:20) presents joy as a way in which God distracts humans from their lives.[5] This is effectively a development of Qohelet's more fundamental idea, that we do not own our possessions, and that enjoyment of what we do is our only "portion." As we observed earlier, though, he also believes that our roles in life are allotted to us according to divine purposes beyond our comprehension, and this idea is also developed here, in a rather different direction. If possessions are essentially props for those roles, allocated by God even to those who have seemingly had to work for them, then they exist at the level of the divine plans; enjoyment, on the other hand, is internal and individual, even if it is, Qohelet suggests, something which itself must be enabled by God. Consequently, it may happen that God assigns wealth but not the ability to enjoy it, because these are quite separate things, and somebody may therefore have all the outward trappings of divine blessing—prosperity, children and long life—but lack the inward gift of enjoyment. As ever in Qohelet's world, appearances may be deceptive.

b. *Pleasure, Ignorance and Judgment*

Such deceptiveness appears to be a key issue in ch. 8, when Qohelet's commendation of pleasure arises not in the context of possessions, but out of a reflection on divine justice. The beginning of this, in 8:10, is rather obscure, but the general point of 8:10–11 clear enough: the wicked enjoy praise and provoke imitation because they are not seen to be punished. Qohelet affirms that ultimately they will be judged and their lives cut short, even if they seem to prolong them, and expresses confidence in the well-being of those who fear God (8:12–13). He concedes, however, that there is a *hebel* in the world, in that the righteous may appear to suffer the proper fate of the wicked, while the wicked may

---

5. The fact that מענה can be derived from verbs referring either to occupation or response has led a number of commentators, since medieval times, to understand this verse as a less theologically problematic statement that God responds to humans by giving them joy; so, for example, Lohfink, "Qoheleth 5:17–19." There is a text-critical issue here: G and the Syriac have apparently read מענהו, with a suffix, but both interpretations can be sustained even if the text is emended, as *BHS* and *BHQ* prefer; indeed, the understanding "occupy" is probably easier. Judging by the reading of G (and a subsequent scholion on the text which may reflect the reading of Symmachus—see Philip S. Marshall, "A Critical Edition of the Hexaplaric Fragments of Ecclesiastes" [Ph.D. diss., Southern Baptist Theological Seminary, 2007], 170–71), it is far from self-evident that the original readers would have understood "respond," as Lohfink suggests, but the issue is not crucial for my broader interpretation.

seem to be treated as though they were righteous (cf. 7:15).[6] It is this which provokes him in 8:15 to another commendation of enjoyment, "and this will accompany them in their work for all the days of their life which God has granted them beneath the sun."

In 8:16–17 this is followed, effectively, by a restatement of his conclusions, derived from his study of wisdom and of human work on earth, that humans cannot really know what is going on in the world, which is apparently what God intends. The discussion continues into ch. 9: the righteous and wise are in the hand of God, and it seems impossible to say what anyone has done when everyone meets the same end (9:1–2). Picking up 8:11, 9:3 again observes that this effectively motivates evil among humans—at least until they die. This leads ultimately to Qohelet's best-known call to pleasure in 9:7–10, but it does so by way of a rather sudden twist: humans may be both confused and motivated to do wrong, but they are better off than the dead. The sense of 9:4 is very obscure, but Qohelet's point seems to be that the dead have nothing, not even emotions, let alone any portion in the world. We should enjoy life, therefore, because we can at least get a portion that way: there will be no opportunity later.

Enjoyment is also tied up with questions of justice, delusion and death much earlier, in 3:16–22. Here Qohelet begins with an observation that there appears to be wickedness in the world even where there ought to be justice and righteousness, but affirms his belief that there will be a divine judgment at the right time. What follows is difficult, but is probably not to be read as an account of some divine test or an assertion that humans really are just animals: the point is more probably that although God will draw distinctions, humans are incapable of perceiving them for themselves.[7] When humans cannot discern a difference between their own

---

6.   I think that the reference here is probably to death rather than general injustice, although it is interesting that נגע אל is used in Job 2:5 of "touching" Job's bone and flesh—that is, injuring or destroying them.

7.   The principal difficulties are the meaning of לברם in 3:18, and the construction of שהם בהמה המה להם, which seems to have been composed with a view more to its assonance and rhythm than its clarity. Briefly, I am inclined to follow the suggestion of Backhaus, *Den Zeit und Zufall*, 136–37, with regard to the derivation and sense of the verb: it is from ברר, with the sense "separate out"; I doubt, however, that it can mean "Gott hat sie ausgesondert," because the construction of the infinitive with -ל would be a remarkable choice for expression of the past tense here, and the future is far more likely. In the second clause, the word order seems more of a problem than the sense, and I understand, literally, "but-going-to-see/that-they-(are)-cattle/(are) they for them." So, "God is going to separate them (humans) out, but what they are going to see for themselves is that they are cattle."

deaths and those of animals, which are visibly identical, and are, in essence, the same, they cannot be expected to appreciate that they really are different (and therefore liable to judgment).

It is apparently in the face of such ignorance that Qohelet commends taking pleasure in one's work at 3:22, and he reinforces the point by asking who can take humans to see what will be after them (a question which he will more or less repeat later in 6:12). Although it is questions of justice which lead him to this point, therefore, it does not seem to be the problem of injustice itself which directly provokes his affirmation of pleasure. The same is probably true in ch. 8 as well, where it is not the injustice, as such, which concerns Qohelet, but the misleading effects of the situation in which judgment is invisible to humans. Correspondingly, both these commendations of pleasure should probably be aligned with that in 3:12–13. There, Qohelet observes that human achievements are limited to taking pleasure, and that to take such pleasure is a divine reward, but he does so immediately after claiming that humans can have no knowledge of God's broader activities.

The issue in ch. 9, then, is rather different: there Qohelet commends enjoyment of life because there will be no enjoyment of death, and this foreshadows the calls at the end of ch. 11, to enjoy life and youth before death and old age arrive. In 3:12–13, 3:22 and 8:15, on the other hand, he commends it because human understanding of divine action, and consequently of the world, is severely restricted. In the latter two of these passages, this ignorance is exemplified by the problem that humans cannot perceive divine action in judgment, but divine justice is not the issue.

c. *Conclusions*

There are a few points at which Qohelet's attitude does come close to *carpe diem*: life is to be enjoyed while it is available. Mostly, though, his commendations of pleasure arise in two contexts. The first contrasts enjoyment with wealth and physical possessions more generally: where such things are not really one's own, pleasure in what one does is something real, which cannot be taken away once it has been achieved. The second sets the human ability to take pleasure over against the human ignorance of what is really happening in the world. Although this may be too general a way of looking at it to be useful, Qohelet seems to be concerned in both contexts to encourage a human focus on what is actually attainable and comprehensible. Just as it is ultimately fruitless to seek physical wealth and possessions, so it is also futile to try to make sense of the world when divine actions, and divine attitudes to human behaviour, are essentially obscure. When the only certain good is the enjoyment which one can achieve in life and work, pursuit of that enjoyment is the only thing certainly worthwhile.

It is apparent from the way that he presents pleasure that Qohelet is not advocating a hedonistic pursuit of pleasurable experiences. Enjoyment is found principally in work, although it is more often than not associated with eating and drinking, and 9:9 includes enjoyment of life with a beloved wife. In 2:9, however, Qohelet himself kept his heart from no pleasure, and we should not try conversely to impose some puritanical definition of pleasure. The issue is not how pleasure itself is to be understood, but rather where one is supposed to be finding it: not least, perhaps, because he doubts our ability to comprehend or control the circumstances in which we find ourselves, Qohelet calls on us not to improve those circumstances, but to embrace them. We are not supposed to be undertaking a search for pleasure, but finding pleasure in what we undertake.

Although he commends enjoyment to all humans, however, it is also apparent that Qohelet does not expect all humans to find it. The power to enjoy what one is doing is clearly distinct from what one is doing, and as something internal to each human, it is separate from the outward role that each human plays in the world. Qohelet stresses repeatedly, however, that it is something offered by God, perhaps as a sort of pay, and in 6:2, especially, he makes it clear that it is something which may be withheld. This is a way in which God can affect the quality of individual human lives without simultaneously changing the roles which humans are playing in the world, and we may reasonably suspect that it is implicated in Qohelet's ideas of divine judgment. Those given outward prosperity but inward misery are, according to 6:1–6, in a very bad way as the result of a divine decision, while pleasure is one of the qualities that God may assign to whomever he chooses in 2:26. When Qohelet talks of the ability to take pleasure as pay or reward from God in 3:13 and 5:18, then, he may mean that it is something offered in return for righteousness, or at least for pleasing God, while the withholding of the ability would constitute an effective punishment. In that case, the pursuit of pleasure is not an alternative to moral or ethical behaviour, but an option open, in effect, only to those who please God.

2. *Right Behaviour*

Just as he seems to be in no doubt that God will judge humans (3:17; 11:9), so Qohelet seems also to be confident that humans can affect God's attitude toward them. This is spelled out with respect to behaviour in the temple and the making of vows in 4:17–5:6 (ET 5:1–7), which allows for the possibility that God may "destroy what your hands have achieved." In 8:12–13, more generally, Qohelet expresses the certainty, despite apparent evidence to the contrary, "that it will[8] work out well for those who fear God, who will be afraid before him, but that it will not work out well for the wicked person; and, like a shadow, he who has no fear before God will not prolong life." The cheery summons in 11:9, to enjoy youth and to "walk in the ways of your heart and in the sight of your eyes," ends with the less cheery warning that "for all these things, God will bring you to a reckoning." In that case, of course, important though it may be for humans to enjoy their lives if they can, there are clearly other things which they should, or should not, be doing.

a. *Action and Attitude*

This question is approached in 7:15 by way of an observation: Qohelet recalls that in his "life of *hebel*" he has seen everything, and there may be "a righteous man who perishes through his righteousness, and a wicked man who lives long in his wrongdoing." This sounds very like 8:14, and it foreshadows the discussion about human perception of judgment in 8:10–14; it also follows a remark about the limitation of human perception by God in 7:14. The point here, though, is different, and Qohelet goes on to talk not about judgment itself, but about proper behaviour in the face of such a situation:

> Do not become very righteous, and do not show yourself wise more than needs be; why make yourself appalled? Do not be very wicked, and do not become a fool: why die when it is not your time? It is good that you grab this, and do not hold your hand back from that, for one who fears God will emerge with both. (7:16–18)

He follows this advice with two remarks which perhaps pick up the mentions of wisdom and righteousness in the first sentence, and the theme as a whole; I translate the first as a question:

---

8. Tomáš Frydrych, *Living Under the Sun: Examination of Proverbs and Qoheleth* (VTSup 90; Leiden: Brill, 2002), 71 n. 45, insists that the verbs relating to the God-fearing and the wicked must be modal here, and are to be translated "should," not "will." That, of course, changes the sense dramatically, so that the verse becomes an assertion of what Qohelet feels ought to be happening even though it is not. It is hardly the most natural reading of the verbs, however, and Frydrych takes no account of the other positive affirmation about fearing God in 7:18. His argument that the following verses preclude a simple future rests on his interpretation of the passage overall, so is essentially circular.

Will wisdom come to the aid of the wise man more than (would) ten powerful men who are in the city?[9]
For there is no person (so) righteous on earth that he can do good and never sin. (7:19–20)

Although Qohelet's reservations about wisdom have been apparent since very early in the book (and we shall explore them in more detail below), it seems extraordinary that he should commend moderation in righteousness, and, similarly, suggest that it is only being "very wicked" which poses the threat of premature death. If moreover, the "this" and "that" of 7:18 refer to righteousness and wickedness, as Rashbam and others have suggested, then Qohelet seems positively to be recommending at least a little wickedness.[10]

The remark in 7:20 offers a clue to the ideas underlying these suggestions. If righteousness were to consist of never sinning, then nobody, in practice, would ever be righteous. Correspondingly, the righteousness or wickedness of people, to the extent that it lies in their actions alone, lies in the sum of those actions. As will become very clear in 8:11, when he regrets the confusion caused by the absence of any immediate punishment for a wrongful deed, Qohelet does not understand judgment to be something triggered instantly by human actions. When he judges humans, therefore, God is presumably not taking account simply of their most recent single actions, but of their behaviour or qualities more generally. This is not itself a radical position in any way, but Qohelet's presentation is unusual in drawing out the consequence, that righteousness will not

---

9. Because of the nature of the concept, the article is very unusual with חכמה, except where the reference is to a specific skill (so 1 Kgs 7:14) or to other specific wisdom which has already been mentioned (e.g. 2 Chr 1:12). It is difficult to judge the original intention where prepositions are pointed as with the article (1:13; 2:3, 13; and 7:23), but the only other explicit appearance in Ecclesiastes is at 7:12, where the reading of G suggests that it may have originated as a doublet of a preceding ה- suffix. It is not unreasonable to suspect, therefore, that in 7:19 the ה- of החכמה may be interrogative: "Will wisdom come to the aid of the wise man more than (would) ten powerful men who are in the city?"

10. As has been observed before, Whybray's argument that אל תהי צדיק must have some special sense of being "self-righteous" seems to founder on the problem that the parallel אל תרשע הרבה has the same form, but can hardly have a sense analogous to that; see his "Qoheleth the Immoralist? (Qoh 7:16–17)," in Gammie et al., eds., *Israelite Wisdom*, 191–204. A similar attempt is made in George R. Castellino, "Qohelet and His Wisdom," *CBQ* 30 (1968): 15–28, esp. 24, which understands "Do not multiply your justice (i.e. in your own eyes)," but runs into the same problem. The common idea that Qohelet is advocating moderation, though, seems to fit badly with the advocacy of action in 7:18, and especially with the later call in 9:10 to act with all one's might.

offer instant protection any more than a little wickedness will attract instant punishment. It is easy to die from being righteous, therefore, as any martyr might attest, and since Qohelet apparently sees no hope of reward after death, then it is pointless to die that way.

This seems consonant with the concluding suggestion, in 7:18, that the human who will emerge unscathed from both righteousness and wickedness is the human who fears God. The same point is made in 8:12–13, and the warnings about angering God in ch. 5 likewise conclude with an admonition to fear him (5:6 [ET 5:7]). Beyond the monologue, indeed, the book as a whole concludes in 12:13–14 with a call to fear God, mindful that he will judge every deed, whether good or bad. Whether or not this is a secondary addition, as many commentators think, it is clearly not wholly out of step with Qohelet's own comments elsewhere. If Qohelet attaches little weight to deeds considered individually, he does, correspondingly, emphasize the need for whatever overall quality of piety or understanding he takes to constitute "fear of God."

This is a difficult expression, and it may have no single, specific sense in biblical usage.[11] Qohelet does not seek to qualify it himself, although he does observe in 3:14 that fear is something which God inspires in humans, perhaps by means of his own unalterable actions. That observation may not throw a great deal of light on the matter, but it does set "fear of God" in the context of divine action, and imbues it with an implication of human awe in the face of the divine. Perhaps there is a model of the implied relationship in Qohelet's account of the proper behaviour toward a king in ch. 8, which itself becomes a reflection on judgment, and on human ignorance and impotence:

> Watch the mouth of a king, and do not be hasty in a solemn undertaking. Leave him, do not hang around at a bad word: for everything he wants, he will do, since a king's word is power, and who will say to him, "What are you doing?" One who keeps a command will know no bad word and time of judgment. The heart of a wise man knows: that for every matter there is a time and judgment, that a person's wrongdoing counts heavily against him, that he cannot know what is going to happen, that when it happens—who will explain it to him? There is no person (who) has power over the wind, to restrain the wind. And there is no control over the day of death. And there is no remission in battle. And wickedness will not save its owner. I saw all this when I applied my heart to every deed which is done beneath the sun, which one person has power over another for harming him. (8:2–9)

11. See my comments in *An Introduction to the Study of Wisdom Literature* (T&T Clark Approaches to Biblical Studies; London: T&T Clark International, 2010), 119–22.

On the face of it, this passage offers advice about the proper behaviour towards a human ruler (8:2–5), and perhaps a reflection on human oppression by humans (8:9); such advice is found sometimes in other literature, and Qohelet himself will touch on the theme again in 10:4 and 10:20. It moves, though, from the "time of judgment" associated with royal displeasure in 8:5, through to a much broader assertion of "time and judgment" in 8:6. Its claim, in 8:7, that nobody knows what is going to happen and nobody else can tell them, is used of a more general human ignorance elsewhere in the book (see especially 10:14), and its description of the king as beyond questioning (8:4) uses an expression employed by other writers to talk in similar terms about God (see Job 9:14; Isa 45:9). We need not go so far as simply to equate the king with God, but it is reasonable to suggest that Qohelet aligns the two here: the power of the king, and the danger which he poses, have a more general parallel in the power of God over human lives, and humans are effectively impotent in the face of each. The best that they can do is to obey the commands that they are given, and to avoid the displeasure that might ruin them.

Whether or not we see such an analogy in 8:2–9, there is no doubt that behaviour before God is the issue in 4:17–5:6 (ET 5:1–7):

> Watch your step, when you go to the temple and draw near to listen.[12] A sacrifice is the payment[13] of fools, for they have no idea how to do wrong.[14] Do not be over-excited out loud, and do not let your heart be in a hurry to force out some word in front of God, for God is in heaven and you are on earth. Accordingly, let your words be few. For a dream comes with a mass of business, and a fool's voice with a mass of words.

12. I doubt that קרוב here can mean "acceptable" (so, e.g., Fox, *A Time to Tear Down*, 230; Seow, *Ecclesiastes*, 194); indeed, it is not clear that it ever has that sense, and when a figurative extension of the normal meaning "near" is employed, the connotation is "near enough to be heard" (e.g. 1 Kgs 8:59; Ps 148:14) or "nearby to protect" (e.g. Ps 34:19 [ET 34:18]).

13. The text is difficult, and G has probably read ממתת, but I take מתת to be original, and probably to be pointed not as an infinitive from the verb with prefixed -מ, but as מַתַּת, the noun which appears in 3:15 and 5:18 (ET 5:19). The sense is presumably that sacrifice is an offering or payment made by fools, not to them.

14. It is hard to understand ידע + ל + infinitive as anything except "know how to," or just possibly "know that one is going to," and there are no grounds for emendation of the text. We would seem to have to read, therefore, "they do not know how to do evil/harm/wrong." Fox, *A Time to Tear Down*, 231, gives up on the sense here, and I am not sure I can do better, but a guess from context (and the common force of אין in such expressions) might be that fools end up making a lot of precautionary sacrifices because they never know whether they are doing the wrong thing—sacrifice, in other words, is a sort of tax on folly.

When you have vowed a vow to God, do not delay in fulfilling it, as nobody has any use for fools[15]—you should fulfil what you have vowed. It is better that you should not vow, than that you should vow and not fulfil. Do not let your mouth get your body condemned, and do not say before the messenger that it was an innocent mistake, (so) why should God be angry with your voice, but destroy the work of your hands? For when there is a mass of dreams, and hot air,[16] and words aplenty, then[17] fear God!

The first verse is very difficult, and it would be dangerous to place too much weight on it. The sense of the passage as a whole, though, seems clear: words which one speaks to God should be no more than required, and vows made to him should be fulfilled. Qohelet is close here to both the thought and the expression of Deut 23:22 (ET 23:21), "When you have vowed a vow to Yhwh your God, do not delay in fulfilling it ..." His broader point is, perhaps, correspondingly related to that of the following verse in Deuteronomy: "it will be no sin in you, should you refrain from vowing" (Deut 23:23 [ET 23:22]). Whether or not Qohelet intends to suggest that only fools engage in the practice of making vows to God and then fulfilling them through votive sacrifices (perhaps because they have no awareness of the risk), he emphasizes unambiguously both that it is unwise to blurt unnecessary words out before God, and that unfulfilled vows are dangerous. This is a way in which one's mouth can cause trouble for one's whole self, and such careless talk is the mark of fools.

The construction of the last verse is difficult, but it relates the need to fear God to the presence of the dreams or aspirations and ill-considered speech which have already been linked to folly. In this context, especially, it is hard not to see some element of real fear, and not mere piety: when exposed to, or tempted to such things, one must be aware that they can in turn bring exposure to severe divine punishment. When he urges his audience not to rush into speaking before God, Qohelet also makes the point that humans are on earth while God is in heaven. That reminder may have a purely physical aspect—one's words are going to have to

---

15. For other uses of the idiom ב- אֵין חֵפֶץ, which seems to have eluded the lexica, see Jer 22:28; 48:38; Hos 8:8. It does not mean that God in particular has no pleasure in fools.

16. הבלים: apparently a play on the literal and figurative connotations of the word.

17. כי is awkward here, as often in Ecclesiastes. It is difficult to take it as an expression of cause with a following imperative, while the absence of a preceding negation, on the other hand, would seem to exclude an asseverative use. Schoors, *Pleasing Words*, 1:103, follows others in seeing the use as emphatic.

travel a long way, so should be properly considered—but it also emphasizes the difference, as well as the distance between God and humans.

As in his remarks about behaviour before a king, what Qohelet seems
to commend above all else here is caution. Prayer and sacrifice are not
welcomed as a way to bring humans closer to God, but viewed as a way
in which the always-distant God can be led to punish humans. That
implies, of course, that God does listen to humans and may act on what
he hears, but it also implies that humans should be very cautious when
they try to catch his ear, and very conscious of the potential penalties.
Later on in 9:2, when Qohelet laments the fact that a single fate befalls
both the righteous and the wicked, those who offer sacrifice and make
oaths are apparently aligned with those who act righteously, so these
activities are probably not being condemned here in themselves. As
when he talks about righteousness more generally in 7:15–20, Qohelet
seems anxious to emphasize rather that the dangers of any activity are
not connected solely to their rightness or wrongness, and also to make
the point that safety lies in fearing God (as in 7:18).

Although we should not reduce its content solely to this issue,
Qohelet's advice in 4:17–5:6 (ET 5:1–7) seems consonant, therefore, with
what we have seen already: he is not concerned to evaluate individual
actions in terms of their moral worth, and to commend or reject them
accordingly, but to point out the dangers even of righteous or commend-
able behaviour. What preserves the individual is not simply doing one
thing or another, but approaching everything with the appropriate "fear
of God." That attitude or quality, as we have noted, is nowhere clearly
defined in the book, but, given his view of the world and of human perception (to which we shall turn again in the next chapter), it seems
unlikely that "fear of God" implies for Qohelet an understanding of the
divine will, as it does in some other literature. The very lack of definition
does suggest, however, that he presupposes some understanding of the
term on the part of his audience, and we should probably not attempt to
imbue it with any novel or overly complicated sense: it involves, perhaps,
no more than a healthy respect for God's ability to judge or destroy, and
a consequent recognition of his power over humans.

b. *Unpredictability*

Since, as we have seen already, it may be difficult for humans to perceive
the consequences of divine judgment, or to associate them with the
actions which provoked them, the very fact of divine judgment is more
something in which Qohelet believes than it is something which he can
demonstrate. Accordingly, when he commends "fear of God" and an
awareness of his judgment, it is against the backdrop of a world in which

no policy or approach seems to guarantee success, even if there are actions which seem to increase the possibility of failure or divine disfavour. As he puts it in 9:11, "…as the race does not belong to the swift nor the battle to the mighty, so also food does not belong to the wise, nor wealth to the intelligent, nor favour to the knowledgeable, because time and circumstance befall them all."

This idea is associated in the next verse with another, more frightening type of unpredictability: "(I also saw) that no person knows his time: like fish which are caught in a terrible net, and like birds caught in a trap; humans are trapped like them at a terrible time, as when it falls suddenly upon them" (9:12). The analogy used here may affirm that the "time" of humans in this second verse is the time of their death, although it could allude more broadly to potential disaster, but in the first verse "time" probably means something more general, and it is paired with the unusual term *pega'*, which refers to "what one encounters." It would be misleading to read this in terms either of fate or of simple chance, because in the broader context of Qohelet's ideas, it is in some sense both. Since humans cannot perceive the place of their actions or existence in the broader processes which characterize the world, those processes may affect them in ways which are far from random, but which may nevertheless appear random to them.

Whether or not Qohelet's view of the world can usefully be called deterministic (and we shall touch on that question later), his interest here and elsewhere is not so much in the character of the underlying processes, as in the consequence for humans of their inability to comprehend what is really happening. It may matter little to anyone except bookmakers that a race will not always be won by the fastest horse, or a fight by the stronger fighter, but when this unpredictability is transferred to more fundamental human pursuits, it poses a serious problem: if it is not always those who have worked to become wise, intelligent or knowledgeable who gain the rewards for such things, why should anyone work to attain those qualities? What inherent value can they have? Of course, this brings us back to the concerns expressed in ch. 2, when Qohelet observed that wisdom, knowledge and skill need not be prerequisites for prosperity (2:21). The issue now, however, is apparently not the unfairness of such a situation, but the uncertainty it inspires. Moreover, humans have to live not only with such uncertainty about the outcome of their choices, but with the ever-present threat of disaster or annihilation.

It is not immediately clear what response Qohelet advocates, and he does not address the problem directly. These observations, however, follow immediately upon his advice in 9:10, associated with the preceding call to enjoyment, that "Everything which your hand finds to do, you should do it with (all) your might. For there is no deed, or answer, or knowledge, or wisdom in Sheol, which is where you are going." It is itself followed, in 9:13–16, by a curious anecdote about a poor wise man who saves his city through his wisdom when it comes under siege from a powerful king (incidentally proving the point that battles indeed do not always go the way of the mighty). The wise man, we may note, is poor in the way that wise men are not supposed to be, but just in the way that 9:11 allows that they may be in this unpredictable world. Despite his rescue of the city, furthermore, "nobody recalls that poor man" (9:15): he is a victim both of poverty despite his wisdom, and of neglect despite his achievement. Qohelet draws the lesson, though, not that the wise man was wasting his time, but that even though he is despised and his words never heard, the episode still proved wisdom to be better than might (9:16), at least in that case.[18] To put it another way, the absence of any reward for his wisdom and of any recognition for his actions does not mean that the man's wisdom was pointless in itself, even if it gave him no special benefit himself, beyond the salvation enjoyed by the whole city.

It would be going too far to suggest that the sequence of observations here constitutes an argument, as such, but it does offer a context in which the concerns about unpredictability are to be read and understood. When Qohelet advises that we should undertake wholeheartedly whatever we find to do, while we still have the chance to act at all (9:10), it may be that our actions will not have the consequences we desire, and we will certainly have no way to predict when we might be overtaken by disaster or death. Even when we do not get what we deserve, however, our actions may still be effective and good in themselves. At the very least, it seems clear that Qohelet does not view unpredictability or unexpected outcomes in the world as a reason for inaction or paralysis, or as an excuse to override his advice that we should throw ourselves into what we do.

That idea might profitably be set in the context of Qohelet's broader perception that what humans do is ultimately not done for themselves anyway, and that what they stand to gain lies only in the experience, not the outcome of their actions. The book does not take the discussion in that direction, however, but switches instead in 9:17 to a series of sayings: this format will dominate the text until the end of ch. 11. Although the links between them are not always clear, however, these sayings do offer some sequences which seem to constitute short discussions in

18. The theme is picked up in the following 9:17–18. If I have understood it properly, 7:19 is more dubious on this point, but it has in mind the rather different context of personal protection.

themselves. The most obvious example of this is 11:1–6, which we shall examine shortly, but it is also noteworthy that Qohelet seems to interrupt the series at 10:5–7 to inject a further observation explicitly from his own experience, and the sayings which follow in vv. 8–11 may pick up that observation with some further remarks about the character of the world.

In 10:5 we are introduced to a problem which is either "like an error proceeding from the presence of the ruler" or "like the error of someone leaving the presence of the ruler" (cf. 10:4). That description is obscure in either case, but the problem seems to consist in the first instance of people being in the wrong place: "The idiot is set in many high places, while rich people sit in lowliness. I have seen servants on horses, and princes walking like servants on the ground" (10:6–7). This is reminiscent of other descriptions in ancient literature of "the world turn'd upside down" and Qohelet may be evoking conventional motifs of societal collapse. The sayings which follow, though, have an absurdity of their own at first, which suggests that they belong with this observation:

> Someone who digs a pit will fall into it,
>> and a snake will bite someone who breaks through a wall.
> Someone quarrying stones will be hurt by them,
>> and someone chopping logs will be endangered by them
> —if the tool is blunt and it has jarred on a surface[19]—
>> but he will improve (his) strength,
>> and wisdom is the profit from making a success.
> If a snake immune to charms should bite,
>> there is no profit for a master of the tongue. (10:8–11)

Of course, there are always going to be risks involved in digging pits and in breaking walls, stones or logs. There is hardly even a slight chance, however, that any attempt to break through a wall will result in a snake-bite, while it would take a long time to dig pits were it really inevitable that the diggers would keep falling into them. The second part of the series seems, therefore, to offer an appropriate qualification: injuries from splitting logs (and perhaps rocks too) arise from faulty tools, and the problem can be overcome (although just how is unclear: the text is very obscure). As the final saying in the sequence comes back to the snake,

---

19. The form קלקל only appears elsewhere in Ezek 21:26, of shaking (cf. the Hithpalpel in Jer 4:24), so although קלל can be used of bronze which has been burnished or polished in some way, it seems unlikely that this form can refer to sharpening, and it is improbable that פנים could mean edges; I emend לא פנים to לפנים: the negative is lacking in G.

though, it observes that even a skilled snake charmer may prove useless when it comes to preventing a bite.

It is difficult to establish precisely what is being said here, but the juxtaposition of social reversal and unexpected injury seem to point once more to unpredictability as Qohelet's theme. The world is not as it should be, either in the ordering of society or in the outcome of actions. The problems arising from actions can be addressed, to be sure, and Qohelet's point may be that there is strength and wisdom to be gained from engagement with them. The extent to which they can be overcome, however, is limited: not every problem is susceptible to a solution. The sequence continues, using the snake charmer's tongue as a link to sayings about the speech of wise men and fools, but moves on from this topic, at least for a while.

Although it occupies little space in the book, and only appears as an explicit concern quite late in his monologue, the unpredictability of human life and action is important to Qohelet because it represents the context in which humans have to live their lives. As we saw a little earlier, false or hidden outcomes can mislead humans, as when the apparent prosperity of the wicked inspires imitation, but human judgment has to contend also with the much more general problem that outcomes do not always, in any case, meet their expectations. Ancient readers might have been less inclined than their modern counterparts to attribute this simply to chance, or the flapping somewhere of a butterfly's wings, and Qohelet, as we have seen, does not reject the view that we can, in some ways, shape our fate by our piety. The outcome of our individual actions, however, is in his worldview contingent on the much broader processes in which they are implicated: if those are beyond our comprehension, then so too are the factors that affect every action we undertake. Correspondingly, there is nothing useful we can do apart from engaging fully in the activities open to us while we are alive, conscious that, if they are effective at all, they may not be effective on our behalf in the ways that we expect.

The practical implications of Qohelet's position are clearest when he returns to the theme one last time, in 11:1–6:

> Scatter your bread across the waters, for in the fullness of time you will come across it. Give a portion to seven, and even to eight, for you do not know what misfortune may happen on earth.
> If the clouds are full of rain, it is on the earth that they will empty themselves, and whether a tree falls in the south or in the north, the place where the tree falls is where it will be.

> Whoever keeps watch on the wind will never sow, and whoever keeps an eye on the clouds will never reap, since you do not know what is the way of the wind. Like the foetus in the womb of a pregnant woman,[20] just so you will not know what God does, he who will do everything.
> Sow your seed in the morning, and do not rest your hand until evening, for you do not know which will prosper, this or that, or if both alike will be fine.

Whatever the origin of the initial image, its sense is probably clear,[21] and there is little here which is difficult or obscure. To begin with, Qohelet commends dividing what one has, perhaps by doing favours which will be repaid—and that is the sense which the expression has come to have in English usage—but at least through some form of physical separation. What follows, when he talks about the rain and the tree, seems to be a statement of the obvious, and that is indeed, perhaps, its point: however unpredictable and unknowable the world—and he will go on to emphasize just how little we understand it—things have to be taken as they come. Worrying about them is worse than pointless if it displaces activity, and although the wind may affect sowing or the rain potentially spoil the harvest, neither the sowing nor the harvest will be accomplished at all if time is spent assessing the conditions rather than getting on with the job: such assessment is pointless anyway, when the way of the wind is beyond human comprehension and prediction. Just as it is wise to distribute what one has in the face of an uncertain future, so one should also sow one's seeds without rest, relying on thoroughness to compensate for one's ignorance of which will succeed or fail. In short, limited knowledge

---

20. I see no good reason to emend כעצמים to בעצמים, which might give the sense "you do not know the way of the spirit in the foetus," but רוח surely belongs anyway with the preceding statement; the analogy is either with the ignorance of an unborn child, or with the human ignorance *about* the unborn child, so the ultimate point is the same.

21. The image is difficult, and traditional interpretations in terms of conducting overseas trade or distributing charity both fail to explain elements of it. The ingenious explanation by Michael Homan, "Beer Production by Throwing Bread into Water: A New Interpretation of Qoh. XI 1–2," *VT* 52 (2002): 275–78, makes the whole passage a *carpe diem* reference to brewing and distributing beer, but the verb here can hardly sustain his translation "because in many days you will acquire it." A connection with *'Onchsheshonqy* 19:10 seems likely, "Do a good deed and cast it in the flood; when it dries you will find it." See Miriam Lichtheim, *Late Egyptian Wisdom Literature in the International Context: A Study of Demotic Instructions* (OBO 52; Freiburg: Universitätsverlag; Göttingen: Vandenhoeck & Ruprecht, 1983), 84. Why it should be bread here remains unclear, unless the implication is that *even* bread, not famous for its waterproof qualities, will be found.

can never overcome uncertainty, and one must respond to this not by trying to improve that knowledge, but by recognizing those things which are at least certain enough to assume, and by hedging one's bets when one can. Any life faces uncertainty and unpredictable ruin, but no life will be improved by indecision and inaction.

c. *Conclusions*

Qohelet distinguishes right from wrong, and believes that there will be a divine judgment of humans before they die, based on their conduct. It is in the power of humans, furthermore, to affect the attitude of God toward them, and so to gain whatever advantage is offered by divine favour. However, they may struggle to recognize what is right not only when God's favour or disfavour are not immediately self-evident in the lives of others, but also when they find that acting properly does not necessarily bring them the material rewards which they expect. Although they are expected to act righteously, therefore, humans face problems in doing so.

Qohelet makes no obvious effort to confront those problems directly, and he sets out no description of what it is to be righteous. Indeed, he seems altogether disinclined to commend righteousness as an end in itself: his interest, as ever, is in maximizing personal benefit. Correspondingly, when it is dangerous for humans to be righteous or wise, they should avoid the danger, although they must also avoid the risks associated with being too wicked or foolish. In their dealings with God, they must likewise be appropriately cautious: it is those who "fear God" who will ultimately enjoy his favour, and it is important for humans to be conscious that they are subject to divine judgment. In an unpredictable world, though, where they have little complete control over the outcome of what they do, caution must not be equated with inaction, and it is no less important for humans to act while they can, and before death forces them to be inactive: if they do not work, of course, they can achieve nothing and experience nothing.

3. *The Limits of Wisdom*

Qohelet's advice about behaviour is not confined to commendations of pleasure, cautious piety and action. It is frequently difficult to know, however, what we should make of the various individual sayings on other themes, which sometimes crop up in unexpected places. Qohelet often seems to use an oblique approach to the issues which he wishes to discuss, and this can make it difficult to determine the point he is trying to make.[22] He is also, sometimes, apparently led to particular statements through a sequence of themes or ideas which may have seemed more coherent to the writer (and perhaps the original audience) than they do to us: the progression of thought is sometimes reminiscent of the use in sentence literature of "catchwords" or other linking devices.[23] On such occasions, there is a danger of trying to impose on to a series of sayings an overall logic or theme which was not originally intended. Perhaps because he addresses it in large part through individual sayings, Qohelet's advice about human wisdom is particularly prone to such interpretative difficulties.

Qohelet speaks often both about his own wisdom and about wisdom in general. Insofar as the two are separable, it is the latter on which I shall focus here, but what are arguably his most significant observations lie in 2:12–26, when he reflects on his business and on the nature of wisdom:

> Then I looked round to observe wisdom, and confusion, and wronghead-edness—for what will the person be who comes after the king, in respect of what he has achieved?[24] And I saw that there was an advantage for the wisdom over the wrongheadedness like the advantage of the light over the darkness: the wise man—his eyes are in his head, while the fool goes along in darkness. But I knew myself that the same turn of events will befall them both, and I said in my heart, "What befalls the fool will befall me, me too, so why was I wise back then, unnecessarily?"[25] Then I said in

22. In 7:21–22, for instance, we are advised "Also, do not take to heart all the words which (people) say, in case you hear your servant being rude about you—for your heart knows too the many occasions when you also have been rude about others." Qohelet will return to the subject of rudeness in 10:20, when he warns against rudeness toward the powerful, even in one's thoughts, and it is tempting to see these as sporadic insertions of a minor theme. The "also" at the beginning of 7:21, though, seems to connect it with Qohelet's previous observation in 7:20, that there is no-one who never sins, and perhaps we are supposed to draw from it the lesson that we may ourselves be guiltier than we think of the shortcomings which we observe in others.

23. In 4:7–12, for example, Qohelet initially observes the sad state of a worker with no son or brother to whom his work may pass, but who works tirelessly for a wealth that can never satisfy him. This picks up a key theme: his work will not only be of no lasting benefit to the worker himself, but it will not even benefit anyone for whom he cares, and in his preoccupation with the work, he will never stop to realize its compete pointlessness. The following verses, though, move on to the theme of companionship, not futility, and their recurring motif of "twoness" may in turn provide a hook for the obscure story in 4:13–16, which mentions a "second youth."

24. See the Introduction, above, for my understanding of 2:12.

25. Both here and at 7:11, perhaps, Qohelet refers to the acquisition of wisdom to an extent which is unnecessary or superfluous, but whereas in 7:11 this idea is

my heart that this also had been *hebel*, because there is no memory of the
wise man forever, along with the fool, since already, in the days which
have come, everything has been forgotten, even how the wise man dies
along with the fool.

There are some difficulties in this passage, but the overall sense seems
clear: wisdom offers an advantage to the wise man, but not in any way an
escape from the extinction that awaits every human, wise or foolish. Its
advantage is limited to a clarity of perception which the fool lacks: the
wise man can see where he is going. Naturally, that seems less than
useful to Qohelet when his concern is with the ultimate outcome of his
life, and he regrets the effort spent on becoming wise, apparently
blaming it on the general forgetfulness which leads humans to forget the
shared fate of all.

The clarity of perception which is offered by wisdom may explain
why it is elsewhere characterized as something uncomfortable, or even
painful: to see where one is going may not be such a good thing if one
has no power to change direction. In certain respects at least, Qohelet
views wisdom as consciousness without control, and for that reason,
perhaps, a source of exasperation and pain (1:18). In the very difficult
6:8–9 he returns to the question of its advantage:

> What advantage[26] is there for the wise man over the fool? What for the
> pauper, (in) knowing that he will depart[27] in the presence of the living?
> The sight of the eyes is better than the departure of life. This too is *hebel*,
> and wishing for the wind.

Again, wisdom seems to be associated with consciousness of death, and
this may likewise underpin the sayings a little later in 7:2–6, which
associate wise men with mourning, sorrow and rebuke, while it is fools
who indulge in laughter and song. Whether or not Qohelet has his tongue

---

very general, with no specific point of comparison, here the context suggests something more precise. Since the wise man shares the fate of the fool, any wise man's
acquisition of wisdom serves no evident purpose: it is redundant, superfluous and
unnecessary—יותר.

26. 4QQohᵃ here reads כמה where the MT has כי מה. To complicate matters, the
original G reading was probably ὅ τι, which supports מה but not כי; cf. Peter J.
Gentry, "The Role of the 'Three' in the Text History of the Septuagint: II. Aspects
of Interdependence of the Old Greek and the Three in Ecclesiastes," *AS* 4 (2006):
153–92, esp. 178–80. In any case, it seems unlikely that we should try to connect
this verse to the last on account of the כי.

27. I take להלך to imply knowledge of future departure, probably death, not
knowledge of "how to walk/act," which would make little sense. I think it is also
likely that הלך should have the same sense in both this verse and the next.

in his cheek,[28] he makes wisdom sound a miserable business there, and folly a great deal more attractive. If 8:1 presents a contrast, then it may also be touching on this issue "…A person's wisdom will light up their face, but their confidence will be dimmed."[29]

Such passages suggest that wisdom genuinely offers insight into the situation of humans, even if Qohelet regards that insight with a certain ambivalence. There are, however, explicit limits on the scope and effectiveness of wisdom, which are spelled out in 8:16–17:

> When I set my heart to knowing wisdom, and to observing the work that is done on the earth—for by day and by night it saw no sleep with its eyes[30]—then I saw all the achievement of God, that[31] no person can discover the achievement which has been achieved beneath the sun, so that[32] a person may work hard to seek, but will not make that discovery. And even if the wise man claims that he is going to know, he will not be able to discover.

The language here echoes 3:11, which speaks about the human inability to discover in its entirety what God has done, and the theme is similar. In 7:13–14 Qohelet attributes the hiddenness of the future to deliberate divine policy, and this passage may also be a more general statement that God actively conceals his activities from humans. In any case, though, human wisdom is not equipped to uncover such things.

---

28. He takes the point to be a little different, but cf. Seow, *Ecclesiastes*, 246: "The sayings are perhaps deliberately ludicrous. By their sheer absurdity, Qohelet challenges the audacity of anyone to tell others what is good and how to have an advantage in life."

29. ועז פניו ישנא: the verb is from שנה (through a quite common interchange of *lamedh–he* and *lamedh–aleph* verb forms), which is used of tarnishing in Lam. 4:1. The expression עז פנים is used in Deut 28:50 and Dan 8:23, where it probably implies ruthlessness, but העז...בפניו in Prov 21:29 seems to mean "proceeds incautiously": I take the basic sense to be one's ability to act without enough, or without too much, consideration, so "confidence" seems appropriate in this context. Goldman's preference for an adjectival form of עז in *BHQ*, 97*, does not take account of the influence on G of its misreading the verb as "be hated" (μισθήσεται); the other versions have *substantivized* adjectives.

30. There is no text-critical warrant for moving or emending this statement, as a number of commentators have attempted to do. I take it to be a parenthetical and figurative reference either to the work or to Qohelet's heart.

31. כי here is probably consequent upon וראיתי: "I saw…, that…"; it does not readily express purpose ("God's work, that…").

32. Expressions similar to בשל אשר generally mean something like "on account of which," "wherefore"; cf. Seow, *Ecclesiastes*, 289–90. A causative sense "because" might be possible, though; see Schoors, *Pleasing Words*, 1:145–46.

Qohelet has probably stated already, in 7:23–29, his own failure in some similar respect, although much of that passage is desperately obscure. Since he frequently refers to his wisdom elsewhere, and even here claims to have "tried all this with wisdom" in 7:23, it is puzzling that he should immediately go on to admit "I said 'Let me be wise!' But it was out of my reach, further than anything which has existed; and who can find the deepest depth?" (7:23–24). In terms reminiscent of his quests in chs. 1–2, he then declares that, "I and my heart turned to know and to research both wisdom's quest and an answer [or 'reckoning'],[33] and how to know the wrongness of folly and foolishness and confusion." The implications of this are not entirely clear, but what Qohelet finds is a dangerous woman, more bitter than death, whom God permits to trap sinners: as some commentators have suggested, it seems likely that this woman is to be connected to the dangerously seductive character in Prov 1–9 (cf. also, for instance, Prov 22:14), who serves as a counterpart to personified wisdom there.[34] What Qohelet is looking into, therefore, may be the sort of ability to distinguish wisdom and folly which is a primary

---

33. On the possible commercial sense of חשבון, see Chapter 1, above.

34. So, for example, Ingrid Riesener, "Frauenfeindschaft im Alten Testament? Zum Verständnis von Qoh 7,25–29," in *"Jedes Ding hat seine Zeit…" Studien zur israelitischen und altorientalischen Weisheit. Diethelm Michel zum 65. Geburtstag* (ed. Anja A. Diesel et al.; BZAW 241; Berlin: de Gruyter, 1996), 193–207, esp. 197. It seems hard to overlook the links with Proverbs, despite Lohfink's assertion (without evidence) that in מר ממות and מצודים and חוטא ילכד בה, "Hier liegen zweifellos sprachliche Klischees aus abwertendem Reden über die Frau vor"; see his "War Kohelet ein Frauenfeind? Ein Versuch, die Logik und den Gegenstand von Koh., 7,23–8,1a herauszufinden," in *La sagesse de l'Ancien Testament* (ed. M. Gilbert; BETL 51; Leuven: Leuven University Press, 1979), 259–87, esp. 263 n. 20. Against Crenshaw, *Ecclesiastes*, 146, it should be noted also that "the theme of the woman who ensnares men," is far from "standard in ancient Near Eastern wisdom," so this is not just some conventional motif that Qohelet has picked up, although the imagery from Prov 1–9 was influential in some later Jewish literature; see Weeks, *Instruction and Imagery*, 131–33, 164. O. Loretz, "'Frau' und griechisch-jüdische Philosophie im Buch Qohelet (Qoh 7,23–8,1 und 9,6–10)," *UF* 23 (1991): 245–64, esp. 246, talks similarly of "die traditionellen altorientalischen Motive von der Bösartigkeit der Frau." D'Alario, *Qohelet*, 148, suggests that Qohelet is recalling a personal experience; cf. Lauha, *Kohelet*, 140, and especially Paul Volz, *Hiob und Weisheit (Das Buch Hiob, Sprüche und Jesus Sirach, Prediger). Übersetzt,erklärt und mit Einleitungen versehen* (2d ed.; Die Schriften des alten Testaments 3/2; Göttingen: Vandenhoeck & Ruprecht, 1921), 249, who speaks of a bitterly painful, transformative experience. While we might allow that the author had encountered such a misfortune, the whole context, for all its obscurity in many respects, seems to be dealing with something more general, and is probably figurative.

concern of that work. In any case, though, 7:28–29 suggest that he failed to find what he sought, and encountered only a human quest for many answers. The wisdom which he employed failed him in some sense, and the wisdom which he sought seems to have eluded him.

Other remarks about wisdom qualify its effectiveness in ways which are not always easy to evaluate. In 7:7, for instance, oppression or extortion may corrupt the wise man, and after 9:16–17 have apparently commended wisdom above might (following the story of the poor wise man who saves his city), 9:18 seems to suggest that its accomplishments are still vulnerable to sin: "Wisdom is good beyond weapons of war, but just one sinner destroys much good." It is not clear whether 10:1, which may be irretrievably corrupt, actually continues that thought or not, but it too may subordinate wisdom to other things. Likewise, 7:19 may be read either as an affirmation of wisdom's superiority to power or, as I think the context suggests, (cf. 7:16), a suggestion that power may sometimes be more helpful.[35] The earlier 7:11–12 are similarly ambiguous, but seem to suggest that the benefits of wisdom are best enjoyed by those who also possess money.

On the other hand, Qohelet certainly aligns wisdom with things that are to be regarded as desirable: like pleasure, it may be given by God to those who seem suitable (2:26), and it is one of the things that will be missed in Sheol (9:10). The wise are like the righteous in 9:1: both are in the hand of God. In 7:16, similarly, righteousness and wisdom are paired when Qohelet warns about the possible dangers of each, and 7:17 correspondingly pairs folly with wickedness. Wisdom is a quality to be admired in the human who has worked with skill to achieve something (2:21), and its potential absence in his own heir stimulates Qohelet's concern that his business will pass to someone who may not deserve it— he himself, after all, employed wisdom in its creation (2:18).

In short, Qohelet has mixed feelings about wisdom: it is important and useful, but also painful and limited. From the contexts in which he emphasizes each aspect, we might judge, perhaps, that he sees it as valuable when applied to the business of living, but not when it is applied to broader questions about life and meaning. We might think in terms of different types of wisdom here, but Qohelet himself perhaps sees it as a question of degree: his regret in 2:15 is not that he has been wise, so much as that he has been wise beyond what was required, the dangers of which are noted in 7:16.

35. See the note to the translation, above.

4. *Summary and Conclusions*

In the world as Qohelet understands it, humans are constrained in various important ways. First, and perhaps most important, is their limited lifespan: they pass from non-existence, through a short period of living, into a death which possesses none of the features of life. There is only a small window in their existence, therefore, for them to achieve whatever they are to achieve for themselves; that achievement, as Qohelet has come to realize, must be something to be found in life "under the sun," since nothing can be taken with them to Sheol. A further constraint is imposed by the nature of their activities, because they are born into a world which stretches far into the past and future: they have only the most limited idea of the part that they are playing in far-reaching processes, and no knowledge of what the future will hold. The course and extent of their own lives, therefore, is unpredictable, and the mark that they will leave on the world unknowable. This ignorance accords with the designs of God, whose own actions and purposes are themselves beyond human comprehension, but shape and incorporate the actions of humans. If this were not difficult enough, humans have also to face divine judgment, and the possibility that their lives may be shortened or ruined by divine intervention.

The only sort of gain which Qohelet can identify in this situation is not a lasting one: the ability to take pleasure in what they are doing is undeniably good for humans, but it is only available while they are alive and active. Since such an ability, moreover, may depend on divine favour, and since divine disfavour may lead to death, or to an inability to find pleasure in life, humans must be conscious always that their actions are subject to God's judgment, while at the same time avoiding destruction or unhappiness from other sources. This can require a careful balancing of considerations: righteousness may please God, but can itself bring risks; wisdom may be important for success, but too much can induce despair. With the clock ticking, however, and their time of death unknown, hesitation and inaction are not realistic options: humans must throw themselves into life, recognizing that their actions will not always lead to the outcomes that they want, protecting their interests so far as they can, and enjoying whatever pleasure their activities can offer before they die.

We shall return to Qohelet's methods and assumptions shortly, but it is important to appreciate that his advice is tailored to his own concerns. If the world is as Qohelet sees it, and human actions really contribute to much greater concerns, then another speaker might argue that a dutiful

subservience to those concerns should be the cornerstone of human existence, or that righteousness and the divine will should never be abrogated
simply to preserve one's life. From a different perspective again, one
could point out that Qohelet seems to have little interest in how humans
can help each other through this complicated life—beyond, at least, his
comments on the value of cooperation to each individual. Notions of
duty and altruism have little place in a discourse which seems rarely to
escape Qohelet's concern with the maximization of personal benefit.
This is a concern, moreover, which seems wholly of a piece with the
more general characterization of Qohelet in the book, as I outlined it
earlier, and we should be wary, therefore, of being swept along into an
acceptance of Qohelet's advice as the only way for humans to negotiate
the world that he portrays.

Chapter 4

OBSERVATION AND ILLUSION

Qohelet himself has a way of summarizing his observations which we have encountered a number of times already: everything is *hebel*, not only in its totality but, judging by the frequency with which he uses the term to describe specific circumstances, also in its parts. As we turn to examine the character and basis of his assessment in this chapter, so we must also engage with the meaning of that term as he uses it, and I shall argue that it serves to link his ideas about the limits of human perception: Qohelet views human activity and human aspiration as based, in large part at least, on serious misapprehensions. Qohelet's own ideas, though, seem to be rooted no less than those of others in observation of the world around him, and his discussion is peppered with anecdotes and claims to personal experience. If he is an empiricist, as sometimes claimed, he seems to be applying his empiricism to a wholehearted attack on the reliability of human perception.

In the light of the insights which he claims, that situation may not be so paradoxical as it sounds, and in this chapter I shall attempt to clarify just what the basis of Qohelet's position is, and how he understands it himself, but will approach the issue by looking first at just what he considers others to be doing wrong.

1. Hebel

Qohelet's preferred term for many of the phenomena which he discusses is usually recognized to be a figure or metaphor, and that has certain implications for the way in which we must approach the question of its meaning. Such figures do not always convey a single, fixed sense, and so it may be quite inappropriate just to seek a meaning that fits every context.[1] At the same time, though, common usage may establish a normal

---

1. See especially Douglas B. Miller, *Symbol and Rhetoric in Ecclesiastes: The Place of* Hebel *in Qohelet's Work* (Academia Biblica 2; Atlanta: SBL, 2002).

meaning or range of meanings, and we cannot overlook such usage. It would seem wise to begin, therefore, by looking at the many other occurrences of *hebel* before we turn specifically to its use by Qohelet.

a. *General Meaning and Usage*

There is wide agreement that the basic, literal meaning of *hebel* is connected in some way with air, or the movement of air, and this sense probably underpins both Isa 57:13, where wind and *hebel* will together snatch something away, and the second part of Ps 62:10 (ET 62:9), where humans are even lighter on the scales than *hebel*. It is difficult to be more precise than that, not least because we have a limited knowledge of the biblical writers' understanding of the physical world. We may reasonably presume, though, that *hebel* must have been differentiated from simple nothingness, or from air (if that was itself a concept[2]) by some quality of movement, temperature or effect.[3] Post-biblical usage, in fact, does suggest that *hebel* is typically exhaled or exuded in some way: the word, or its Aramaic cognate, is used of breath, vapour, the hot air from cooking, and the lethal miasma of a pit or a marsh. The notions of hot air, breath or exhalation are not excluded by the passages from Isaiah and Ps 62, and there may even be a play between literal and figurative meanings in Job 35:16, where it is *hebel*, "hot air," that is said by Elihu to open Job's mouth, when "without knowledge he multiplies words." There is no good reason to suppose, therefore, that the underlying idea in biblical usage was very different from that in post-biblical Hebrew, and the sense is affirmed by Aquila, Theodotion and Symmachus, who all seem to have used the Greek words ἀτμίς or ἀτμός in their translations of Ecclesiastes—these similarly refer to vapours of various sorts.

Strictly speaking, then, Qohelet is declaring everything to be "hot air," or something similar, and perhaps a translation in those terms would fit

---

2. The term אויר = ἀήρ enters Hebrew only in post-biblical usage, and הבל may be, in fact, the closest biblical equivalent. We should not assume, however, that the writers conceived of air in the way that we do, as a single substance subject to changes in temperature or humidity and capable of movement.

3. This is one good reason, I think, that renderings in terms of emptiness or nothingness are inappropriate, and miss the point of the metaphor. Among recent commentators, see, for example, Gianfranco Ravasi, *Qohelet* (2d ed.; La Parola di Dio; Cinisello Balsamo: Paoline, 1991), who prefers "vuoto," "emptiness," "perché non è troppo astratta e occidentale come 'nulla' ma d'altra parte non è troppo corposa come fumo o soffio, essendo il 'vuoto' espressione di nulla, di assurdo, di inconsistente" (p. 23). Konrad Ehlich, "Hebel–Metaphern der Nichtigkeit," in Diesel et al., eds., *"Jedes Ding hat seine Zeit... "*, 49–64, defends "Nichtigkeit" in terms of philosophical usage.

quite well with the other idiosyncrasies of Qohelet's style. If we do retain
his metaphor in translation, then the opening declaration may be a little
less grand than in the King James version ("Vanity of vanities..."), but it
has an attractive bluntness:

> "Complete hot air!," says Qohelet, "Complete hot air! It's all hot air!"

It may be as misleading, however, to leave figures untranslated as it may
be to substitute an interpretation. At least outside a very restricted
agricultural context, for instance, words like "hogwash" simply do not
mean what they appear to say, and there is surely nobody outside France
who cares to be called a "little cabbage" by their lover. If *hebel* has
similarly acquired a fixed sense or connotation other than "vapour" in
biblical Hebrew, then by leaving it untranslated we risk opening the term
up to a wider range of interpretations than the author would originally
have intended. Some such consideration presumably motivated the
(otherwise very literal) LXX translator to substitute "vanity" (ματαιότης)
for "vapour," and it means that we cannot ignore other figurative uses of
hebel.

Such figurative uses are, in fact, more common than literal uses of
hebel in the biblical literature and we regularly encounter it used as a
poetic metaphor or simile. The noun is also used polemically in places to
describe idols or foreign deities, especially in Jeremiah, and that usage is
common enough to suggest that it had become something of a cliché.[4] At
the same time, however, it is clear that *hebel* did not settle down to
convey any single meaning. Where certain of the contexts in which it
appears do seem to demand a particular understanding, that understanding can never be transferred to all other contexts. So, for example,
Ps 144:4, "A human is like *hebel*: their days are like a passing shadow,"
would seem to be using *hebel* as a figure for transience and insignificance: human life is so short as to be inconsequential in the eyes of
God. In Isa 30:7, however, that meaning would be quite inappropriate.
The text declares, "Egypt is *hebel* and offers empty help": here the point
is to emphasize the uselessness of Egyptian aid, so the issue is not transience, but worthlessness or a lack of substance. Of course, we cannot
always recognize the precise implication in a given case, and it is doubtful that we can or always should specify single, specific connotations:
figurative language does not work that way. When, for example, Prov
31:30 contrasts beauty in a woman with piety, calling it *hebel*, the image
surely evokes not only insignificance but transience as well: in contrast
to piety, physical beauty is both superficial and passing. Although *hebel*

---

4. See, e.g., Jer 8:19; 10:8.

may have come to have certain particular connotations or extended meanings, the biblical evidence suggests that, on the whole, it remained very much a live metaphor, through which writers could use the figure of breath or vapour to convey, separately or simultaneously, a variety of ideas.

Certain of these ideas do dominate the usage, to be sure. The fact that *hebel* is ephemeral and dissipates rapidly, which is illustrated most vividly in Prov 13:11 ("Wealth dissipates [faster] than *hebel*, but he who sets [some] aside will prosper"), is probably the notion uppermost in the characterization of human life as *hebel* in the Psalms. The fact that it is without solid form, on the other hand, is probably the spur to the other common use of the imagery, in assertions of insubstantiality or inefficacy. In such contexts, it can almost suggest something close to nothingness, as in Jeremiah's dismissals of idols, or on the two occasions when *hebel* is used in the context of comforting or consoling, and the comfort of *hebel* is said to be no comfort at all (Job 21:34; Zech 10:2). Such imagery may also be associated both with futility, as when Job sees the task of defending himself as *hebel*, since he is certain to be condemned (Job 9:29), and with the disappointment of expectation, as when foreign help is watched for in vain by the speakers in Lam 4:17. In such contexts, however, the implication is not really that something is non-existent or without meaning, so much as that it is ineffectual or incapable of being accomplished.

While *hebel* is used principally to convey these ideas of transience and ineffectiveness, there are a few places where it seems to have a further sense. In Job 27:12 it is apparently used to suggest that Job's friends are misguided or intellectually confused, rather than that they are "breath" or "vapour," and the characterization of human thoughts as *hebel* in Ps 94:11 seems similarly best understood as a reference to intellectual confusion or limitation. Although Ps 39:6 (ET 39:5) seems to suggest that humans are themselves *hebel*, because they are short-lived, this same sense of confusion seems to be at play in the next verse, which associates *hebel* with their inability to discern who will gather what they pile up (and this verse, incidentally, is sometimes linked to Eccl 2:26). It is also possible that in some of the passages which are usually considered references to idolatry, *hebel* rather represents sin or wasteful preoccupation more generally. So, for example, in 1 Kgs 16:13 and 16:26, where the people of Israel are said to have provoked God "with their *hebel*s," nothing in the context demands a narrow understanding in terms of idols, and the first verse explicitly picks up the prophecy of Jehu in 16:1, where Israel's provocation of God is "with their sins," suggesting a broad equivalence between the terms. It is interesting, in this respect, to observe that a denominative verb developed from the noun *hebel*, and this seems to connote confusion or deception: it is used of being misguided (Ps 62:11 [ET 62:10]) or of misleading others (Jer 23:16), and the noun perhaps takes on this connotation where it is used with the verb (2 Kgs 17:15; cf. Jer 2:5; Job 27:12). The verb itself does occur once in rabbinic sources, where it refers to the effect of hot air,[5] and that may be the idea behind this biblical usage: the prophets of Jer 23:16, for instance, are perhaps "blowing hot air" at their listeners.

We must be cautious in claiming that any of these are "meanings" of *hebel*: they are implications inherent more in the contexts where the figure is used, than necessarily in the scope of the term itself. What we can say of *hebel* is that its principal biblical use is in figurative descriptions, which use the physical characteristics of *hebel* to evoke notions of transience, uselessness or misguidedness. While the interpretation of various passages remains open to debate, and while there has been lively discussion about some aspects of the sense, none of this seems especially doubtful or problematic. The difficulties arise when we try to apply it to Ecclesiastes.

b. *The Uses of* Hebel *in Ecclesiastes*
From the opening and closing pronouncements that "everything is *hebel*," we can reasonably suppose that Qohelet's repeated characterization of situations as *hebel* is a way of illustrating this general claim through specific, comparable instances. Indeed, as if to affirm the connection between his different cases, Qohelet most commonly uses *hebel* in an almost formulaic way, describing a phenomenon or situation, and then remarking that, "This (also) is *hebel*." Such descriptions are to be found some nineteen times in the book (in 1:14; 2:1, 11 [twice], 15, 17, 19, 21, 23, 26; 4:4, 8, 16; 5:9 [ET 5:10]; 6:2, 9; 7:6; 8:10, 14). There is, to be sure, some variety in his usage, and this distinctive wording is sometimes not used even when *hebel* is the predicate of a description, as in the mottoes of 1:2 and 12:8, and in 11:10, when youth is called *hebel*. There are other variations as well: 11:8 claims that "everything which comes is *hebel*," and 3:19 uses "for everything is *hebel*" as support for an assertion, rather than as a description; 4:7–8 and 8:14 introduce a situation as *hebel*, and then subsequently describe it again, using the more formulaic comment. Rarely, Qohelet also makes pronouncements using the "this

---

5. See *b. Šabb.* 17b: "bundles of wet flax may not be put in an oven אלא כדי שיהבילו while it is still day." Since this is the restrictive Beth Shammai rule, the sense of the Hiphil here is probably "dry out," or "give off all their moisture," rather than "begin to steam" (as the Soncino translation prefers).

(also) is..." wording, but without using *hebel* at all (cf. 1:17; 5:15 [ET 5:16]). We can hardly, then, speak of a fixed and completely formulaic approach. There is sufficient continuity, however, to suggest that the *hebel* characterizations within Qohelet's discourse form part of a broader theme, cumulatively affirming that everything is indeed *hebel*.

Matters are complicated a little by the fact that Qohelet uses *hebel* in other contexts as well, and not merely in pronouncements that something is *hebel*. In the difficult 5:7, the plural is used in conjunction with dreams and words, and 6:11 also identifies *hebel* as a product of speech. In 6:12, 7:15 and 9:9, we find *hebel* used attributively to characterize lives, or the days of one's life, and in 6:4 it is associated with the circumstances into which a premature child is born. Even if we set aside those other uses, however, it is difficult to understand the meaning of *hebel* in Ecclesiastes simply in terms of its meanings elsewhere. One obstacle lies in the association of *hebel* with statements that something is bad or painful in 2:21, 4:8, and 6:2 (all places where the concern is with failure or inability to enjoy one's own possessions). Despite Douglas Miller's unconvincing claim that "foulness" is a possible referent of the metaphor elsewhere,[6] and despite the fact that to be *hebel* is never a good thing, there is a certain tension between describing a situation as *hebel* and describing it as bad. In none of these instances does Qohelet appear to be saying "it is bad but that doesn't matter, because it is shortlived or without real effect." More generally, although it is easy to point out places where *hebel* might indicate transience, uselessness, or both, it is difficult to reconcile either of those common connotations with all uses of the term in the book, or with other material in the book. Even if we allow the possibility that the book uses the word or image to align phenomena which are all *hebel*, but *hebel* in different ways, this merely eases the difficulties, and does not resolve them. Passages that are hard to explain in terms of transience may be no easier to explain in terms of uselessness or misguidedness.

That would suggest that *hebel* in Ecclesiastes may have connotations which are not attested elsewhere. Occasional turns of phrase, moreover, might be taken to imply that the book sometimes loses sight of the word's literal meaning altogether, so that the usage is no longer consciously metaphorical: Qohelet claims in 4:7 to have "seen (a) *hebel* under the sun," and in 8:14, he speaks of "a *hebel* which is done on the earth." Together, these considerations can be used to justify a different approach to *hebel*, essentially setting aside the literal meaning and the usage elsewhere, in favour of examining the use of the term solely within Ecclesiastes. Some scholars, accordingly, have identified new meanings

6. Miller, *Symbol and Rhetoric*, 95–97.

for the word, ones which are derived from broader interpretations of the book, and which correspondingly fit well into all or most contexts of its use there.

Any such approach, however, has to explain how the original readers were supposed to recognize this new meaning of a term or figure which was, after all, probably quite familiar and established already. So, for instance, Michael Fox's influential interpretation of *hebel* as "absurdity," which we shall examine more closely in a moment, provides a meaning which is plausible in itself, and which provides an interesting way to read the book.[7] It is difficult to see, though, how such a sense could have arisen, either as a new metaphor or as the extension of some existing connotation. Breath, or hot air, after all, is not an obvious image for irrationality, or an offence to reason, and *hebel* never seems to have been used that way before or after Ecclesiastes. Furthermore, we cannot simply ignore the fact that *hebel* was used elsewhere, and that readers would have approached Ecclesiastes with certain presuppositions about its potential meanings. If those readers were being invited to modify or discard such presuppositions, we might expect to find some clearer indication. Without wishing to downplay the poetic character of much language in the book, it is one thing to extend the meaning or scope of a familiar term, but quite another to lure readers into a serious mis-reading, by replacing its meaning with a new one.

What we can say with some confidence, then, is that the original readership would itself have required some guidance. On the evidence from elsewhere, someone reading the pronouncement in 1:2, even at the time the book was written, would not immediately have known precisely what Qohelet meant when he declared that "everything is *hebel*": was he saying that everything was transient? Insignificant? Misleading? What,

---

7. See especially Fox's "The Meaning of *Hebel* for Qohelet," *JBL* 105 (1986): 409–27. The idea is elaborated also in his commentaries, *Qohelet and His Contradictions* (JSOTSup 71; Sheffield: Almond, 1989), 29–51, and *A Time to Tear Down*, 27–49. The rendering "absurdité" had been used earlier by André Barucq, in *Ecclésiaste. Qohéleth. Traduction et Commentaire* (Verbum Salutis; Paris: Beauchesne, 1968), who makes a greater distinction between what he means and the tenets of existentialist philosophy: "En proposant la traduction 'Tout est absurdité' nous n'entendons pas placer dans la pensée de Qohéleth un jugement sur le sens métaphysique des choses, mais bien sur la façon dont elles apparaissent à son esprit. Il se voit dans l'impossibilité d'en donner une explication intelligible. La seule explication du monde est à chercher dans le plan de Dieu sur lui et cela échappe à l'investigation humaine. C'est là que gît l'absurdité. Il faut s'accommoder d'un monde sans en comprendre le sens... Qohéleth n'est pas un précurseur des philosophes de l'absurde" (p. 27).

for that matter was the scope of "everything"? The statement is provocative: what follows is surely intended not only to justify it, but also to explain it, and 1:2 is qualified in the next verse with Qohelet's question about the profit that humans can take away from what they accomplish in life. This juxtaposition implies not only that Qohelet's "everything" is (at least) the totality of human work, but also that what makes this *hebel* is the human inability to take a profit from it. At the same time, it effectively excludes a reading of "everything" as "everyone," and an understanding of the initial claim as a general statement of human transience.

Because 1:3 is phrased as a question, albeit a rhetorical one, the following verses are most naturally read as an answer or further qualification. As they set out Qohelet's view of the world, the lack of profit in human work is itself associated with the world's continuation beyond the span of human lives, and the limits which this places on human understanding: there is a mismatch between the permanence of the world, with its eternal processes, and the short lives of humans. Everything is *hebel* because there is no profit to be gained from any human work in life, and that lack of profit lies somehow in the fact that humans exist impermanently within a permanent world. After Qohelet has introduced himself in 1:12, the following verses, 1:13–15, then reiterate the general conclusion, and make similar associations in a different way: Qohelet examines "everything which is done beneath the heavens," asking whether what God has given humans to do is a bad business, and concludes that everything achieved beneath the sun is *hebel*. At this point, then, the reader can have been left in little doubt that when Qohelet is talking about *hebel*, he is talking in relation to human work within the world—work which is set within the context of, on the one hand, human impermanence, and, on the other, divine intention. Qohelet adds the further information, though, that everything achieved in the world is not just *hebel*, but "wishing for the wind," or possibly "a wishing of the spirit" (*rĕ'ût rûaḥ*: we shall examine the phrase shortly); it is crooked beyond straightening, and an incalculable loss.

In the first chapter, then, Qohelet does not define *hebel* explicitly, but he does provide for his audience a context within which the claim of 1:2 and 1:14 is to be understood. Shortly afterwards, in 1:18, his study of wisdom and its counterparts leads him to the conclusion that it is "worrying for the wind" or "worrying of the spirit" (*ra'yôn rûaḥ*), because wisdom is painful, and he characterizes pleasure as *hebel*, declaring that fun is mindless, and pleasure useless (2:1–2). After looking around at his own achievements, in 2:11 he finds that it was "all *hebel*, and *rĕ'ût rûaḥ*, and there was no profit under the sun," once again linking *hebel* to the absence of gain from work, and to *rĕ'ût rûaḥ*.

It would be difficult to conclude from any of this that Qohelet has in mind the transience of *hebel*: it is applied in these first chapters with some consistency to things that humans do, such as working, being wise or having fun, and it associates these things not with transience, but with a lack of gain or function. More than that, though, they may entail a positive loss, and the idea that they are useless seems intertwined with the alliterative descriptions of them as *rĕ'ût rûaḥ* or *ra'yôn rûaḥ*, terms which Qohelet uses a number of times here and in the next few chapters.[8] "Futility" may be closer to the mark than transience, but, again, Qohelet seems to imply more than just ineffectiveness.

The second word in each of these expressions, *rûaḥ*, is a common word, itself used of breath, but also of wind and spirit; the link with *hebel* suggests that a similar metaphor of air or wind is being used. Neither *rĕ'ût* nor *ra'yôn* appears as a Hebrew word elsewhere in biblical literature, but both do appear there as Aramaic words: *rĕ'ût* with reference to royal and divine wishes or decisions in Ezra (5:17; 7:18), and *ra'yôn* referring to thoughts or worries in Daniel (2:29, 30; 4:16 [ET 4:19]; 5:6, 10; 7:28). Since there are many other Aramaisms in Ecclesiastes, it is hard to ignore these established uses, and they point to *rĕ'ût rûaḥ* meaning something like "wishing for/by (the) wind," and *ra'yôn rûaḥ* either the same, or "worrying by/about (the) wind."

The more precise implications of these expressions may be apparent from other usage: 5:15 (ET 5:16) uses a similar figure of "toiling for *rûaḥ*" either to describe the zero net gain of a human at death, or with ironic reference to their (ultimately pointless) reasons for working. This understanding is compatible with the one occasion when *ra'yôn* appears in Ecclesiastes without *rûaḥ*: in 2:22 the *ra'yôn* of a human heart is set beside physical toil, in a context which suggests that it means mental labour, ambition, or anxiety. This verse might be compared with 4:6, which does not use *rĕ'ût rûaḥ* as a simple comment on a situation, in the normal way, but again links it with physical toil, counting both as less desirable than a little tranquillity. Such references suggest that we are dealing with a way of talking about human motivation and pre-occupation, and both expressions apparently connote some sort of pointless anxiety or desire. When Qohelet talks about human activities in the opening of the book, then, it is in terms not only of profitless futility, but also of aspirations which are not going to be met.

I have mentioned Michael Fox's understanding of Qohelet's "vanity" in terms of absurdity. According to this, Qohelet finds a mismatch between the actual world and his expectations of that world, which leads

8.   See 1:14; 2:11, 17, 26; 4:4, 6; 6:9; and 1:17; 4:16.

him to a critique of phenomena as unreasonable and unexpected.[9] As we have already observed, though, this understanding runs into the problem that such a sense is unattested elsewhere, and is not readily derived from the image itself—in what sense is a vapour or breath of air absurd and unexpected? That difficulty seems to be affirmed by the usage in the first two chapters, where Qohelet seems to be complaining not about the failure of an absurd world to meet reasonable human expectations, but about the failure of human expectations to comprehend the realities of the world. The nature of the world, and of temporary human existence within it, means that any work or effort undertaken with the expectation of gain is likely to be disappointed. Fox is surely right to see such disappointment of expectation as central to Qohelet's use of *hebel*, but wrong, I think, to suppose that the term refers to the disappointment rather than to the expectation. Throughout 1:1–2:11, *hebel* is aligned with human efforts, and if Qohelet does not wish his readers to perceive the term as conveying its common implication of futility, the only direction in which he guides them away from that sense is toward an additional nuance of pointless aspiration.

c. *The Meaning of* Hebel *in the Monologue*
If we read beyond the very beginning of the book, then that nuance starts to play a more prominent role. In 2:15–16, the *hebel* lies in the fact that Qohelet has made the effort to become wiser than a fool, and is explained in terms of both ultimately being forgotten: his effort seems to have gained him nothing.[10] In 2:17–21, Qohelet hates life, because everything achieved under the sun is *hebel* and *rĕ'ût rûaḥ*, and hates all his own work because his accomplishments must pass to some unknown successor. The reference is explicitly to work, and the problem seems to be that the results of labour do not belong permanently to the labourer. As he goes on to emphasize in 2:22–23, which picks up the question posed in

---

9. As Fox himself puts it in his "Meaning of *Hebel*," 426, "Underlying Qohelet's *hebel*-judgments is an assumption that the system should be rational, which, for Qohelet, means that actions should invariably produce appropriate consequences. In fact, Qohelet stubbornly expects them to do so. Qohelet believes in the rule of divine justice. That is why he does not merely resign himself to the violations of equity he observes. He is shocked by them: they clash with his belief that the world must work equitably. These violations are offensive to reason. They are absurd."

10. Fox, "Meaning of *Hebel*," 420, sees Qohelet's point here as being "that it is *unjust* for such different causes (ways of life) to have the same outcome (death)" (his italics), but 2:16 explicitly identifies forgetfulness as the problem, and may be understood, indeed, as referring to forgetfulness about the shared fate of the wise and foolish.

1:3, the worker has no gain for all the work done under the sun, while "through each of his days, pains and exasperation have been his job; at night, too, his heart has not relaxed." It is not merely the lack of gain which seems to be *hebel* here, but the fact that so much has been expended.

In 2:26, the *hebel* lies in the fact that humans are assigned desirable things like pleasure or undesirable work for others according to divine choice, and for the first time it is not applied directly to an effort or undertaking. In the broader context of his ideas, moreover, it is difficult to maintain that Qohelet sees such distinctions as objectively problematic. Fox has to read this in the context of Qohelet's previous concern about succession—it is "still an absurdity" even "if the toiler is offensive to God and the beneficiary is one who enjoys divine favour."[11] Qohelet is talking about the need for pleasure now, though, and it is unclear why he would revert to the previous issue merely to emphasize some special circumstance. In 4:4, again, the *hebel* seems to lie not in work, but in the fact that work is motivated by envy.[12] It is difficult to see any objective futility—or absurdity—here, but both passages do seem to address issues of false motivation: the workers of 2:26 do not understand that the rewards of their work depend not on the work itself, but on divine favour, while the envy noted in 4:4 seems utterly misplaced in a world where one should work for the pleasure to be found in work and the material prosperity of others has little meaning. In 4:8 we find something comparable: the *hebel* of a man who works neither for the benefit of anybody else, nor to his own satisfaction, but never stops to ask why he is denying himself any pleasure. Only in the first of these sayings, which represent a sequence of pronouncements, is it possible to identify *hebel* strictly with the disjuncture between expectation and reality, and in all of them Qohelet seems to be addressing primarily the problem of false or misplaced human motivation. We are coming close, in such instances, to the uses of *hebel* in other literature with reference to intellectual confusion.

It is difficult to know what constitutes the *hebel* of 4:16b, which follows the very obscure story of the king and the youth in 4:13–16a, but

---

11. Ibid., 418.

12. This is one of the passages that most clearly demonstrates the problems in Daniel Fredericks' attempt to view the usage of הבל throughout the book in terms of transience, an interpretation which he thinks portrays a much more orthodox character to Qohelet's thought than is usually allowed. See his *Coping with Transience: Ecclesiastes on Brevity in Life* (The Biblical Seminar 18; Sheffield: JSOT, 1993), 59: "Qoheleth is convinced that much effort is motivated by envy, and…ends in what is merely transitory." There is nothing in the text, though, about the results of the labour, and they are not what is being described as הבל.

it is also characterized as *ra'yôn rûaḥ*, and the point is perhaps about the effort required to attain the kingship when kings stand in a limitless line, and will soon be forgotten. In any case, though, 5:9 (ET 5:10) once again describes as *hebel* what is clearly a problem of human motivation or aspiration, that those who seek wealth will never be satisfied by it, and it is again difficult to see this in terms of something being wrong with the world or with reality: these individuals suffer not because the world fails to supply what they legitimately expect, but because their expectation has no limit, and can never be fulfilled.

In 6:2 Qohelet finds *hebel* (and terrible tragedy) in the case of the man who is granted material prosperity by God, but not the power to enjoy ("consume") it: it is instead consumed by a foreigner. Here we are back in territory close to that of 2:26, but there is no reference to effort or, explicitly at least, to expectation. Fox sees *hebel* in "the whole situation described: God gives wealth, then takes it away (by misfortune or by death) and gives it to another. This absurdity is divinely ordained."[13] It is difficult to understand the situation wholly in those terms, however, since the man is apparently unable to enjoy his wealth even while he has it, and we are told that "his appetite is deprived of nothing which it desires." The passage is also set in a context which focuses upon the ability to enjoy what one has, and this verse presents a case which is virtually the opposite of the ideal situation described in 5:17–19 (ET 5:18–20); 6:3–4, moreover, continue the theme in their description of a man who fathers many children and lives many years but finds no satisfaction or ultimate rest. Loss, therefore, is hardly likely to be the issue here in 6:2, and the *hebel* seems to lie in the inability of the man to take advantage of what he has got. He epitomizes Qohelet's idea of a disconnection between material prosperity and actual reward or happiness, and the problem is the gulf between what he seems to have and what he actually has.

It is also difficult to identify just what is being called *hebel* and *rĕ'ût rûaḥ* in 6:9, especially since it is hard to judge the sense or potential relevance of the following verses, 6:10–11. It seems likely, though, that the theme has been set in 6:8, and that Qohelet is talking about the limitations of wisdom: the wise man has no real gain because there is none in knowing that one will die, when being alive is better than dying; any (wise) attempt to override the fixed constraints of the world will merely generate a lot of words and hence a lot of *hebel*, without yielding any profit. There is an apparent link, in any case, to lack of gain, and probably a reference to unrealistic expectations of wisdom. In 7:6, part of Qohelet's series of sayings about the wise and foolish, it is difficult to

13. Fox, "Meaning of *Hebel*," 418.

say whether it is the laughter of fools which is *hebel*—because they are happy when they should not be—or whether Qohelet is reflecting on the saying or the series as a whole, and referring to the solemnity of the wise.

Finally, Qohelet describes things as *hebel* twice in ch. 8, both in connection with his discussion of judgment, and the failure of humans to perceive that it is happening. In 8:10–13, the *hebel* lies in human forgetfulness about the behaviour of the wicked, or perhaps more generally in the facts that delayed judgment leads humans to want to do wrong, and that the sinner apparently prolongs his life, even though it is those who fear God that will really survive. The point is driven home by two uses of *hebel* in 8:14: "There is a *hebel* committed on the earth, that there may be righteous people to whom something happens as if for the deed of the wicked, and there may be wicked people to whom something happens as if for the deed of the righteous. I said that this too is *hebel*." From what has gone before, though, it is clear that Qohelet does not believe this to be a problem of divine inconsistency, or an absence of divine judgment. His concern is rather that the way in which judgment works does not preclude suffering for righteousness or prosperity in conjunction with wickedness (as was pointed out earlier in the similar 7:15); correspondingly, there is a mismatch between what is actually happening and what humans can perceive to be happening, which influences their behaviour for the worse.

When Qohelet singles out particular situations as *hebel*, then, he is clearly not referring to the same sort of issue in every case. Only with considerable difficulty, moreover, can we identify each *hebel* as an instance of some more general absurdity in Fox's terms, especially when Qohelet seems to be talking about misguided human motivations rather than a specific difference between human expectations and reality. What the various uses do seem to have in common might be characterized as a problem of human perception or aspiration: an activity or a phenomenon is *hebel* when humans are driven to think or act in some way by a false or faulty apprehension of what they are doing. Typically, it is the misguided action or effort itself which attracts the description, but Qohelet also uses *hebel* to describe situations which can or do cause such misguidedness, because humans misinterpret what they see in them—the prosperity of a man when he has no pleasure, for instance, or the continuing good health of the wicked, which conceals the fact of divine judgment.

This understanding suits some of the passages where Qohelet uses *hebel* outside his formulaic characterizations of situations. In 3:19, for instance, *hebel* seems to be used of whatever differentiates, or fails to differentiate, humans from animals, and in 6:4 it describes the situation into which the man is born who has long life and many children, but no pleasure: he arrives in *hebel* and departs in darkness, worse off than the stillborn child who never saw the sun. In this context, set beside darkness and in contrast to sight, *hebel* is surely itself a reference to what obscures or deceives the man's perception.

Some of the same language is present in 11:7–12:2, but the reference and sense is less clearcut:

> And, the light is sweet, and it is good for the eyes to see the sun. For if a person lives many years, he should rejoice in them all—and should remember the days of darkness, that they will be many. All that comes is *hebel*. Rejoice, young man, in your youth, and let your heart make you content in the days of your being young: walk in the ways of your heart, and with the sight of your eyes; and know that, for all these things, God will bring you to a reckoning, but remove vexation from your heart, and let trouble pass away from your body, for youth and dawn are *hebel*. And be mindful of who created you in the days of your youth, when the bad times have not yet come, or the years approached of which you say "I have no pleasure in them"; when the sun and the light have not yet dimmed, or the moon and the stars, or the clouds returned with the rain.

This passage is not a single closed unit, and the last verse leads in to the description of death or old age with which Qohelet ends his monologue. The verses are held together, though, both by the imagery of light and darkness (associated with life and death) and by the theme of their advice. In 11:7–8 the man who lives many years should rejoice in them all, bearing in mind that he will die; in 11:9–10 the young man should enjoy his youth, bearing in mind that he will be judged for his actions, and in 11:10–12:1 he should further set aside his worries, while bearing in mind his creator. In what amounts to his closing advice, Qohelet summarizes his concerns that humans should find pleasure throughout life, but also that they should be aware of death and divine judgment as realities. It is not surprising that he should return to his characteristic metaphor in this context, even though he has not used his "this is *hebel*" formula for some time, since 8:14.

The first use of *hebel* here refers to "all that comes," and its position suggests that Qohelet is talking about the "days of darkness," which will be many, and are usually understood to be death. The second occurrence of the word, however, clearly refers to youth, and it is difficult to reconcile the two if we understand it as a statement of transience or ephemerality, as commentators are generally inclined to do: can Qohelet really be saying, in the space of a few sentences, both that the endless darkness of death is *hebel*, and that youth (probably linked to "dawn") is *hebel* because it passes quickly? I think it is more likely that in both places he is affirming the need for his recommendations: everything one faces in life, and perhaps especially in youth, leads humans toward the sort of false motivations and futile activities which he has described as *hebel* throughout his monologue, and so, one last time, he reminds them of the real need to find pleasure and to do those things in which it can be found. They must remember, at the same time, both that there will be an end to this opportunity, and that God will influence their ability to take advantage of it.

Something similar may be true of 9:9, where Qohelet commends the reader to "See life with the woman whom you love all the days of your life of *hebel*, which he has given you beneath the sun, all the days of your *hebel*, for that is your portion in life." This is followed, to be sure, by a warning in 9:10 about Sheol as one's future destination, but 9:9 itself emphasizes *hebel* twice as a characteristic of human living, without any obvious implication that life is transient.[14] Although this verse does not point us toward any particular interpretation of the term, in fact, its use here may reasonably be read, against the background of Qohelet's other references to *hebel*, as contrasting the pleasure to be sought with the character of the life within which it is to be sought. There are two other occasions when Qohelet refers to life as *hebel* in such a way: in 7:15 he is talking about his own life, without further specification, and in 6:12 about the difficulty of knowing what is good for a person in life, and what will come after them, noting that "The days of his life of *hebel* are finite, and he will spend them in shadow." Transience might be the theme in the latter, but so might the limits of human knowledge, and it is hard to press a single interpretation on any of these passages.

d. *Conclusions*

As has sometimes been argued, if Qohelet meant lots of different things by *hebel*, this would undermine his attempt to link so many phenomena together as manifestations of a single problem: "everything is *hebel*" would have less impact if some of his examples were clearly only futile, others insubstantial, and still others simply transient.[15] His use of a metaphor, though, does allow Qohelet to draw related issues together in a way that would be difficult were he using less figurative language, and this

---

14. There are some text-critical problems in 9:9, most notably the omission of כל ימי הבלך from some Masoretic manuscripts, the Targum and the Syriac version; its status in G is unclear, although it is attested by Aquila. It is difficult to say whether the repetition in the Hebrew is original and caused the confusion, or is itself an error.

15. So Fox, "Meaning of *Hebel*," 413–14.

becomes very apparent when we try to translate the word or to abandon the metaphor ourselves.

It is difficult to exclude additional nuances in some places, but what *hebel* seems principally to represent for Qohelet is bound up with a misapprehension of the world, and their place in it, by humans: they invest effort for things they cannot gain, or for reasons which are false, and fail to pursue or to accomplish the only truly beneficial option which is open to them—pleasure in their activities—either because their concerns lie elsewhere, or because they have been misled into behaviour which may shorten their lives or prevent their enjoyment. What confronts humans is *hebel* because it is misleading or illusory, but what they typically do in response to it is also *hebel* because it is misguided or deluded. So, for instance, in 2:21 and 2:23 *hebel* describes both sides of the same coin: the reality that one's work will pass to someone else, and the consequent futility of the pain and effort which one has put into it. Qohelet perhaps has in mind the fact that *hebel* is something which humans may both encounter and produce (maybe explicitly through speech in 5:6 [ET 5:7] and 6:11), but the principal advantage for him of *hebel* as a figure is that it represents something which can be felt, although not held or kept, but which can also touch one without effect: it is simultaneously misleading, insubstantial and ineffective. These are not distinct qualities, but different ways of regarding *hebel*'s basic nature, and the ways of interacting with it. They are also associations with *hebel* that were probably familiar to Qohelet's readers from other literature. It may have required the contextualization offered by Qohelet's initial claims and questions for them to have a clear sense of the way he is using the term, and of the scope of his claim in 1:2, but there is nothing radically new in the force of the metaphor here.

Without an equivalent, established metaphor in English, it is difficult to translate *hebel* in a way that reflects the different nuances,[16] even if we are willing to sacrifice the continuity of Qohelet's usage by adopting different terms in different contexts. The idea of an illusion, however, and of corresponding human delusion, comes close to catching the sense of *hebel* both in Ecclesiastes and in many of the other texts where it is used, and that may provide the best basis for translation. Of course, "illusion" does not really capture the aspects of futility and loss, which are also important to Qohelet, and for that reason a strong case could also be made for retaining the traditional translation, "vanity," despite the

---

16. I have a fondness for Burkitt's idea of הבל as equivalent to "a bubble," expressed as an afterthought to "Is Ecclesiastes a Translation?" (p. 28). As a translation, though, "Everything is bubbly" lacks a certain *gravitas*.

modern shift in that word's primary usage. Whatever term we choose, though, it is important to appreciate that *hebel* serves to summarize and to connect many of Qohelet's ideas about human action in the world, but it does not wholly encapsulate or define them.

2. *Qohelet and the Problem of Perception*

The principal limitations of human understanding, according to Qohelet, may be summarized as follows:

- *Humans do not learn lessons from the past.* This is explained in terms of a forgetfulness that arises from the constant turnover of human generations in the world (1:11; cf. 2:16; 9:5), although it is also manifest in more short-term forgetfulness (9:15, and perhaps 4:16).
- *Humans cannot know the future.* Ecclesiastes 3:22; 6:12; 7:14 and 10:14 refer in similar terms to the inability of humans to know what lies beyond them in the world, and the unpredictability of life means that they can have equally little idea of what will happen to them while they live (see especially 9:12). The problem is apparently not a simple inability to predict the future, but is tied up with their lack of control over outcomes.
- *Humans cannot see the differences which underlie apparently identical phenomena.* This point is made most clearly in 3:18–22 and 8:10–15, and is arguably a subset of the next.
- *Humans cannot discern the nature of divine activity.* The simplest statement of this is in 11:5, "you will not know what God does, he who will do everything." In other places, human ignorance seems to be portrayed as the result of some divine purpose (see 3:10–15; 7:13–14; 8:17), although it is not entirely clear to what extent God is deliberately blocking human understanding, and to what extent this is merely a side-effect of his activities.

The last point is especially important, because divine activity for Qohelet embraces not just those tasks in which God is directly involved, like judgment or the punishment of vow-breakers, but all the activities in which humans are involved as well: as we saw earlier, he envisages human work as contributing to processes that are under God's control. Correspondingly, because humans do not know what God is doing, they do not understand what they themselves are really doing.

These limitations combine to make it difficult for humans to develop any autonomous understanding of their situation. Except perhaps in the case of the wise, however, who do see some or all of the problem,

Qohelet does not portray them as searching for such understanding, conscious that their information is inadequate. Rather, they more typically act on their own beliefs and perceptions, leading them into the situations which Qohelet regards as *hebel*. What they are doing is not always unreasonable, as such, and one might quite properly and logically, for example, look to the behaviour of the prosperous as a clue to God's will, if one were unaware that they were actually unhappy, or about to face punishment for that behaviour. Reasonable or not, though, the actions of humans are always founded on faulty information, or on a failure to appreciate the significance of factors which might affect them.

Since he regards it as impossible to achieve adequate knowledge, Qohelet commends to his fellow human beings an approach which does not rely on such knowledge: they should do what they find to do, and take what pleasure they can from it. His critique of their present actions, though, is rooted both in his own observations, which are presumably subject to the same limitations, and in certain beliefs which, as he appears to concede himself, may not always correspond to the perceptible evidence. Perhaps especially because so much of what he says seems so potentially controversial, it is important to understand the nature of the authority he claims, allowing him to pronounce so many things *hebel*, but his own advice sound.

a. *Qohelet's "Empiricism"*

Here it may be helpful to recall that there is a diachronic, autobiographical aspect to the monologue. In particular, when Qohelet describes his thoughts about his business and his wisdom in 2:11–26, it is in terms of a strong reaction arising from a new realization: he is driven to hate life and his work (2:17–18), and he regrets, or at least questions, the effort which he has put into both becoming wise and creating his business (2:15, 20–23). To the extent that Qohelet believes his eyes to have been opened and his previous activities misguided, we have correspondingly to suppose that there has been some change in his outlook. If, as I suggested much earlier, the enquiries described in 1:13–2:2 are to be considered as separate events, which precede this change, then we may have to reckon with, as it were, "early" and "late" Qohelet. The key issue here, however, is not that he has undergone some radical change of opinion—only his views about pleasure seem notably different—but rather that Qohelet presents himself as a man transformed by reflection upon his own experience, whose exceptional wisdom, however much he might now regret it, also offers exceptional insight into the lessons of that experience.

Qohelet also sometimes presents himself as unusual in other respects. In 7:15, for instance, he asserts that "I have seen it all, in the days of my *hebel*," which is a claim to extensive experience, even if it should probably not be taken to mean that he has seen literally everything (although see 1:14), and in 9:15, he appears to be the only man who remembers the poor wise man. He also continues, though, to present his ideas as the product of his own investigations and reflections, so that what he "sees" is not always merely what he observes. This serves a rhetorical function, in that it engages the audience in his deliberations,[17] but it does have another, significant consequence: there is no suggestion that the conclusions reached by Qohelet are those that would be reached by just anybody on the basis of their own experience.

For that reason and others, the description of Qohelet as an "empiricist," which has gained some traction in recent scholarship, is useful only up to a point, and it has generally been presented with due caution.[18]

17. As Michael Fox, "Qohelet's Epistemology," *HUCA* 58 (1987): 137–55, esp. 150–51, puts it, "the introspective report, though contrary to the usual claim of traditional authority, strengthens the speaker's ethos. Qohelet interposes his consciousness between the facts and his readers, for he seeks to persuade by empathy. He bares his soul in all its twistings and turnings, ups and downs, asking his readers to join him on an exhausting journey to knowledge. If the readers can replicate the flow of perception and recognition as it developed for Qohelet, they will be more open to accepting the author's conclusions as their own."

18. See especially ibid. A. P. Hayman, "Qohelet and the Book of Creation," *JSOT* 16 (1991): 93–111, cites Fox, but goes rather further in affirming "a thoroughly empirical epistemology" (p. 98). Crenshaw, "Qohelet's Understanding," 212–13, is inclined to see empiricism as fundamental to wisdom thought more generally (which I doubt—see my *Introduction*, 114–16), and notes that "few interpreters would deny the overwhelming experiential basis of Qoheleth's teaching" (p. 212); he goes on, however, to note the many assertions which seem to have no such basis, and to conclude that, "The simple truth is that Qoheleth accepted an astonishing variety of transmitted teachings without submitting them to the test of experience" (p. 213). On the other hand, M. Patrizia Sciumbata, "Peculiarità e motivazioni della struttura lessicale dei verbi della 'conoscenza' in Qohelet. Abbozzo di una storia dell'epistemologia ebraico-biblica," *Henoch* 18 (1996): 235–49, looks at Qohelet's vocabulary associated with knowledge and perception, to affirm a conclusion rather stronger than Fox's—that Qohelet is using "un sistema epistemologico di tipo empirico-induttivo" in deliberate, polemical contrast to the non-empiricism of other wisdom traditions. Annette Schellenberg, in her wide-ranging study *Erkenntnis als Problem. Qohelet und die alttestamentliche Diskussion um das menschliche Erkennen* (OBO 188; Freiburg: Universitätsverlag/Vandenhoeck & Ruprecht, 2002), examines Qohelet's empirical side (pp. 161–91) in the context of a broader consideration of his epistemology, and understands his appeals to individual experience in terms of his belief that human knowledge is limited to what happens within the world, where only experiential and empirical enquiries are possible (p. 196).

Although he seems to be granting himself exceptional knowledge, Qohelet places himself under most of the same constraints as other humans: he draws explicitly upon no tradition of knowledge from the past, he makes no claim to knowledge of the future (cf. 8:17), and he concedes the limits of his own wisdom in understanding what is really going on (7:23–29). Placed in that predicament, he appeals to experience and observation as the basis for understanding, and, although there is nothing in the monologue which resembles an explicit epistemology, this comes close to reflecting key empirical principles. One might equally suggest, though, that the reasoning and understanding of other humans, about which Qohelet is so often bitterly critical, is no less empirical in that respect. It is not his empiricism, as such, but the certainty that he has better information, and a better ability to analyse it, which differentiates Qohelet's opinion—and this certainty introduces elements which are far from empirical.

As has often been observed even by those who view the basis of his thought as primarily experiential, Qohelet asserts that some things are true which cannot possibly be deductions from his own experience. Foremost among those, perhaps, are his ideas of divine judgment as equitable and inevitable: the perceptible evidence that would seem to contradict such ideas leads him not to discard them, but to characterize the evidence as misleading. Furthermore, Qohelet presumably has no evidence for the actual condition of the dead, which is asserted with such vehemence as a reason for the living to take full advantage of their lives: his view of Sheol may reflect a common assumption, but it is no less an assumption. If his statements about divine activity in, say 3:10–15; 5:18–19 (ET 5:19–20) or 7:14 are not simply assertions, then they too are at best based on other assumptions, and 8:17 seems deliberately paradoxical: Qohelet claims to have seen God's achievement in concealing his achievements. At other times, his claims may be less central to his key themes, but are straightforwardly statements of opinion: 5:11 (ET 5:12) asserts, for instance, that "Sweet is the sleep of a servant, whether it is a little or a lot that he eats, but the satedness of a rich man—it does not let him sleep"; this may or may not be true (I have my doubts, personally), but it is a sweeping generalization, backed by no argument or explicit observation. Qohelet's belief that wisdom is better than might is actually presented in 9:15 as standing in contradiction to his observations that the poor wise man has been forgotten, his wisdom despised, and his words ignored.

Commentators usually note the presence of such assertions, but less often observe that Qohelet's experiential statements are not only combined with such dogmatic statements, but also frequently themselves shaped by assumptions and criteria which are introduced without argument or evidence. As we saw earlier, to take the prime example, Qohelet has ideas about gain and profit which might not be shared by everyone, but which become a yardstick for his claims about human work and motivation. Human labour is not inherently or objectively *hebel*, but Qohelet views it as such because it does not deliver what he would like, and what he feels others should be working for. Correspondingly, his idea that effort without pleasure must be counted as loss lead him to declare in 6:3–6 that an unborn child is better off than the man with outward prosperity but no enjoyment—just as the unborn are better off than those who have already seen what terrible things can happen in the world (4:3). Right or wrong, such statements embody value judgments even where they are presented as the conclusions of observations.

Finally, it is important to point out that Qohelet may present his observations as evidence upon which he has reached a conclusion (e.g. 7:15–20), but he also uses them as a way to illustrate his opinions (e.g. 9:13) and as the starting-point for problems (e.g. 4:1). Furthermore, he presents judgments or opinions as observations (e.g. 6:18; 8:17), and it can be difficult in any given case to say just what he is doing. The examples drawn from nature in 1:5–7, at the very start of his discourse, demonstrate some of the issues. They are, on the face of it, significant natural processes from which Qohelet extrapolates his ideas about the way the world works. When we consider the many non-continuous events which might be mentioned in connection with the world, though, it seems more likely that these are actually selected illustrations of an opinion about the world. The drying and flooding of a wadi, say, or the burning of a fire might lead one to a very different understanding. In 5:13–17 (ET 5:14–18) we are offered Qohelet's remembrance of a man who loses everything, departing the world with as little as he brought to it, which might lead to conclusions about unpredictability or risk. This instead, however, proves to be a sort of story about the ultimate fate of all humans and their need to find pleasure: it is not evidence so much as a parable, and the same might be said of other such stories, like 4:13–16 or 9:13–16.

If all this is an attempt to smuggle assertions in as facts proven by experience, then it is an extraordinarily inept one. The "early" Qohelet, who stuffs himself with pleasure to examine it, and who builds his business to learn about human work, is at least in part an experimentalist, and it would not be improper to describe him as an empiricist. For most of the monologue, though, it would be difficult to retain that description of Qohelet without stretching it to the point of being meaningless. Qohelet does not typically extrapolate ideas from experience, but places his experience in the context of his ideas. Even when he is set on this path by his traumatic reactions in ch. 2, these reactions are triggered not by what has happened, but by his realization that what will happen at some future date does not accord with what he wants to happen, and that this undermines his basic assumptions about, among other things, ownership of his possessions and the role of prosperity as a reward.

Rather than seek some epistemological basis or agenda in Qohelet's discourse, and then assume that this has not been carried through properly, we may do better to remember that he has adopted the format of a memoir, not a philosophical essay. Since he is, however loosely, offering us a narrative of his experience, we should expect him to be linking his ideas to that experience, but that does not imply that he must be grounding those ideas in experience. We shall return to some of these issues, but for the moment it is enough to say that Qohelet is probably not to be regarded as a thoroughgoing empiricist, either in terms of his practice, or in terms of any underpinning theory of knowledge.[19] That means that we do not have to address the problems which might be raised by trying to reconcile even a very loose empiricism with Qohelet's ideas about human perception and the uselessness of trying to understand the world. It does not really explain, though, how Qohelet seems to claim a level of knowledge and insight which he believes to be lacking in other humans, and it leaves open some important questions about the ways in which other humans are supposed to gain knowledge.

b. *Wisdom and Perception*

If Qohelet himself cannot really be called an empiricist, the label may not, as we have noted, be entirely inappropriate for other humans in the world which he describes. This world may be illusory and human perception of it faulty, but these humans apparently operate according to what they see within it or deduce from it, uninfluenced by forgotten episodes from the past or by such distinctions as wealth which can and cannot be enjoyed. To the extent that they seem less concerned about things which seem invisible, like divine judgment or the incomprehensible divine purpose, it could be argued, indeed, that their behaviour is more rooted in their experience than are Qohelet's ideas in his own. Furthermore, although he may imply that they are too attached to such notions as a link between divine favour and material wealth, too reluctant to address their own motives, or too optimistic about their ability to control their lives and the future, Qohelet does not attack his fellow

---

19. I think that Craig Bartholomew's description of Qohelet's epistemology as "autonomous" may be both more accurate and more helpful; see Bartholomew, *Ecclesiastes*, 271.

humans for replacing reason with dogma. It would imply too theoretical a basis for what they do if we were actually to call them empiricists, but humans do generally come across from Qohelet's monologue as pragmatists, at least, and not as fantasists or idealists.

What Qohelet actually wants to change seems not to be the basis upon which humans act according to their perception of the world, but key aspects of that perception. If someone undeserving can become prosperous through inheritance, for instance, their prosperity cannot be regarded as a sign that individuals are deserving, and so humans should not evaluate it as such when making decisions about their own aspirations or behaviour. Such arguments tend to chip away at the observable aspects of existence: humans must appreciate that what lies behind the visible world is something much more complicated than they can see. Conversely, though, there is an undeniable benefit in pleasure, even if it is "useless" (2:2), and a corresponding loss involved in discomfort. As he emphasizes the impossibility of using incomprehensible externalities as the basis for human behaviour and motivation, so Qohelet also falls back on those things which humans can sense without the need for interpretation: they can rely on such things because they are not implicated in the world that lies beyond human control or understanding.

If this seems rather Cartesian at first blush, it must also be recalled that Qohelet does insist on certain externalities which are not perceptible to humans. We could plausibly substitute a concept of chance or fate for God in Qohelet's ideas about the world without significantly altering his conclusions about the inability of humans to influence or understand that world. Qohelet insists, however, that humans are judged and can influence that judgment, which means that if they are to achieve the pleasure to which they should aspire, they must do so in a way that is acceptable to an external arbiter. Of course, this raises problems of its own when human actions are constrained by divine plans, and Qohelet commends an attitude of caution and fear of God, rather than a set of rules: to that extent, he is again looking to the controllable sphere of the human heart rather than to external behaviour. His emphasis on what we can own or control within ourselves, however, is driven strongly by Qohelet's belief in forces outside us. God and the world may be incomprehensible or misleading, but they are very real.

Viewed from a modern perspective, Qohelet's certainties about judgment seem to sit awkwardly beside his many reservations about human knowledge of the world, and that has undoubtedly contributed to a widespread suspicion that they have been introduced by some secondary editor of the book. It is not easy just to extract them, however, without changing in important respects what he is saying. Like certain other aspects of his thought, in fact, they are probably to be regarded as fixed points in his understanding of the world. Qohelet is not an atheist, and atheism in the modern sense may not have been an intellectual option for him. He believes also in a God who is active, and who exercises control over affairs in the world: this too was probably a standard assumption among his contemporaries, along with the idea that such a deity would judge. These are assumptions, to be sure, and we might be inclined to view them as dogmatic, from a perspective in which they are not universally held. They are no more remarkable in an ancient context, though, than are basic scientific principles in our own. Correspondingly, although they are hardly instances of empiricism, we should probably not view Qohelet's maintenance of such ideas as an attempt to inject particular religious views into his argument: divine action is one of the fundamental factors in (or constraints on) human understanding of the cosmos, alongside such things as the certainty of death.

Qohelet implies that humans do not always take proper account of such things, but his insistence on their significance does not itself constitute the foundation of his claim to speak with unusual insight: he is not bringing some fresh religious perspective to bear on the issues, but integrating common assumptions into his account. That foundation is more probably to be understood as the exceptional wisdom which he asserts at the beginning of the monologue, and which is mentioned occasionally thereafter in connection with his observations. As we saw much earlier, Qohelet does not believe that wisdom offers a way to transcend the limits of human understanding, but what it does provide is a painful clarity, expressed in terms of sight in 2:14. It is this clarity that enables him to "see" better than others the reality of the human predicament, rather than any knowledge that is unavailable to them, or any better method of acquiring knowledge.

If so, then Qohelet probably perceives what he is saying and doing not in terms of a new approach to knowledge or as the introduction of new data into human calculations, but as the clarification and correction of assumptions which are based on faulty perception and reasoning. Humans behave in certain ways because they do not properly understand the nature of their activities within the world, or the limits of their control and influence. This is *hebel*, an illusion or delusion which arises not from what is intrinsic to reality, but from the human failure to grasp what is intrinsic. Informed by his wisdom, Qohelet's examination leads him to realize that humans are placing too much dependence on things which neither they nor he can properly understand, but the complexity of which he, at least, can appreciate. Humans must move, as it were, to safer ground, and give priority to those things about which they can be more certain—notably the enjoyment which they can experience for themselves, the avoidance of unnecessary pain, and the activity of God (which is itself the cause of uncertainty in other areas).

c. *Authority and the Past*

One thing that is notable by its absence in all of this is any claim to authority beyond Qohelet's assertion of his wisdom and insight. He does not evoke any teaching, revelation or tradition, and he does not explicitly portray others as doing so. This is, of course, the flip side to his focus on human experience, and an aspect of his "empiricism." It is curious in itself, however, not only because most comparable ancient literature has no such exclusion—as we shall see in the next chapter—but also because it is difficult to imagine how it would have been acceptable to his audience as a premise of his argument.

Of the limitations which Qohelet sets on human understanding, that which denies knowledge of the past is perhaps the most questionable, and of all the assertions that he makes in his introduction, that of 1:11 seems the most immediately open to challenge: in a world of books and stories how can there really be "no memory of the earlier times, and likewise of the later"? The source of Qohelet's wisdom is not specified, but he nowhere presents it as an accumulation of human experience, and he may even exclude the past as a proper consideration for wisdom (cf. 7:10). More generally, human knowledge seems to be cut off between generations in a way that suits Qohelet's presentation of the world, but hardly, on the face of it, the realities of his context. So striking is this contradiction between assertion and experience, especially in a monologue which places a high value on experience, that we can hardly pass it by without attempting some sort of explanation.

There are a few options for such an explanation. It could be, for instance, that Qohelet is thinking only in terms of a very distant past and a very distant future. That, however, would hardly suit the case he is trying to make. If he means to say, alternatively, that information from the past is inherently unreliable, then that would itself be a problematic claim—and it is, anyway, hardly what he says. We should not ignore the further possibility that this simply is a highly questionable assertion, which either invites or hopes to elude the scepticism of the reader, but I think the most plausible explanation is altogether more straightforward: when Qohelet speaks about memory, he really does mean just memory. Books and records may preserve particular ideas and information, but they do not transmit experience in a more general way, susceptible to the sort of examination that characterizes Qohelet's analysis. Correspondingly, when we try to make sense of the world on the basis of what we have encountered, we cannot just reach into the records of others as though they were a part of our own experience, and others may not have preserved the information that we might need. Human memory is indeed short, even if human records go back a very long way.

If that is in fact Qohelet's point, it throws an even harsher light on to the absence of authoritative tradition in his discussion, since that absence cannot then just be subsumed into a more general denial of useful information from the past. Indeed, if Qohelet is suggesting that the past would only be of use in understanding the world were we able to tap into it as though into our own memories, he seems altogether to be disdaining the possibility that there might be value in the conclusions reached by previous generations. That would not be surprising, however. If Qohelet's greater insight is derived from his greater wisdom, then opinions from the past would be more insightful than his own only if they were the opinions of yet wiser individuals. As the text stands, Qohelet believes himself wiser only than those who preceded him in Jerusalem (1:16), and so might theoretically value the opinions of wiser men from bigger cities, but whether or not we see this as a secondary limitation linked to his identification with Solomon, it seems clear that in practice Qohelet sees no need to consult the opinions of any other such wise men. We shall pursue some of the implications of that a little later, but may observe here that, whatever we make of his attitudes to the past, Qohelet's neglect of advice from the past throws considerable light on the nature of his wisdom. However acquired, it is apparently not a body of knowledge and conclusions, incorporating the insights of many individuals or eras, but a practical, analytical tool—not so much a science as a technology.

A rather different sort of issue arises from Qohelet's rejection, or more precisely his neglect, of non-human authority. It would be no more than a circular argument to say that he rejects revelations of the divine will because he regards the divine will as hidden, and it would also, perhaps, be something of a misrepresentation: God's broader actions and activities are certainly concealed, according to Qohelet, but some aspects of his will are apparent—he does not, for instance, seem to care for the breaking of vows (5:3–5 [ET 5:4–6]). Qohelet's God is not sealed off from humanity, and there is nothing in the monologue's descriptions of God which would necessarily exclude the possibility of revelation. Those descriptions do, however, betray Qohelet's belief that what God shows to humans may be shown to suit his purposes, not to enhance their understanding. God is not an enemy, and if he acts in such a way that humans fear him (3:14), that may only be to their advantage (7:18; 8:12–13). Qohelet does, however, believe that God deliberately misleads or obscures human understanding for his own reasons (7:14; 8:17).

Consequently, even if he were to accept that some oracle or text had impeccable credentials as divine revelation, that does not mean that Qohelet would consider it a helpful contribution to his quest for understanding. In that respect, it is interesting that he links dreams—widely regarded in the ancient world as a potential source of revelation—with *hebel* and unhelpful words (5:2, 6 [ET 5:3, 7]).

In short, then, Qohelet might recognize the authority of other humans if he thought they were wiser than him, and he might recognize the authority of divine revelation if he thought its purposes corresponded to his own. He ignores both, however, and in doing so affirms that he has a very specific idea of proper human understanding, not as a sort of communal effort between humans, and certainly not as something to be acquired in the form of information from God, but as the application of the finest mind—his own—to the problems thrown up by experience. Qohelet considers himself to see further, but assuredly not by standing on the shoulders of giants.

3. *Summary and Conclusions*

To address Qohelet's use of the term *hebel* at this stage might seem like no more than an exercise in tidying up. In the preceding chapters, we have, after all, gained a fair idea of how he believes the world to work, and how he thinks that humans ought to live in it. When we look closely at the metaphor which he uses to sum up so much, however, it becomes apparent that *hebel* represents for him not just some general or particular wrongness in the world or in humans, but a more basic problem that stands in the way of human understanding. Human actions and motives are *hebel*, and some aspects of the world in which they live are likewise *hebel*, because all are implicated in a misperception of reality. This leads humans to misunderstand their situation, and to place their confidence in things about which they should not be confident, so that much of what drives and shapes them is no more than an illusion.

Qohelet's repeated, emphatic use of this metaphor suggests both that he sees himself as more perceptive than others and that he attaches significance to overcoming their misperceptions. His own understandings of the world, though, seem constrained by the same limitations which he believes to constrain all human understandings. This pushes him toward an analysis rooted in experience, since such limitations permit little else, and that has itself given rise to descriptions of Qohelet in modern scholarship as an empiricist. He does not really adopt a recognizably empirical approach to knowledge with any consistency, though, and is probably no more or less an empiricist in this respect than are the humans whose ideas he views as *hebel*. His issue is not with the methods that they employ to understand the world, which are founded in their own observations and experiences, but with the conclusions that they draw.

Qohelet's own reflections, influenced by his own concerns but enhanced by his considerable wisdom, lead him to believe that certain common suppositions are false. It is not the case, for instance, that humans can gain anything meaningful as a product of their labours, that they can shape the future in any usefully predictable way, or that they can readily judge a human's standing with God from their material wealth. Such considerations lead him to commend instead the prioritization of things about which humans can have greater confidence: in particular, nobody can deny that there is a genuine benefit of some sort in the experience of pleasure, and that benefit should therefore be pursued. No less weight is to be given, however, to things like divine judgment, even when the indubitability of their existence seems belied by the virtual invisibility of their operation. Qohelet believes himself to be offering a solid handhold to people who, though they do not know it, are grasping at air.

What he offers them is, however, an interpretation which makes no appeal to authority beyond Qohelet's claim to exceptional wisdom. The monologue is by no means devoid of rhetoric, and certainly seeks to persuade, but it disdains to offer its audience any good reason why they should accept it apart from the plausibility of its claims and arguments. Even if we allow that there was some original attempt to link it with Solomon, and so to imbue it with the authority of his reputation, that link was only ever at most implied. In this respect, as in others, Qohelet's speech is highly unusual, and its distinctiveness will become more apparent, but also perhaps more explicable, as we turn to look at its relationship with other ancient literature.

Chapter 5

QOHELET AS A SCEPTIC

"Hey Johnny, what are you rebelling against?" "Whaddya got?"
(The Wild One, 1953)

Qohelet sets himself against the *hebel* of human endeavours, though not against any named, coherent system of thought or belief. He does not ask explicitly, moreover, to be placed on the side of, or against any, particular tradition or school of thought, and we are invited to consider his a lone voice, speaking from his own reflection on his own experience. Insofar as he has a single target, it appears to be any assumption by his fellow humans that they can themselves influence or properly understand the world in which they live. If his positive proposals can be condensed down to a single idea, on the other hand, it is that humans must be active, not with a view to the outcome of their actions, but because it is only in those actions that they can find enjoyment, and it is only enjoyment which offers them any gain from their lives. Both the attack and the proposal sound radical, but it is difficult to evaluate them in isolation, and we risk allowing our understanding of Qohelet's significance to be established largely by his presentation of himself.

If it seems obvious to many commentators that Qohelet is a sceptic in some sense, even if that sense is not always clearly defined,[1] then we

---

1. As Schellenberg, *Erkenntnis*, 45–50, has pointed out, there is much discussion of Qohelet's scepticism without much definition of the term, or agreement about its meaning—she singles out Martin A. Klopfenstein, "Die Skepsis des Qohelet," *TZ* 28 (1972): 97–109, as "ein Paradebeispiel für die Art der Probleme in der Diskussion," because the article discusses Qohelet's scepticism throughout, without once defining it (p. 47). That may be a little harsh, because Klopfenstein is hardly the only culprit. She goes on, though, to acknowledge that it is difficult to pin down a single definition (pp. 60–62), and turns to approach the matter through an investigation of Qohelet's ideas, rather than by measuring them against a fixed yardstick. This is sensible in many respects, and my own approach, although very different in other respects, takes much the same starting-point. Over-definition can be unhelpful in itself: in his pair of studies, "What is Scepticism and Can It Be Found in the Hebrew Bible?," *SJOT* 13 (1999): 225–57, and "Ironic Correlations and Scepticism in the

should perhaps bear in mind also that scepticism may be a matter of perspective:[2] in our own day, after all, it is not unusual for people hold-ing particular religious or political views to believe themselves to be attacking an entrenched scientific establishment, while that establishment includes scientists who may perceive themselves to be sweeping away centuries of religious dogma. If the essence of scepticism, broadly understood, lies in the expression of doubt, then in such situations we are hardly dealing with a clear-cut case of received wisdom, on the one hand, and scepticism on the other. Indeed, if we allow that there may be some truth in the self-understandings of each, then both sides are "sceptical." Obviously, though, they are not on the same side, and it is important for us to understand that, outside some particular technical uses in philoso-phy (to which we shall come later), scepticism need not itself unite sceptics—it is an attitude or approach, not a set of conclusions.[3]

In addition, and perhaps more importantly, we must also be careful about extrapolating from expressions of doubt the existence of any corre-sponding certainties. To take a simpler case, I am sceptical about the idea of the moon being made from blue cheese, but you would be unwise to draw from my doubt the inference that any adult actually holds that idea. Even when they are talking about the same matters, then, sceptics may have nothing more in common than their sceptical attitude, while scepti-cal attitudes to an idea do not in themselves indicate the acceptance of that idea by others.

Joy Statements of Qoheleth?," *SJOT* 14 (2000): 67–100, William Anderson finds relatively little use for his elaboration of the modes of scepticism after he has turned to the much more interesting question of its relationship with irony.

2.   Robert Johnston makes the interesting suggestion in this respect, with regard to Qohelet, in his "'Confessions of a Workaholic': A Reappraisal of Qoheleth," *CBQ* 38 (1976): 14–28, that, viewed from the point of view that wisdom literature is supposed to be about the living of human life, Qohelet's message is not a sceptical assault, but a call to return to core values.

3.   I think that this is a problem in Crenshaw's treatment, which understands scepticism in terms of a loss of faith; see, for example, "The Birth of Skepticism in Ancient Israel," in *The Divine Helmsman: Studies on God's Control of Human Events, Presented to Lou H. Silberman* (ed. James L. Crenshaw and Samuel Sand-mel; New York: Ktav, 1980), 1–19, esp. 9: "On the one hand, skepticism addresses itself to a specific theological situation; in short, it signifies a crisis of faith in God. On the other hand, the skeptic also isolates a wholly different kind of bankruptcy—the loss of faith in human beings." He goes on (p. 12), to talk about admissions concerning the "bankruptcy of knowledge" resting "ultimately upon convictions about God." To a great extent, as is clear at the outset of his essay, Crenshaw is furnishing his own idea of scepticism, and that idea is of a body of beliefs, albeit negative ones. See also the comments of Schellenberg, *Erkenntnis*, 47–48.

It is important to emphasize two such seemingly self-evident points in part because there is a tendency in some scholarship both to talk of scepticism in wisdom literature as though it were a single phenomenon,[4] and to presume that it arose in response to some particular orthodoxy. A conventional distinction between "sceptical" and "orthodox," or "pessimistic" and "optimistic" wisdom literature does have its uses as a broad and loose way of classifying texts, and it also draws attention to certain common features. If we are not alert to the risks, however, then it can lead us both to blur the distinctions between some texts and to overestimate the differences between others. With respect to Qohelet in particular, though, we need to be conscious that his possible scepticism in some areas does not imply that he must have been sceptical in others, even where the attitudes expressed in other texts might lead us to expect him to have been. We must also recognize that some of the expectations which he attacks would not necessarily have been common expectations, and that certain of his doubts might have been very widely shared. Qohelet's relationship with other "sceptical" and "orthodox" texts is itself something which needs to be examined, and not presumed from the outset on the basis of broad generalizations or suppositions.

Correspondingly, if we are to understand Qohelet's place in ancient literature and thought, his supposed scepticism should not be the point at which we start, but the point at which we finish, and it is our understanding of his ideas in context which should define that scepticism, if the term is appropriate at all, not *vice versa*. I want to begin, however, by returning briefly to the question of Qohelet's presentation in the book, before looking at particular areas of his thought.

1. *Qohelet in the Literary Tradition*

It hardly needs to be said again that Qohelet's monologue is founded in an autobiographical account, and his words presented as personal conclusions rather than as received wisdom. Before we are too swept away, however, by Qohelet's claims to have developed his ideas from his own experience and insight, it might be salutary to look at something written along rather the same lines, but by a very different author:

---

4. So, for instance, E. J. Dillon, *The Sceptics of the Old Testament: Job, Koheleth, Agur: With English Text Translated for the First Time from the Primitive Hebrew as Restored on the Basis of Recent Philological Discoveries* (London: Isbiser & Co., 1895).

Οὐδείς, Κύρν᾽, ἄτης καὶ κέρδεος αἴτιος αὐτός,
ἀλλὰ θεοὶ τούτων δώτορες ἀμφοτέρων·
οὐδέ τις ἀνθρώπων ἐργάζεται ἐν φρεσὶν εἰδὼς
ἐς τέλος εἴτ᾽ ἀγαθὸν γίνεται εἴτε κακόν.
πολλάκι γὰρ δοκέων θήσειν κακὸν ἐσθλὸν ἔθηκεν
καί τε δοκῶν θήσειν ἐσθλὸν ἔθηκε κακόν.
οὐδέ τωι ἀνθρώπων παραγίνεται ὅσσ᾽ ἐθέλησιν·
ἴσχει γὰρ χαλεπῆς πείρατ᾽ ἀμηχανίης.
ἄνθρωποι δὲ μάταια νομίζομεν, εἰδότες οὐδέν·
θεοὶ δὲ κατὰ σφέτερον πάντα τελοῦσι νόον.

Nobody, Cyrnus, is himself responsible for loss and profit,
but gods are the givers of both these things.
Nor does any human labour knowing, at heart,
whether he is moving to a good conclusion or a bad.
For often, expecting to do badly he does well,
and expecting to do well he does badly.
Nor do as many things come to a man as he wants:
for he holds the means of terrible hardship.
We humans value vanities, knowing nothing,
but gods bring everything to a conclusion
according with their own purpose. (Theognis 133–42)[5]

Theognis was a Greek lyric poet of the sixth or late seventh century B.C.E.: although these lines are generally considered authentic (not least because they are addressed to his friend Cyrnus), much was ascribed to him in antiquity that was probably not, and "Theognidea" were widely cited in classical literature.[6] Ranston noted many years ago that there are numerous correspondences of thought or expression between his verses (or those attributed to him) and Qohelet's speech,[7] and it is certainly difficult to read Theognis without frequently being reminded of Qohelet, as some other examples may indicate:

Πάντων μὲν μὴ φῦναι ἐπιχθονίοισιν ἄριστον
μηδ᾽ ἐσιδεῖν αὐγὰς ὀξέος ἠελίου·
φύντα δ᾽ ὅπως ὤκιστα πύλας Ἀΐδαο περῆσαι
καὶ κεῖσθαι πολλὴν γῆν ἐπαμησάμενον.

5. My translations are from the text in M. L. West, *Iambi et Elegi Graeci* (2 vols.; 2d ed.; Oxford: Clarendon, 1989–92), 1:180, 194, 221, and 231.

6. There is an extensive literature; see most recently Hendrik Selle, *Theognis und die Theognidea* (Untersuchungen zur antiken Literatur und Geschichte 95; Berlin: de Gruyter, 2008).

7. See especially H. Ranston's *Ecclesiastes and the Early Greek Wisdom Literature* (London: Epworth, 1925), 13–62, 142–50; also "Ecclesiastes and Theognis," *AJSLL* 34 (1918): 99–122; and "Koheleth and the Early Greeks," *JTS* 24 (1923): 160–69.

The best of all things for humans is not to be born,
nor see the rays of the dazzling sun
—but once born, to pass as swiftly as possible through the gates of Hades
and lie with much earth heaped over. (Theognis 425–28)

Ξυνὸν δ᾽ ἀνθρώποις ὑποθήσομαι, ὄφρα τις ἥβης
ἀγλαὸν ἄνθος ἔχων καὶ φρεσὶν ἐσθλὰ νοῆι,
τῶν αὐτοῦ κτεάνων εὖ πάσχεμεν: οὐ γὰρ ἀνηβᾶν
δὶς πέλεται πρὸς θεῶν οὐδὲ λύσις θανάτου
θνητοῖς ἀνθρώποισι:

I'll make one suggestion to all humans: while you still are young,
having a bright bloom, and soundness of mind at heart,
enjoy what you have. For there is no growing young
twice comes from the gods, nor release from death
for mortal humans... (Theognis 1007–11)

Κύρνε, θεοὺς αἰδοῦ καὶ δείδιθι: τοῦτο γὰρ ἄνδρα
εἴργει μήτ᾽ ἔρδειν μήτε λέγειν ἀσεβῆ:

Respect and fear the gods, Cyrnus, for it is this that restrains a man
From doing or speaking impiety. (Theognis 1179–80)

Although they are frequently rather general, such resemblances led Ranston himself to see Theognis as a major, although probably indirect, influence on Ecclesiastes. That is not impossible, in fact, unless we wish to date Ecclesiastes very early, but the more important point is that much of what seems radical in Ecclesiastes, when it is read as part of the biblical canon, seems much less unusual when it is considered in the context of ancient literature more broadly. Theognis is not a radical sceptic, and Greece was not somehow cut off culturally from the rest of the eastern Mediterranean, even long before the Hellenistic period, so it is not at all unlikely that some of the sentiments which he expresses had much wider currency.

To take a quite separate example, we also find strong resemblances to some of Qohelet's other themes in an Egyptian text from a much earlier period which describes itself as a harper's song from the tomb of King Intef, although its actual date and origin are disputed:[8]

8. My translation is based on the transcriptions of Papyrus Harris 500 (BM Papyrus 10060), col. VI, 2–VII, 3, and of the fragmentary copy from the tomb of Paatenemheb (the Leyden fragment), in Michael Fox, "A Study of Antef," *Orientalia* 46 (1977): 393–423, esp. 405–6. For the sake of clarity, I have taken considerable liberties with the presentation of the text. For collected translations of harpers' songs, see especially Miriam Lichtheim, "The Songs of the Harpers," *JNES* 4 (1945): 178–212, and Edward F. Wente, "Egyptian 'Make Merry' Songs Reconsidered," *JNES* 21 (1962): 118–28. Fox also gives a translation and a transcription of

The song which is in the tomb of Intef, the justified, which is in front of the harpist:
This noble is flourishing: fate is good, perishing good.
A generation has been going, another staying on,
Since the time of the ancients.
The divine dead who existed long ago, are at peace in their pyramids;
Nobles, become spirits, likewise buried in their pyramids.

Those who built tombs—their places are no more:
see what has been done with them!
I have heard the words of Imhotep and of Djedef-Hor,
widely quoted as their sayings.
See the places belonging to them, their walls crumbled away—
their places are no more, as though they had never existed.
None comes from there
to say how they are doing, to say what they are doing
until he has made our hearts whole,[9]
until we pass swiftly to the place they went.

But be happy in your heart:
Forgetfulness performs the spirit-making rite for you.[10]
Follow your heart while you exist,
put myrrh upon your head, dress yourself in fine linen,
anoint yourself with true wonders of divine stuff.
Keep adding to your happiness, let your heart never slacken.
Follow your heart and your happiness, do your things on earth.
Let your heart never perish, until[11] there comes to you that day of lament:
the Weary-Hearted One doesn't hear their lament,
weeping doesn't save a man from the netherworld.

Papyrus Harris in his *The Song of Songs and the Ancient Egyptian Love Songs* (Madison: University of Wisconsin Press, 1985), 345–47, 378–80.

　9.　The text reads *stm.tw=f*, with Fox, I understand this to be a writing of *r stmt=f*. This would seem to align the clause with what follows, although Fox translates "and thus to heal our hearts." David Lorton, "The Expression *šms-ib*," *JARCE* 7 (1968): 41–54, esp. 47, prefers to read in accordance with the preceding, as *stm=f*. The verb is otherwise unattested, although it appears to be a causative form; most commentators understand it as "make complete," Lorton as "make to cease."

　10.　I divide *wḏꜣ=k ib=k rs mhꜣ ib ḥr sꜣḫ n=k*, as Lichtheim, *Ancient Egyptian Literature*, 1:197. Lichtheim disowns her previous rendering, "May thy heart be cheerful to permit the heart to forget the making of (funerary) services for thee" ("The Songs of the Harpers," 92)—presumably reading *r smhꜣ*—as "overlong and unbalanced." Fox also divides *r smhꜣ*, but refuses to construe *wḏꜣ=k* with *ib=k*, rendering, "Be hale! while your heart is directed toward self-forgetfulness."

　11.　There are significant differences between the sources here. I read *m wḏ ib=k*, with Papyrus Harris (as Fox), where the Leyden text has *m ḥd ib=k* (or *ḥdt*: Fox, *Song of Songs*, 380); cf. Lichtheim, "as your heart commands." Immediately afterwards, though, it is probably the Leyden text which is right to read *r* before *iw n=k*.

Refrain: Have a holiday—never tire of it!
No one can have his things go with him.
There is none who goes comes back again.

This song is unusual in its insistence not that one should rejoice in the afterlife, or perhaps in the context of specific funerary celebrations, but that life should be enjoyed because death is unknown—quite a radical position in the Egyptian context, which itself attracts criticism in another song.[12] Much of the content, though, is highly conventional, and found in other harpers' songs and funerary inscriptions—not least the initial reference to the coming and going of generations, which is sometimes linked elsewhere to natural phenomena. Just before it too commends rejoicing in life, for instance, the *Song of Khai-Inheret* remarks that:

(As) the waters go downstream
And the north wind goes upstream,
(So) every man (goes) to his (appointed) hour.[13]

Of course, the reference here is to the Nile, and the theme seems to be very different from that expressed by Qohelet in 1:6–7, but there are enough points of contact with Egyptian harpers' songs more generally that Stefan Fischer sees them as a major influence on Ecclesiastes.[14] That is questionable, at least if we are to envisage anything close to direct influence, but these texts again show that what seems so strange in the biblical context may have been much more commonplace in reality. Certain of the themes in the Intef song recur many centuries later in tomb autobiographies from the Late Period. For example,

O my brother, my husband,
Friend, high priest!
Weary not of drink and food,
Of drinking deep and loving!
Celebrate the holiday,
Follow your heart day and night,
Let not care into your heart,
Value the years spent on earth!
The west [i.e. the place of the afterlife], it is a land of sleep,
Darkness weighs on the dwelling-place

---

12. See Lichtheim, "The Songs of the Harpers," 197–98, and *Ancient Egyptian Literature*, 2:115–16.

13. From Lichtheim, "The Songs of the Harpers," 201.

14. See Stefan Fischer, *Die Aufforderung zur Lebensfreude im Buch Kohelet und seine Rezeption der ägyptischen Harfnerlieder* (Wiener alttestamentliche Studien 2; Frankfurt am Main: Lang, 1999), and "Qohelet and 'Heretic' Harpers' Songs," *JSOT* 26 (2002): 105–21.

Those who are there sleep in their mummy-forms.
They wake not to see their brothers,
They see not their fathers, their mothers,
Their hearts forgot their wives, their children.[15]

One final example may suffice. The Sumerian *Ballade of Early Rulers*, as Alster titles it a little quaintly, bears a resemblance to the harper's song from the tomb of King Intef, but can claim transmission rather closer to Israel: copies of a version are known from Ugarit and Emar, and another version is attested in Assurbanipal's library in Nineveh.[16] The version from Syria, as reconstructed by Alster, reads in translation:

With Eni the plans are drawn.
According to the decisions of the gods, lots are allotted.
Since time immemorial there has been [w]ind!
Has there ever been a time when you did not hear this from the mouth of a predecessor?
Above them were those (kings), (and above) those kings were others.
Above (are) the houses where they lived, [below (are)] their everlasting houses.
Like the remote heavens, no hand, indeed, has ever reached them.
Like the depth of the underworld (lit. earth), one knows nothing (about it/them).
All life is an illusion.
The life of mankind was not [intended to last for ever].
Where is Alulu, the king [who reigned 36,000 years?]
...
Where are those great kings, from former days till now?
They are no longer engendered, they are no longer born.
Life onto which no light is shed, how can it be more valuable than death?
Young man, let me truly instruct you about your god!
Chase away grief from depression! Spurn silence!
Instead of a single day's joy, let there come a long day of 36,000 years
<of silence!>
As for her little child, may Siraš rejoice over you!
These are the regulations of righteous mankind![17]

15. From the Stela of Taimhotep. Translation from Miriam Lichtheim, *Ancient Egyptian Literature: A Book of Readings*. Vol. 3, *The Late Period* (Berkeley: University of California Press, 1980), 62–63. See also Burkes, *Death*, 190–97; Burkes' excellent study considers more generally the developments in attitudes to death that are reflected both in such texts and in Ecclesiastes.

16. For a general description with translations, see Lambert, "Some New Babylonian Wisdom Literature," 37–42. Editions of the three known versions are given in Alster, *Wisdom of Ancient Sumer*, 288–322.

17. Translation from Alster, *Wisdom of Ancient Sumer*, 312–17. Sayings in other versions are often strikingly reminiscent of Qohelet; note, for example, from the

Although they are not always linked to each other, or to other ideas, in the same ways as in our work, references to human transience and calls to enjoy life can be found in a very wide range of ancient Near Eastern and classical literature. Indeed, Christoph Uehlinger has assembled a very impressive array of texts to demonstrate the close relationship between Ecclesiastes and other ancient Near Eastern literature in many different respects.[18] To that extent, far from being a lone voice, Qohelet may have echoed themes and ideas which were well known already to his audience, and it seems increasingly clear that the book, for all its idiosyncrasies, stood well in the mainstream of ancient literature, and perhaps also ancient popular culture (if that can be generalized). It is important, in other words, to appreciate that Qohelet may have seemed far from shockingly new and radical to the original readers of the book.

Neo-Assyrian text, lines 5–6: "Whatever the heart('s desires[?]) are on earth, they are no good, [they evaporate (?)] in 'wind(?)'' / The task of a scholar's pupil does not yield a joyous heart" (p. 321). Having earlier noted that the Syrian texts show signs of struggling with the original (pp. 292–93), Alster himself comments (p. 297), that "It should now be clear that the spiritual atmosphere of Qohelet was not inspired by Greek influence alone. The inspiration came, at least in part, from Sumerian texts of the early second millennium B.C.E. So far one would have thought that the most likely channel through which they might have passed to the biblical world is through the Syro-Mesopotamian area of the Late Bronze Age (thirteenth century B.C.E.). We can now dismiss that possibility, because the scribes of that area evidently had so many difficulties in coping with the original sources that they were unable to understand them fully, or even seriously misunderstood crucial points. So the transmission is more likely to have happened much later, during the exile through learned circles in Babylon itself." I think we should more probably draw the conclusion that, whether the origins are ultimately Sumerian or not, the Near East and Eastern Mediterranean regions were familiar over a very long period with the sorts of themes and ideas found in Ecclesiastes.

18. Christoph Uehlinger, "Qohelet im Horizont mesopotamischer, levantinischer und ägyptischer Weisheitsliteratur der persischen und hellenistischen Zeit," in *Das Buch Kohelet. Studien zur Struktur, Geschichte, Rezeption und Theologie* (ed. Ludger Schwienhorst-Schönberger; BZAW 254; Berlin: de Gruyter, 1997), 155–247. The principal concern of this important study is to demonstrate that, "Das Qoh-Buch ist— historisch betrachtet—zunächst einmal ein Teil der *altlevantinischen Literaturgeschichte*. Die Primärquelle für die Erhebung der 'zeitgenössischen Diskussion' ist dann aber die mesopotamische, ägyptische und levantinische Weisheitsliteratur der persischen und hellenistischen Zeit in ihrer ganzen Breite, nicht nur die ältere alttestamentliche Weisheit und/oder die griechisch-hellenistische Popularphilosophie" (p. 156). Other studies include Loretz, *Qohelet und der alte Orient*, and Johan Yeong-Sik Pahk, "Qohelet e le Tradiziuoni sapienzali del vicino oriente antico," in Bellia and Passaro, eds., *Il Libro del Qohelet*, 117–43.

It is possible also that Ecclesiastes drew more directly on existing literature, and there is nothing new or especially problematic in the notion that Qohelet may be citing other sources; after all, we saw earlier that 5:3 (ET 5:4) seems to allude to Deut 23, and most commentators also recognize an allusion to, or even a borrowing from, Gilgamesh in ch. 9.[19] Furthermore, the epilogue to Ecclesiastes seems to suggest itself, at 12:9, that Qohelet was in some sense a collector of sayings. From that point of view, we should be conscious that less of a premium was placed on originality in ancient Near Eastern literature, and that materials were often recycled or re-contextualized in new compositions.

We may be reasonably confident, on the other hand, that such materials as the author did borrow or adapt from elsewhere did not originally include the sort of comments which tie them into Qohelet's broader themes about *hebel*, or his own experience. To an extent that we cannot clearly define, Qohelet's monologue seems to be a re-working of existing ideas and materials, which sets them in the context of Qohelet's over-arching themes and narrative. That draws attention to the essentially facilitatory nature of that presentation, but it does not in itself detract from the originality of the work overall. Indeed, it suggests that we should be looking to the broader aspects of the presentation if we are to understand the distinctiveness of the book.

a. *Instruction and the Individual*

As we may recall from much earlier in this study, instructional literature, especially in Egypt but also elsewhere, was usually attributed to a named author, in contrast to most other pre-classical Near Eastern literature. The convention may go back to an original association of such works with tomb biographies, but these attributions were commonly fictional. In many cases, they were apparently intended to lend authority and prestige to the advice which they offered, by linking it to some famous man, perhaps from the distant past, whose example was worth following. Alternatively, or in addition, the attribution sometimes provided a narrative context within which the content was to be understood, and such late instructions as *Ahiqar* or *'Onchsheshonqy* set their advice within quite complicated stories.[20] Although it is not an instruction itself, the general

---

19. See, for example, Loretz, *Qohelet und der alte Orient*, 116–22. Uehlinger, "Qohelet im Horizont," 180–92, rightly questions whether the author of Ecclesiastes could have drawn this directly from *Gilgamesh*.

20. *Ahiqar* may bear some responsibility for this development, and Lichtheim has argued plausibly that it exercised a significant influence on *'Onchsheshonqy*; see Lichtheim's *Late Egyptian Wisdom Literature*, 13–22.

presentation in Ecclesiastes can probably be understood in broadly similar terms, and the use of a fictional speech to frame ideas is very widespread in Near Eastern literature.

Although linked to an individual in this way, however, instructions often also claimed or sought a place in some much longer tradition. One of the earliest Egyptian examples, for instance, the *Instruction of Ptah-hotep*, has the elderly vizier pass on to his son advice that is his own, but that has also been passed down to him through the generations, from ancestors who once listened to the gods.[21] In Mesopotamia, *Šuruppak* claims a legendary, antediluvian origin, and in Jewish literature, the unnamed but individual father who speaks in Prov 1–9 is careful to show how his words go back to teaching from his own father (Prov 4). Rather later, the prologue to the Greek version of Ben Sira points out that the book was written in the light of much reading of the Torah, which concurs both with Ben Sira's own association of wisdom with law, and with his strong emphasis on inherited instruction. A sense of age and tradition is important for many such works, and one Egyptian composition, apparently a collection of admonitions, styles itself simply *The Instruction According to Ancient Writings*.[22] In this respect, Qohelet's monologue is clearly very different: to whatever extent it actually made use of older material, it makes no actual claim to antiquity beyond the dubious association with Solomon, and Qohelet's words are avowedly his own, not lessons passed down from of old.

The monologue is not entirely without parallel in this respect. Tradition is not explicitly at the heart of all ancient advice literature, and the specific experience of the protagonists may indeed sometimes have an explicit role to play in their advice. For instance, two Egyptian instructions attributed to kings—*Amenemhet* and *Merikare*—do anchor part of their content in experiences attributed to those kings,[23] and it would be wrong to view advice as wholly disconnected from individual experience in other texts. Instructions are never presented, however, as radical

21. Papyrus Prisse, col. 5, lines 4–6; see the translation in Parkinson, *The Tale of Sinuhe*, 250.

22. See my *Early Israelite Wisdom* (Oxford Theological Monographs; Oxford: Clarendon, 1994), 169–70. The Egyptian text is now published in Fredrik Hagen, "'The Prohibitions': A New Kingdom Didactic Text," *JEA* 91 (2005): 125–64. The ostracon preserving the title (OBM EA 5631 [*verso*]) does not certainly belong to the rest of the work, which is an unusual collection of negative admonitions, but the fact that it does contain the beginning of one such admonition makes it unlikely that we are dealing with a freestanding "literary doodle," to use Hagen's term (p. 152).

23. Translations in Lichtheim, *Ancient Egyptian Literature*, 1:97–109, 135–39; Parkinson, *The Tale of Sinuhe*, 203–34.

re-evaluations of received traditions, and conformity with those traditions is clearly valued more highly in such compositions than is independence of mind. Correspondingly, references to personal experience
should not generally be understood as references to real personal
discovery. When the writer of Prov 24:30–34, for example, tells of how
he passed the overgrown field of a lazy man, sat down and considered it,
and reached the conclusion that laziness is a bad thing, we are being
offered an illustrative story, not an account of a new philosophical
insight—and it is telling that the conclusion reached is no different from
that found without such a story, but in almost identical words, at Prov
6:10–11. It is, perhaps, no less telling that Ben Sira looks for wisdom in
study and prayer (Sir 39:1–11) or in instruction (51:13–22), not in personal experience. Although, as we have seen, Qohelet cannot be called
an empiricist without significant qualification, the presentation of his
ideas as the consequence of experience and observation, without reference to tradition, does stand out in the wider context of ancient advice
literature.

One consequence is that the authority of the advice devolves entirely
on to Qohelet himself, and the reader's response to it is bound up,
therefore, with the credibility of the character. In this respect, Qohelet
occupies a role more like that of the individual characters in dialogues,
and it may be no coincidence that a few ancient texts use separate voices
to explore questions about the usefulness or validity of traditional advice.
This exploration can take several forms, and perhaps the simplest is
found in the Egyptian *Instruction of Any*, when Any's son replies to the
instruction given by Any, protesting at his inability to learn so much.[24] A
similar, but much more interesting device is used in the Mesopotamian
work, *Šūpê-amēlī*, where a father again presents what seems to be quite a
conventional instruction. The son's response does not convey either his
gratitude or a protest against learning. Rather, he seems to talk about
uncertainty over who will enjoy the proceeds of his land, about his
father's leaving his wealth behind when he dies, and about the shadow of
death hanging over humans, who will be cut off from the living when
they have died.[25]

---

24.   Translation in Lichtheim, *Ancient Egyptian Literature*, 2:135–46. See also
Michael V. Fox, "Who Can Learn? A Dispute in Ancient Pedagogy," in *Wisdom,
You Are My Sister: Studies in Honor of Roland E. Murphy, O.Carm., on the
Occasion of His Eightieth Birthday* (ed. M. L. Barré; CBQMS 29; Washington:
Catholic Biblical Association of America, 1997), 62–77.

25.   See especially Hurowitz, "The Wisdom of Šūpê-amēlī."

Although comparisons have been drawn between Qohelet and the son in *Šūpê-amēlī*, it is difficult to say whether the son's reply even constitutes a rejection of the father's instruction, let alone a sceptical assessment of instruction in general. The preamble to the work, in fact, seems to commend the father as a man who has been given divine insight, and we are not offered a specific basis for the son's objections—unless it is in his initial claim that humans are restless. This makes it difficult to say precisely how the reply is supposed to relate to the father's instruction, and what we are supposed to make of the piece overall. What we can say, though, is that the detachment of advice from tradition, and its attribution more strictly to individuals, offered an occasional way for writers to present separate, perhaps critical viewpoints.

Although it is not so straightforwardly described as "advice literature," the so-called *Dialogue of Pessimism* in Mesopotamia also shows, in a rather different way, how traditional sayings can be used to formulate an argument for quite contrary courses of action—perhaps pre-empting a tenet of Greek sophism[26]—as a servant justifies the different, and contradictory proposals of his indecisive master.[27] Here, the dialogue is not between characters with opposing viewpoints, but instead a single character is made to express different views. The late Demotic instruction on Papyrus Insinger famously sets up contradictory sayings to show the limitations of conventional advice in the face of divine power, and if the whole content was originally attributed to one speaker, as seems likely (the beginning is lost), it is using a similar technique within a rather different format.[28]

Links with Qohelet have been suggested on other grounds for all these "sceptical" compositions, but the key point here is that they reflect a degree of vitality in the literary conventions employed. When Qohelet attributes his ideas not to tradition but strictly to his own experience, in a fashion that seems unremarkable to a modern reader, he is also detaching them from any implication of established authority. The presentation of the character in this way gives him a different sort of voice, and the few loose analogies in the context of advice literature suggest that other authors may have exploited such techniques to talk more critically about advice.

26. Diogenes Laertius says of Protagoras, καὶ πρῶτος ἔφη δύο λόγους εἶναι περὶ παντὸς πράγματος ἀντικειμένους ἀλλήλοις: οἷς καὶ συνηρώτα, πρῶτος τοῦτο πράξας, "And he was the first who said that there were two contradictory cases to be made about every matter; and he would propound them, being the first to do so" (*Lives and Opinions of Eminent Philosophers* 9:51)

27. Lambert, *Babylonian Wisdom Literature*, 139–49.

28. See Lichtheim, *Late Egyptian Wisdom Literature*, 107–234.

b. *Cumulative Argument*

The detachment of Qohelet from claims to traditional authority makes Ecclesiastes different from most other advice literature in respect of its attribution, but is not without parallel. Something similar might be said also of its attempt to prove general points, which go beyond the particular aphorisms and observations which it offers, and here again we may turn to Papyrus Insinger for an analogy. I shall have more to say about the thought of that text a little later, but for now it suffices to note that it shares with Qohelet's monologue an unusual aspect of presentation: repeated affirmations of a single point in relation to many different themes.

This Ptolemaic work is more regularly structured than Ecclesiastes, organizing its predominantly one-line sayings by subject matter into separate, numbered teachings. Except for the last, furthermore, each of the preserved teachings closes with a comment that (in Lichtheim's translation) "The fate and the fortune that come, it is the god who determines them," or some minor variant on that. The point is often preceded by other comments about divine action, or by the inclusion of sayings, as noted above, which contradict sayings already presented in that teaching. What appear to be a lot of miscellaneous aphorisms, when they are considered separately, are deployed in this way to demonstrate a single overall point, that human fortunes and affairs are under divine control.

Clearly, Ecclesiastes does not have a comparable sequence of separate sections or, for that matter, such regularity of form in its sayings. The characterizations of different phenomena as *hebel*, however, serve a similar purpose, both marking the conclusion of many observations, and cumulatively affirming Qohelet's point that all is *hebel*. Again, they provide a framework for the interpretation of many different items, the implications of which would not always be clear otherwise, and they are not merely a structural device, but integral to the design of the book. Although there is no good reason to suppose any direct influence of one upon the other, Ecclesiastes and the Demotic instruction share a common mode of argument, if it can be called that.

Perhaps a better way of looking at this, however, is not in terms of rhetorical technique, but in terms of the way both understand individual pieces of advice or observation as contributions to a broader idea. Obviously, Qohelet's speech is already far from being just a compilation of aphorisms, but he owes a clear debt to literary traditions of sayings collection, especially in chs. 7, 10 and 11, when series of sayings take the place of continuous discussion. Even elsewhere, the set pieces, the many sudden breaks and the apparent changes of direction all serve to remind us that Qohelet is delivering neither an essay nor a sustained argument, but a lot of essentially individual items. That these are supposed to add up to something more than the sum of their parts, however, is indicated not only by specific resemblances between many of them, but also by the way he links them to his overall theme. Indeed, when the motto of 1:2 is repeated in 12:8, we may well understand this as an effort to show that an initial proposition has been clarified and proved.[29] Qohelet has a point to make, and he conscripts his many observations of *hebel* to make it.

Of course, Qohelet does not make his point only in this way, and there are times at which he does seem to be using something closer to what we would recognize as reasoning. In 2:18–22, for example, he would seem to be making the point that:

- ownership does not depend on worthiness or hard work
- therefore worthiness and hard work do not imply ownership
- therefore worthiness and hard work are a waste of effort

Of course, the argument hinges on the second step here, which is rather questionable—and that may be why Qohelet does not state it explicitly, but apparently allows the conclusion to follow from a double statement of the initial premise. This is indicative, however, of a general tendency not to set out arguments completely, or even to indicate their nature. To put a point made earlier in a different way, are we supposed, for instance, to take the natural phenomena of 1:5–7 as the basis for an inductive argument, which extrapolates the existence of other processes from these examples, or are they just illustrative of an existing belief? The distribution of related discussions across the monologue, along with this apparent lack of concern to form clear arguments, make it difficult to view what Qohelet is saying in terms of a treatise, but it is also clear that the book makes an effort not only to link its ideas, but to develop and extrapolate from them, albeit in what appears to be a very disjointed way.

Papyrus Insinger furnishes a parallel to the use of accumulation, but not obviously to such development, and in this respect Ecclesiastes is very unusual as advice literature. That probably does not mean that we should regard it instead as philosophy, at least if that were supposed to imply that argumentation in itself creates a link to Greek philosophical texts[30]—and it is not clear that the distinction would be especially useful

---

29. See, for example, William H. U. Anderson, "The Poetic Inclusio of Qoheleth in Relation to 1,2 and 12,8," *SJOT* 12 (1998): 203–13.

30. Peter Machinist, "Fate, *miqreh*, and Reason: Some Reflections on Qohelet and Biblical Thought," in *Solving Riddles and Untying Knots: Biblical, Epigraphic, and Semitic Studies in Honor of Jonas C. Greenfield* (ed. Ziony Zevit, Seymour Gitin and Michael Sokoloff; Winona Lake: Eisenbrauns, 1995), 159–75, suggests

otherwise.[31] For all that it includes, however, more conventional series of sayings, along with a certain amount of material which is, at best, tangential to its key themes, Qohelet's monologue seems to involve a deliberate attempt to demonstrate a more general point than its contents can show individually.

c. *Poetry*

Because we have focused on Qohelet's main ideas, we have had little reason to look at some of his "tangential" material at all. Some of this

that "if we are to consider Greek, specifically, Hellenistic, influence on Qohelet's use of *miqreh*, and I think we may, we must be circumspect, for the influence may reside not so much in the use of *miqreh* for fate per se, as in the ability to write about *miqreh* in a way that indicates both a rational process at work and, even more, a reflection on what that rationality consists of. We have here, in short, a concern for 'second-order' thinking such as marked Greek thought from the pre-Socratics onward and that otherwise is hardly to be noticed in the written remains of the pre-Hellenistic Near East" (p. 174). Whether or not that overstates the degree of argumentation in Ecclesiastes, I am sure that it misrepresents the type. For the sort of thinking which Machinist has in mind, see especially G. E. R. Lloyd, *Magic, Reason and Experience: Studies in the Origin and Development of Greek Science* (Cambridge: Cambridge University Press, 1979).

31. I do not intend to address the broader question of Qohelet's affinities with Greek philosophical thought. Attempts to associate ideas in Ecclesiastes with Greek philosophy have a long and mixed history, and even the most ardent proponents of such an association might admit that the issue has too often been confused by a focus on superficial resemblances rather than underlying purposes or assumptions: this is a criticism which might be levelled in particular at Rainer Braun, *Kohelet und die fruhhellenistische Popularphilosophie* (BZAW 130; Berlin: de Gruyter, 1973), which is very learned but somewhat eclectic, although there is a similar tendency visible in some other works. Carol Newsom, "Job and Ecclesiastes," in *Old Testament Interpretation: Past, Present, and Future: Essays in Honor of Gene M. Tucker* (ed. James L. Mays, David L. Petersen and Kent H. Richards; Nashville: Abingdon, 1995), 177–94, esp. 185, notes that "parallels alone do not constitute an argument for influence, especially when the ideas or expressions in question may just as easily be traced to native Semitic wisdom traditions." A useful overview appears in Burkes, *Death*, 91–108, but it is difficult to get a proper handle on the subject because the links which individual scholars perceive depend to a great extent on their understanding of what Qohelet is saying, so there is no single set of claims which can be addressed. In principle, it is unlikely that the date of Ecclesiastes would preclude contacts with early Greek philosophy (although associations with the more developed philosophical systems are probably to be excluded on that basis), but we should not neglect the extent of the cultural links between Greece and the Levant long before that date: resemblances may indicate relationships without demonstrating dependencies.

consists of sayings like those in 4:9–12, which seem to pick up the point about working only for oneself made in 2:7–8, but to carry it in a quite different direction, which is of questionable relevance to Qohelet's theme. Obviously, what counts as tangential or irrelevant is going to depend on what one takes to be the theme and meaning of different passages. The most significant example, however, is probably the most unarguable as well: even if death or old age are important considerations at other points, it is difficult to see how the long and problematic sequence of images in 12:2–7 might have been included to prove any particular point. Their function, indeed, seems not to be argumentative but evocative, and they bring the monologue to a close among scenes of the dimness, grief and brokenness which will mark also the close of every human life.

Elsewhere, the sequence of pairs in 3:2–8 fits more closely into the particular point that Qohelet is trying to make. Whether any of the sequence is needed to make that point might be debated; it would be hard to argue that it is all needed, however, or that the many different pairs each express some different nuance of his argument. Similar questions, indeed, might be asked about, say, the analogies presented in the pro-logue at 1:5–9, or the sayings presented in series by ch. 7. Whether or not the author of Ecclesiastes composed them himself (and I see no good reason to suppose that he did not) such set-pieces have clearly not been included solely, or perhaps even primarily, for the purpose of argumen-tation. Without either getting involved in problems of definition, or sug-gesting that we must read them as verse, we can speak very broadly of these materials as poetry, and some or all are often actually considered poems.[32]

---

32. Hertzberg, *Der Prediger* (Kommentar zum Alten Testament 17/4; Gütersloh: Gütersloher Verlagshaus Gerd Mohn, 1963), 73, for instance, takes the prologue ("ein Meisterstück") to be "in schlichter, edler Sprache geschrieben, lauft es in rhythmisch freier Form ab, meist in Dreiern und Zweiern, die zwanglos und doch in metrischer Absicht geordnet sind," and Verheij suggests that the passage "is at a rather blurred part of the borderline between poetry and prose"; cf. Arian J. C. Verheij, "Words Speaking for Themselves: On the Poetics of Qohelet 1:4–7," in *Give Ear to my Words: Psalms and Other Poetry in and Around the Hebrew Bible. Essays in Honour of Professor N. A. van Uchelen* (ed. Janet Dyk; Amsterdam: Societas Hebraica Amstelodamensis, 1996), 183–88, esp. 183. Verheij notes the pervasive use of assonance and repetition which is characteristic of vv. 4–7, and similar devices are explored in the more wide-ranging study by Wong Tin-Sheung, "Qoheleth 1:3–11: Prose or Poetry?," *Jian Dao* 14 (2000): 25–47. In 3:1–9, Athalya Brenner, for example, takes it for granted that we are dealing with "a poem which lists human actions and reactions in contrasted pairs," although she argues that Qohelet has re-used (or "misused") an existing love poem; see "Some Observations on the Figurations of Woman in Wisdom Literature," in *A Feminist Companion to*

Just as it is not obviously helpful, however, to call Qohelet a philoso-pher because he argues, so it is doubtful that we should speak of him as a poet because he uses poetic language. This is one respect, indeed, in which he has much in common with the protagonists of other ancient advice literature, who (contrary to rumour) characteristically have little time for simple and lucid exposition. As the citations from Theognis at the beginning of this section may suggest anyway, however, it is not easy or desirable to impose strict categories of that sort on ancient literature. The presence of these materials, on the other hand, does go some way to offset any impression that demonstration of its key ideas is the only concern of the monologue.

We may be pushed a little further in the same direction, if we observe that the most obvious biblical analogies to some of Qohelet's themes and ideas are to be found in the Psalms. For instance, Ps 39:5–7 (ET 39:4–6) not only draws on the imagery of *hebel* to emphasize the transience of human life, but also declares that "one collects, but knows not who will gather in"—apparently a reference to the idea that we are forced by mortality to pass our work on to others we do not know. Psalm 49 makes the same point, that wealth must be left to others, while at the same time emphasizing that the wise and the foolish must both die (v. 11 [ET 10]), and that all humans, indeed, must die like animals (vv. 13, 21 [ET 12, 20]), joining their ancestors in Sheol, where they will never again see the light (v. 20 [ET 19]).[33] Psalm 73, on the other hand, concerns itself with the problem that the wicked seem prosperous and healthy, which leads others to praise them, and to doubt divine justice.

Of course, there are differences too, and if we can talk of any direct influence passing between Qohelet and such psalms, then the direction of that influence is difficult to establish—as is the cultic significance, if any, of the particular poems. Such questions, however, do not really change the fact that key themes in Qohelet's monologue are best attested else-where in Hebrew poetry, and we might also bear in mind that the book of Job, commonly linked with Ecclesiastes in discussions of sceptical and pessimistic literature, is itself primarily poetic. Poetry and poetic

---

Wisdom Literature (ed. Athalya Brenner; The Feminist Companion to the Bible 9; Sheffield: Sheffield Academic, 1995), 50–66, esp. 50, 57. J. A. Loader, "Qohelet 3:2–8—A 'Sonnet' in the Old Testament," *ZAW* 81 (1969): 239–42, goes so far as to declare that in 3:2–8 we have "an exact parallel to the Petrarchan sonnet" (p. 241). More generally, see Loretz, "Poetry and Prose."

33. See Holger Delkurt, *"Der Mensch ist dem Vieh gleich, das vertilgt wird": Tod und Hoffnung gegen den Tod in Ps 49 und bei Kohelet* (Biblisch-theologische Studien 50; Neukirchen–Vluyn: Neukirchener Verlag, 2005).

language have to be considered not only as a component of our book, but as a significant characteristic of the works which seem to stand closest to it in Hebrew literature.

d. *Conclusions*

We observed much earlier in this study that there are some distinctive aspects to the presentation of Qohelet as a character. Clearly, there are also some distinctive features in his monologue itself, and we have noted in particular here both its conscious detachment from any idea of ancient or traditional authority, and its attempts to develop particular themes, associating specific instances with a general conclusion. Along with both the autobiographical and the observational aspects of Qohelet's discourse, the former highlights the obvious concern to present his words as those of an individual, arising out of individual experience. We have also seen, however, that such individualism and detachment from tradition is attributed to characters in some other, comparable literature, and that what looks like a break with the usual conventions may be no more than a literary exploitation of those conventions.

There are similar indications of both continuity and distinctiveness in Qohelet's accumulation of *hebel* statements to affirm that "all is *hebel*." The only close parallel, on Papyrus Insinger, stands very clearly in the traditions of advice literature, even if it is bending the conventions to a new purpose. Qohelet's speech stands further from the standard collections of sentence literature, and can aspire to a more complicated development of its ideas. It is not an essay, though, and there is a lack of continuous discussion within most of the monologue that both recalls the normal atomism of ancient advice literature, and inhibits serious argumentation. We observed, finally, that there are also materials present in the book which have clearly not been included only—or at all—for their contribution to development or elucidation of the key themes, and that it seems difficult not to discern in some of them a quality that is more poetic than argumentative.

It is undoubtedly difficult to point to any other ancient composition that looks quite like Ecclesiastes overall, and its presentation is also clearly unusual in certain particulars as well. Of course, we possess only a limited corpus of other texts for comparison, and the problems over dating make it difficult to assess the relationship even with those. I think, though, that we have enough indications to suggest that the original readers would probably have found more here that was familiar than radically new in the book's presentation. We need to distinguish, however, between claims and reality in such matters—between, one might say, the authorial assertions to which a reader consents, and the reader's own knowledge and recognition.

It seems difficult to doubt that the author of Ecclesiastes sets up Qohelet as a radical thinker of some sort. From both his self-presentation and his attribution of his conclusions to personal experience, rather than to tradition, it may have been apparent to readers from the outset that Qohelet did not want to be heard as just another tradent of ancient wisdom. From his challenging initial claims and his subsequent attempts to demonstrate them, moreover, it would probably also have been clear that he was offering more than just a collection of advice. Going back to our earlier discussion, we might add that things like his dialect and commercial vocabulary would probably also have shaped a strong initial perception that Qohelet was supposed to be different. Of course, as the book progresses, such initial indications are rapidly affirmed by the narrative of rejection and regret in ch. 2, and by Qohelet's subsequent self-presentation as a man who sees clearly in a world of delusion.

As we have seen, however, there are grounds to suspect that many of Qohelet's themes, and even certain of his words, would have been familiar already to the original audience, and, in looking at the distinctiveness of the presentation, we have also seen much that is conventional, or at least not unprecedented. Setting aside the message of the book itself for the moment, we must appreciate that although readers probably understood that Qohelet was being presented to them as something new, it was as something new within the confines of the familiar—a character who reacts against convention in a text which is steeped in convention, and who bares his soul while dressing his words as traditional sayings, or perhaps sometimes as poetry. In certain ways, indeed, Qohelet is a counterpart to the more common protagonists of advice literature, whose words actually may be novel, even though they are presented as ancient tradition. At the very least, there is too much in the book that is familiar even to us from elsewhere for us to presume that its original audience would have taken its self-presentation at face value.

Accordingly, it would seem no more wise to assume that Qohelet's words really are radical, just because they are presented as such, than it would be to assume that they are genuinely the *cri de coeur* of a man who has been through the experiences he describes. This is a literary work, intended to be read against a background of conventions and expectations about which we know very little. Certainly, what evidence we have suggests, on the other hand, that readers might well not have expected to find in a work like this the relative consistency of theme that the monologue exhibits, and they may have been surprised by the way in which possibly familiar motifs of transience and enjoyment, for example, are tied together. The fact that much may have been conventional does not mean that nothing in the book was new.

2. *Key Themes*

As we turn to the place of Qohelet's ideas, then, it is important to recognize that they too may have roots much deeper in existing literature, and that what Qohelet associates with his own experiences and observations may well have been derived by the author from elsewhere. Again, though, we find an interesting combination of the old and the apparently new, and here the inter-relationship of new ideas begins to give us a clearer picture of the book's distinctive contributions.

a. *The Problem of Divine Sovereignty*
Various limitations are placed on human knowledge and ambition in ancient advice literature. *Ptahhotep*, for example, recognizes that some individuals may simply be incapable of learning what they are supposed to do, and finds in this a distinction between those deemed suitable and unsuitable by the god—an idea that is a little reminiscent of Qohelet's ideas in 2:26.[34] The debate between father and son in the *Instruction of Any* also raises questions about the human ability to learn what is supposed to be learnt, although in a rather different way. The most important and commonly cited limitation, though, is the ability of gods to overrule human plans. As two examples from Proverbs put it:

> Many plans are in the mind of a man, but what will occur is what Yнwн has planned. (Prov 19:21)

> There is no wisdom, and no understanding, and no plan that stands in the way of Yнwн: a horse is readied for the day of battle, while the victory is Yнwн's. (Prov 21:30–31; cf. Ps 33:17)

At the heart of such ideas there lies not a rejection of advice, but an acknowledgment that divine action cannot be constrained by human action. The *Instruction of Amenemope* famously contrasts human words with divine deeds,[35] but also points to various ways in which humans can incur divine anger, and in this respect it is probably typical of an emphasis on personal piety which became widespread in New Kingdom

34. See Papyrus Prisse, col. 16, lines 3–13; translation in Parkinson, *The Tale of Sinuhe*, 262–63.
35. *Amenemope* XIX.16–17: "The words men say are one thing, the deeds of the god are another"; Lichtheim, *Ancient Egyptian Literature*, 2:157.

Egypt.[36] Put simply, the unconstrainable power of the divine means that humans can never guarantee a particular outcome on the basis of their own behaviour, but can nevertheless behave in ways that improve their chances of success and minimize their chances of incurring divine punishment.

Although such limitations are not always stated explicitly, they are probably understood even in much earlier literature. Correspondingly, there may never actually have been any purely "optimistic" advice literature, if by that term we mean to imply that writers considered themselves to be offering cast-iron guarantees of success to those who followed their advice about specific behaviour. The issues are drawn out very effectively in the biblical book of Job, which does not focus specifically on advice, but which shows how the situation of an individual may not actually reflect an anticipated divine response to their behaviour. Arguably, in fact, Job's sufferings come about not *despite* his piety but *because* of it: whether or not Job's friends and community would usually be right to interpret the situation in terms of divine punishment or discipline, they are wrong to do so in this case—as both Job and the reader are well aware. When God intervenes, moreover, it is not to explain his actions, but to affirm that he does not need to explain them: the issue is not that humans should perceive no relationship between their behaviour and what happens to them (cf. 38:13), but rather that God is not bound to the maintenance of such a relationship by any commitment or debt.

The recognition of divine sovereignty does not in itself imply the inadequacy of advice, and, likewise, does not exclude the probability that common understandings of a situation may be correct. In Job, divine retribution is normally operative, which is why it is presumed by others to be the reason for the hero's suffering, and Job's prosperity, both before and after the events addressed by the main story, is associated with divine favour. It is because retribution usually functions that the exceptions pose a problem, and we may observe that the statement of divine freedom in Prov 19:21 ("Many plans are in the mind of a man...") is preceded, just a few verses before, by an assurance that God can indeed be constrained: "He who's kind to a poor man puts YHWH in his debt—and he will pay him back what's owed" (Prov 19:17). Papyrus Insinger, mentioned already above, puts conventional advice into perspective by adding contradictory statements, but there is no reason to suppose that the advice is considered to have been rendered useless for

---

36. See, for example, J. Assmann, "Weisheit, Loyalismus und Frömmigkeit," in *Studien zu altägyptischen Lebenslehren* (ed. E. Hornung and O. Keel; OBO 28; Freiburg: Universitätsverlag; Göttingen: Vandenhoeck & Ruprecht, 1979), 11–72.

that reason. In literature which emphasizes the power and freedom of gods, then, we do not usually find some corresponding belief that humans can do nothing to control their own situation. This is rather, one might say, a theoretical limitation that explains unpredictability in human affairs, and that sustains a theological presupposition of divine sovereignty. In many texts it is effectively ignored while in others it provides a key focus for concern, but what we are probably seeing is not a difference of fundamental belief between such texts, so much as a difference in concern or emphasis.

Read in relation to such issues, Jewish literature offers some interesting complications, especially in respect of both the covenantal ideology which runs through many historiographical and other materials, and the associated idea of commands ("instruction") about behaviour given by God. There may be a sideswipe at notions of covenant, indeed, in Job 40:28 (ET 41:4), and if a belief in divine self-limitation through covenants is not strictly incompatible with ideas of absolute divine sovereignty or freedom, it does at least sit a little uncomfortably with them. I have argued elsewhere that the ideas put forward in Prov 1–9 try to incorporate Deuteronomic themes into what is essentially the framework of instructional literature,[37] and that attempt gives rise to a very distinctive approach: for this work, the task of humans is apparently not so much to conform to a preset idea of right and wrong behaviour, but to gain through instruction, and then to internalize, a wisdom that permits them to recognize in any situation the behaviour which is expected of them by God. We do find, therefore, at least one specifically Jewish response to the problem.

In some important respects, this is very distinctive. An emphasis on discernment and differentiation in Prov 1–9 effectively nurtures the idea that righteousness lies in understanding the divine will, rather than in following a set of specific admonitions. Although the work is not trying directly to address the problem of divine sovereignty, therefore, it superficially removes from God the constraint of having to reward or punish behaviour in accordance with such admonitions. Indeed, the presentation shifts a great deal more away from God, since humans, as depicted in Prov 1–9, are typically not judged directly, but destroy themselves by following the wrong paths: without wisdom, the limits on their perception turn the world into a sort of minefield, and even that wisdom has to be told apart from other, more dangerous would-be guides (see especially 1:10–19; 7:1–27; 9:13–18). By elaborating an idea of discernment forged by instruction, Prov 1–9 offers what may be a more confident assurance

---

37. See my *Instruction and Imagery.*

of conformity to the divine will, but places the onus on humans to adapt themselves, not on God to constrain himself.

This may be a version of the idea which Qohelet himself promotes— that it is those who fear God that will survive—and such an idea may be found elsewhere in Proverbs as well (e.g. 14:27; 19:23): wisdom literature has broader concerns with attitude and character, which make it inappropriate to focus solely on actions as the trigger for divine response. Qohelet's ideas about divine sovereignty, however, are not related solely to those in Proverbs, but seem broadly to echo ideas found very widely in other wisdom literature: God is beyond human constraint, which imposes limits on the effectiveness of human behaviour; despite that, however, the God-fearing may expect to survive. If he doubts that humans can assure their well-being through their own actions, this a doubt which seems to have been very widely shared.

Qohelet's approach to questions in this area, though, becomes much more distinctive when we consider his rejection of a simple link between actual wellbeing and material prosperity. Although God does apparently reward humans, as we saw earlier, it may not be by granting them rewards that are physical, or even visible; accordingly, if such things are what humans seek when they behave in a certain way, they may find themselves rewarded, but not with what they thought they wanted. Conversely, those who appear to be prospering may actually be suffering, or at least awaiting punishment. Without fundamentally challenging the idea that righteousness and wickedness will usually elicit an appropriate divine response, Qohelet nevertheless detaches that response from human expectations about deed and consequence in a much more radical way than does other literature, and understands it in terms of his more general doubts about the correspondence between perception and reality, tied up with his ideas about the world.

b. *Fate and Process*
Before we pursue that further, it is important to look a little more closely at other understandings of divine action. To the passages about divine sovereignty cited above from Proverbs, we might add the following examples, which do not so much contrast as integrate human actions with divine plans:

A human's mind may plan his route, but it is YHWH who places his steps. (Prov 16:9; cf. Jer 10:23)

The steps of a man are from YHWH, and a human—what can he understand of his way? (Prov 20:24)

These rather similar sayings seem to suggest that God may not merely overrule human plans, but actively exploit them: humans can believe they are acting according to their own design when their deeds are actually being controlled by God, or may simply be led along in a particular direction without understanding that their route is planned by God.

Although its ideas in this respect are a little different from those of Qohelet, Papyrus Insinger illustrates another way in which the divine plan may run counter to the human understanding of a situation:

> A lifetime is given to the impious man, in order to make him encounter retaliation.
> Property is given to the evil man in order to deprive him of his breath through it.
> One does not understand the heart of the god until what he has decreed has come. (30.23–31.1)[38]

And we can compare also some lines from a Sumerian/Akkadian bilingual text found at Ugarit:

> People do not by themselves know their doings.
> The plans for day and night rest with the god.[39]

It is clearly not novel in itself for Qohelet to suggest that what God is doing in a situation may not be what humans perceive themselves to be doing in that situation, or that human activities may form, in effect, a part of divine activities. In practical terms, indeed, that may be the implication of a great many general statements about divine action in a wide range of literature, when divine ends can only be achieved through the unconscious manipulation of human actors.[40] If we are right, however, to understand that Qohelet sees all human activities in terms of much broader processes beyond the control of the actors, then this seems to represent something rather different from *ad hoc* interventions by God in the lives of individuals.

Quite what it does represent for humans, though, is more difficult to specify, particularly if we try to understand Qohelet's ideas on the subject in terms of freewill and determinism. We saw earlier that the discussion

---

38. Translation from Lichtheim, *Late Egyptian Wisdom Literature*, 229.

39. Translation from Alster, *Wisdom of Ancient Sumer*, 325. See also M. Dietrich, "'Ein Leben ohne Freude…'. Studie über eine Weisheitskomposition aus den Gelehrtenbibliotheken von Emar und Ugarit," *UF* 24 (1992): 9–29; and Nougayrol, "Textes Suméro-Accadiens," 291–300 and pls. 164–66.

40. I doubt that Qohelet has the historical consciousness imputed to him by Staples, "Profit in Ecclesiastes," 94–95, but that study discusses several interesting biblical examples.

of times in 2:26–3:11 very definitely portrays human actions—and even emotions—as divinely approved in some sense, and that is probably also the implication of 9:7: "Go, eat your bread with pleasure, and drink your wine with a happy heart. For God has already approved your work."[41] Such ideas seem to suggest some sort of determinism, and it is possible to read much of the monologue in such terms.[42] His strong affirmation of divine judgment would seem to suggest, nevertheless, that Qohelet believes humans themselves to be liable for their actions, and that surely seems implicit also in, say, the advice about righteousness in 7:16–20, or about the dangers of breaking an oath in 5:3–5 (ET 5:4–6).

This apparent tension between determinism and free will is surely present in the text, but it is not clear that it is a tension of which Qohelet ever shows himself to be aware, and here we may be imposing categories or drawing distinctions that would have been alien to the author of the book, or at least to his character. Qohelet's own way of describing God's relationship to human activities is in terms of employment and the setting of tasks: humans are workers doing for God a job which they do not understand, and which they may not be aware even that they are doing. If they do anything, however, then they are effectively doing this job, and they are employed until they die. To all intents and purposes, though, this is irrelevant to humans themselves in the conduct of their lives: ignorant of the fact that what they do is contributing to some much greater design, they simply pursue their own plans and ambitions. Of course, those ambitions are at the heart of Qohelet's claims about *hebel*, and *hebel* would not be a problem for him if human motives were not distinct from divine plans.

The same distinction, however, is one way in which to understand his belief that humans are liable to judgment even though their actions form part of a divine plan or process. According to such an explanation, Qohelet regards the human will to do good or bad as the determining factor in judgment: a murder may suit the divine will when it happens,

---

41. We could probably understand this alternatively in terms of Qohelet's ideas about restrictions on pleasure, with the very possibility of such enjoyment indicating approval.

42. The most comprehensive discussion is by Dominic Rudman, in *Determinism in the Book of Ecclesiastes* (JSOTSup 316; Sheffield: Sheffield Academic, 2001). Rudman concludes that Qohelet is a determinist "in the truest sense of the word" (p. 202), although he allows that there is a degree of free will involved in the seeking of pleasure, and sees kings as free agents, courtesy of a sort of divine delegation of authority. As will become clear, I think that this study, valuable though it is in many ways, imputes a greater thoroughness and consistency to Qohelet's thoughts on the matter than can actually be found in the text.

but a murderer is still a murderer. Even if everything is right in its time, to put this more generally, there are still right and wrong actions at the human level, and those who wilfully do what they believe to be wrong are displaying defiance toward God, rather than fear of him. If, however, Qohelet really does achieve a *modus vivendi* between his ideas in this way, by separating the morality of actions on the human level from the role of those actions on another level, then he is ignoring a point which is crucial to discussions of determinism: the mechanism of divine action. If God's plan or process needs a murder, then how is that achieved without motivating someone to commit the crime? The other main possibility, I think, is that we may be imposing too strong an idea of determinism on Qohelet's talk of times and processes, and that we should envisage something much more adaptive. On that reckoning, the processes which Qohelet envisages are not fixed and predestined, but feed, as it were, off anything that comes their way—more like the wind than the sun, to use his own illustrations, never ceasing but endlessly shifting. The most important point, though, is that the book itself does not offer an explanation, and in seeking to understand for ourselves how Qohelet reconciles his ideas we are in danger of overlooking the possibility that he (or the author) simply does not see the problem.

All this is important here because determinism is often adduced as one of the most distinctive characteristics of the book, and it would do much to help us place its thought were that true. In particular, determinism has probably been the single most important consideration in a number of attempts to link Ecclesiastes with Stoicism, which also struggled with issues of free will in respect of wrongdoing, but which held a fundamentally deterministic view of the universe.[43] Without going into all the difficulties that are involved in making such a link, however, it may be apparent that the gaps and problems in Qohelet's account of human subordination are no less eloquent than his assertions on the matter: this is not self-evidently the work of a writer familiar with the issues involved.

Indeed, it is not clear that Ecclesiastes marks a significant advance on Proverbs in this respect. The passages cited above, from Prov 16:9 and 20:24, seem deterministic to us, but lie in the context of a sayings

---

43. Among modern scholars, see, for example, John G. Gammie, "Stoicism and Anti-Stoicism in Qoheleth," *HAR* 9 (1985): 169–87. Otto Kaiser, "Determination und Freiheit beim Kohelet/Prediger Salomo und in der Frühen Stoa," in *Gottes und der Menschen Weisheit. Gesammelte Aufsätze* (BZAW 261; Berlin: de Gruyter, 1998), 106–25, makes a more heuristic comparison. The issue is studied in detail by Rudman, *Determinism*, 173–99, who sees significant parallels, and suspects at least an awareness in Ecclesiastes of Stoic ideas.

collection which contains numerous non-deterministic sayings. They exhibit also a concern with the problem of human comprehension that matches Qohelet's own emphasis very well, and suggest that discussions in this area were linked more to the general issues of divine sovereignty and inscrutability than to any doubts about free will. Qohelet's extrapolation of "processes," illustrated by natural phenomena, is much more distinctive than any deterministic ideas linked to those processes, but it is difficult to see Qohelet's ideas of divine governance overall as any sort of a coherent attack on existing conceptions. Furthermore, although a perception of determinism in the book was certainly a problem for some later commentators, the practical implications of any such determinism are limited so long as Qohelet continues to assert also the reality of divine judgment and the independence of human motives. It is doubtful that anyone could use Qohelet's assertions on the matter to justify the sort of fatalism that blames God for human sin, and is attacked in Sir 15:11–20.

c. *Human Knowledge*

We are surely touching on issues more important to the book itself when we return to Qohelet's ideas about knowledge, and we have already observed their centrality both to his thought and to his message. It also appears to be in this area that Qohelet most deliberately challenges established practices or ideas, portraying the common activities and assumptions of humanity as misguided, and putting his own insights forward as the only reliable source of guidance. If it is doubtful whether we can usefully describe as sceptical his rather commonplace views about the limits on human action, the term does surely seem more appropriate for at least some of his views about human knowledge and perception.

Of course, it is not so easy to separate the two areas, and we have already noted that the sentence literature in Proverbs makes its own observations about the limited human knowledge of divine plans; questions about knowledge of God, in particular, seem closely related to problems of divine sovereignty, and no less common. Even without looking beyond the biblical wisdom literature, we may recall that human ignorance is a key issue also in Job, where the reality of the hero's situation cannot be known by his companions, and that Prov 1–9 is deeply concerned with problems of perception and discernment. Such issues are not confined either to wisdom literature or to the Bible, and *Ludlul Bêl Nêmeqi*, to take one example from many in the ancient world, asks,

> Would that I knew these things were acceptable to the god!
> That which is good to oneself may be a sacrilege to the god,
> That which is wretched to one's heart may be good to one's god.
> Who can learn the plan of the gods in the heavens?
> Who understands the counsel of the deep?
> Where did humanity learn the divine decree of the gods?[44]

Qohelet's interest in divine inscrutability and human ignorance of God is not novel in itself, then, and we have no reason to suppose that he was addressing any common assumption that divine action was transparent, or that there were no limits on human knowledge of God.

In fact, though, Qohelet seems less interested in divine hiddenness and human ignorance than in the misperceptions and misunderstandings which result not just from the inadequacy of the information available to humans, but from a deliberate divine intention: humans do not merely misinterpret what they see, but are positively misled—or, at the very least, kept in the dark. This is a much more sophisticated idea, and although the possibility that gods could mislead as well as conceal was hardly unknown in the ancient world, Qohelet's interpretation of the consequences has no close parallel in the extant literature. Again, commentators have sometimes turned to Greek philosophy as a potential influence, and Qohelet does show a superficial resemblance to the early sceptical philosophers, who were concerned with the impossibility of certain knowledge. Their reasons for this concern, though, were very different, and in both his dogmatism and his empiricism Qohelet displays certainties about knowledge and the senses which would have been quite alien to that tradition.[45]

---

44. Tablet II, lines 33–38; translation from Annus and Lenzi, *Ludlul bēl nēmeqi*, 35.

45. Hans-Peter Müller, "Kohelet im Lichte der frühgriechischen Philosophie," in *Weisheit in Israel. Beiträge des Symposiums "Das Alte Testament und die Kultur der Moderne" anlässlich des 100. Geburtstags Gerhard von Rads (1901–1971), Heidelberg, 18.–21. Oktober 2001* (ed. David J. A. Clines, Hermann Lichtenberger and Hans-Peter Müller; Altes Testament und Moderne 12; Münster: Lit, 2003), 67–80, rightly doubts the dependence of Qohelet's scepticism on Greek thought (p. 79), and, from the pen of an expert on Greek scepticism, there is an even stronger rejection, worth citing in full: "…y a-t-il des ressemblances entre la pensée de l'Ecclésiaste et celle des philosophes grecs sceptiques? Peut-on postuler l'influence du monde hellénistique sur l'auteur juif? La réponse à cette question n'est pas difficile à trouver: n'étant pas sceptique, l'Ecclésiaste n'a pas été influencé de façon positive par le scepticisme grec. Il n'existe aucune raison pour croire que l'Ecclésiaste ait eu une connaissance directe du scepticisme grec: aucun verset ne suggère un intérêt, favorable ou défavorable, pour la philosophie sceptique; aucune phrase ne suggère une connaissance, directe ou indirecte, de Pyrrhon ou d'Arcésilas. (J'irais volontiers

It is important to observe also that human knowledge of the world and of the divine is not the only type of knowledge dealt with in the monologue. When he considers wisdom in those terms, Qohelet freely asserts its limitations, but, as we have seen, wisdom is not simply ineffective. In fact, it offers practical advantages in the accomplishment of objectives, and a degree of insight which, if not great enough to overcome the limitations set on human knowledge, is at least sufficient to bring about an understanding of those limitations, and so to cause pain. This is, again, a long way from the ideas about knowledge found in philosophical scepticism, and it must be emphasized that the possibility of certain knowledge in itself is not rejected by Qohelet, merely the possibility of accurate knowledge about particular things.

In fact, there is so very little in common between Qohelet and Greek scepticism that it seems pointless to speculate about any possible historical connections: most scholars would date Ecclesiastes late enough for its author to have known of that tradition, or at least of its forebears, but if he did know of it, he clearly knew little or nothing about it. The differences do, however, help to point up some important aspects of Qohelet's own position on human knowledge. In particular, epistemological uncertainty evoked for the philosophers a suspension of judgment and a corresponding tranquillity. Insofar as ignorance is linked to his belief that humans can do no more than enjoy what they do (e.g. 3:11–13, 22), Qohelet's position bears a superficial resemblance to this—but ignorance is quite different from uncertainty, and it is not itself supposed to be the source of joy, merely an obstacle to other potential sources of gain for humans, which obliges them to fall back on enjoyment. The limitations on human knowledge which explicitly attract his attention, furthermore, are not general but very particular, and we outlined them earlier. Obviously, there are much broader concerns about perception involved in his ideas of *hebel*, but we can do a certain amount to delimit Qohelet's own scepticism in this area over and against the Greek variety: he does not doubt the ability of humans to know except in defined areas, and so does not doubt the possibility of knowledge itself; he does not differentiate certainty from knowledge; he does not see uncertainty as a good, but regards the limits on knowledge as a problem. In fact, we may reasonably draw from all this—and also, perhaps, from our earlier discussion of his "empiricism"—the inference that Qohelet has no significant interest in epistemology as such, or any apparent knowledge of the

un peu plus loin: l'Ecclésiaste ne s'intéressait pas à la philosophie grecque, qu'il ne connaissait pas du tout…)"; see Jonathan Barnes, "L'Ecclésiaste et le scepticisme Grec," *RThPh* 131 (1999): 103–14, esp. 114.

epistemological problems which so intrigued early Greek philosophers of various schools. His doubts are not about the ability of humans to know, but about their ability to apprehend their situation when they have, and can have, no knowledge of particular things.

Those particular things include divine activity, and the limitations that he sets on knowledge in that area more probably place Qohelet in the majority than in some special sceptical camp, although it is very possible that he was actually defending that majority position, if there really were wise men claiming to know more than was commonly allowed (8:17). In other matters, however, especially his rejection of human memory, he seems to have been stating ideas much less familiar to his contemporaries. These do not arise from general preoccupations with proof and certainty, but from his basic beliefs about the world, and we must return to those if we are to understand them.

d. *Humanity and the Changeless World*

As we have observed, Qohelet's claim in 1:2, that all is *hebel*, is followed and qualified by his rhetorical question about the profit available from human work: the false human expectation of an unachievable gain is the very starting-point of Qohelet's speech. The nature of this gain is not spelled out, but the subsequent narrative in ch. 2 suggests that it consists in some way of the material accomplishments from human labour: the problem for humans is that what they think they are making for themselves turns out not to be theirs. To borrow the vocabulary of business ourselves, humans think that they are working for capital, but receive only a salary.

I have questioned already whether most of Qohelet's audience would have seen human life in quite these terms, but if we accept that it is the falsehood of this expectation which Qohelet himself begins by lamenting, then his doubt is focused not on human capacities, but on the very notion of human ownership. The impossibility of true ownership, moreover, is itself tied up both with his ideas about the essential continuity of the world, from which nothing can be removed, and with his proposal to find a sort of gain in pleasure, which is non-material. Since, as we have seen, the distinctive aspects of his ideas about retribution and human knowledge seem also to be founded in his beliefs about the very nature of the world, their centrality to his thought can hardly be denied. The expression of those beliefs at the beginning of the monologue, moreover, before Qohelet has even introduced himself, affirms the importance that he attaches to them.

Although we can and have explored the character and consequences of these ideas, however, it is much harder to place them in any sort of context outside the book itself. In part, they are a statement of the obvious, that the world goes on after us, but there are more controversial elements, most notably the idea that:

> What will be, will be whatever is,
> and what will be done, whatever is done—
> and with nothing new beneath the sun.

Again, this is reminiscent of some statements in Greek philosophy, such as Parmenides' influential denial of change, that what exists is without beginning or end:

οὐδέ ποτ' ἦν οὐδ' ἔσται, ἐπεὶ νῦν ἔστιν ὁμοῦ πᾶν, ἕν, συνεχές[46]

> Neither was it ever in the past, nor will it be in the future, because it is all together now, single, continuous.

There is no indication, however, that Qohelet's idea is rooted in the sort of concerns that gave rise to such statements in early Greek philosophy, or that he understood it to have the same ramifications. Parmenides argues for a changeless world from an ontological denial of non-existence, and this changelessness stands in contradiction to the senses in a way that calls the senses into question—it is not merely concealed by the transitoriness of human life.[47] More generally, although it is not difficult to find philosophical statements about the world in ancient sources which resemble what Qohelet is saying, it is much harder to find in Qohelet's monologue anything like the context of discussion which gave rise to such statements. We cannot exclude the possibility that the author knew of philosophical claims about continuity and changelessness, but if he did, he shows no sign of sharing or of understanding the reasoning which gave rise to them.

When we look at the Jewish religious context as a possible background, the problem is rather the opposite: it is not difficult to see, at least in broad terms, how Qohelet's ideas might stand in line with or in opposition to other ideas, but he does not make explicit statements about such relationships. His endless processes, for example, seem anti-teleological, and difficult to reconcile with, say, the periodization of history in apocalyptic literature, or with concepts of an eschaton. Beyond his statements about memory, though, Qohelet has nothing to say about history, and his depiction of the world as everlasting does not wholly and

---

46. Fragment 8, lines 5–6. See Hermann Diels, *Die Fragmente der Vorsokratiker: Griechisch und Deutsch* (2d ed.; Berlin: Weidmannsche Buchhandlung, 1906), 1:119.

47. The argumentation in Parmenides is discussed in Lloyd, *Magic*, 69–71.

specifically exclude ideas of an ultimate transformation—just as his God, who promotes an ignorance which inspires fear, does not seem likely to be a source of prophetic or apocalyptic revelation, but such revelation is never positively denied. If there is supposed to be an attempt here actively to combat any particular cosmological, historical or theological ideas, it must surely have lain in allusions which are now obscure to us.

Rather than seeing a statement of opposition to some unidentified worldview, however, I think that we might do better to understand Qohelet's purpose in terms of his own alignment of ideas. What is important to him in the prologue, and what he will draw out through the rest of the monologue, is the disparity between the world and the lives of humans. Humans actually do come and go, and so are themselves, in a sense, each something new, and each ultimately something which will be removed from under the sun: their actions and achievements belong to the world, but they are detached from those. Accordingly, the permanence of the world points up the brevity of humans, and its continuity shows how temporary is their ownership or control of anything within it. Qohelet talks about the world in the context of humans and their work, and what he chooses to emphasize about the world may be understood as a necessary component of what he has to say about humans. In that case, he is not promoting a cosmology so much as an anthropology.

The transience of humanity is a long-established theme in ancient literature, and although it is harder to find precise parallels to Qohelet's claims about gain and ownership, they accord with ideas about the limited value of worldly goods which go back into the earliest literature:

> Nothing at all is to be valued, but life should be sweet. You should not serve things; things should serve you.[48]

48. This is the translation of lines 242–43 of *Šuruppak* in Jeremy Black, Graham Cunningham, Eleanor Robson and Gábor Zólyomi, *The Literature of Ancient Sumer* (Oxford: Oxford University Press, 2004), 290; cf. Alster, *Wisdom of Ancient Sumer*, 296, where it is lines 252–53, and translated as "Nothing at all is of value, but life should be sweet-tasting. Don't appreciate things (too much); (because then) things will evaluate you (i.e., you will become dependent on their evaluation)." The first line also appears as the opening of a series of inter-related Sumerian compositions, which are presented by Alster under the heading "Nothing is of Value" (níŋ-nam nu-kal, versions A, B, C, in *Wisdom of Ancient Sumer*, 266–87). In these texts, it is followed by another disavowal of the value of material goods: "Whenever a man does not own some piece of property, that man owns some property." These texts, incidentally, include a number of sayings which resemble Qohelet's words in general terms, including commendations of joy. Note also in *Enlil and Namzitarra* (lines 19–20) Enlil's rhetorical question: "You may acquire precious metals, you may acquire precious stones, you may acquire cattle or you may acquire sheep; but the day of a human being is always getting closer, so where does your wealth lead?"

What seems to make Qohelet stand out, is not that he is presenting concepts that would have been unfamiliar or unpalatable, but that he is presenting them in a way that seems especially harsh and bleak. Viewed from his perspective, the world is incomprehensible and impermeable, above all a source of frustration and disappointment to those humans who cannot accept their temporary and limited role within it. It is difficult, however, to see anything in this which is actually sceptical of established ideas, and if it is novel, then the novelty lies more in the presentation than in the thought.

e. *Pleasure and Material Prosperity*

Finally, it is important to say a few words in particular about Qohelet's detachment of material prosperity from actual wellbeing, which is, as we have noted already, a very distinctive aspect of his message. In certain respects, though, it is also a very difficult one, not least if we attempt to regard it as a sceptical reaction against assurances in other literature that righteousness or wisdom can assure wealth, and other desirable possessions. The speech by personified wisdom in Prov 8 is the classic biblical example of such assurance, and, although we should bear in mind that the promises made there must be read in terms of the very specific ideas put forward by Prov 1–9, there is no reason to doubt that most advice literature expected material rewards—subject to the hazards posed by divine sovereignty. It is less clear, however, that Qohelet is actively attacking the substance of this idea.

When he first touches on the issue in 2:18–23, it is interesting to observe that Qohelet does not deny that wisdom and work may lead to prosperity; that is, after all, how he built up his own business. Rather, it is the inheritance of prosperity which undermines for him any simple link between material reward and proper behaviour, and although this drives him to see possessions as something assigned by God, and potentially taken away by God, he seems never wholly to abandon the idea that humans can earn material prosperity—or, indeed, fail to earn it (4:5; 11:4). How we reconcile these ideas will depend, of course, on how we understand Qohelet's ideas about human employment by God more generally, and this is, perhaps, another indication that he is something less than a wholehearted determinist.

We must emphasize here, however, that although humans do have the ability to create wealth for themselves, it is integral to Qohelet's ideas

Translation from Black et al., *The Literature of Ancient Sumer*, 113. The text was edited in M. Civil, "Enlil and Namzitarra," *AfO* 25 (1974): 65–71; cf. also Alster, *Wisdom of Ancient Sumer*, 327–38.

that this wealth is essentially worthless, because it does not belong to its owners. Correspondingly, it would be very unlikely that Qohelet could conceive of material prosperity as a reward, because it would be a reward without value. On the other hand, he does see real value in pleasure, and if the granting of pleasure by God potentially constitutes a form of reward, as we suggested earlier, then this is Qohelet's equivalent to the assurances in Proverbs and elsewhere. The fact that prosperity may be assigned to the undeserving, then, provokes Qohelet to a realization that divine reward cannot lie in material wealth, but that leads him in turn not to a rejection of reward, but to a re-evaluation of its character. If he is sceptical about traditional ideas of reward, it is only about the form that that reward takes, not the general principle of retribution.

What seems more interesting here is the identification of joy as something which stands outside the valueless realm of the material. In 3:4, 8, after all, weeping, laughter, love and hate were all included in the list of actions which humans undertake as part of their employment, and the pleasure which Qohelet has in mind is clearly not just an emotion or an emotional reaction, like these others, but something more like a sensation. Naturally, this has led to further comparisons between Qohelet and Greek philosophy, although the obvious comparison with Epicureanism founders rapidly, not just on the problem that Qohelet's joy bears little resemblance to the moderate asceticism of that movement, but also on the fact that Epicureanism embraced many other ideas, including non-involvement by the gods in human affairs, that are hardly compatible with Qohelet's outlook. Early hedonist schools, such as the Cyrenaics, stand closer to Qohelet's ideas, although it is again difficult to reconcile with his theology the relatively little that is known of their broader ideas. While it would be difficult to deny the possibility of a limited influence from that direction, Qohelet's ideas may rest on no more than a development of the *carpe diem* motif, which was widespread in ancient literature.

3. Conclusions: Qohelet's Scepticism

Far too few texts have survived from antiquity for us to speak with any confidence about what views were normative and commonplace in any given context, and the works that we do possess have often survived more through chance, or through their connection to later interests, than because they were necessarily typical. It is not a simple task, therefore, to assess the extent to which any text was truly radical or different. In the case of Ecclesiastes, however, there are sufficient parallels to many of its key ideas that we must clearly be cautious about setting too much store by its own presentation of Qohelet as a radical questioner of human expectations. He is, certainly, set apart from tradition, and given distinctive characteristics and experiences: we are supposed to see him as a lone individual, embittered by the realization that all he did for himself proves not to be his at all, and we are supposed to take from his words the clarity of vision which comes from a man of exceptional wisdom reflecting on his world. When it comes down to it, though, it is difficult to find in Qohelet's monologue a scepticism that is genuinely new, and its original audience may have seen much that was positively familiar to them behind the presentation.

If we are going to call Qohelet a sceptic at all, then it must be with the recognition that he is neither adopting a position of uncertainty in some general sense, nor apparently trying to set limits on human knowledge and control which went significantly beyond those widely acknowledged in a range of other literature. On some particular points, to be sure, what Qohelet has to say may well be new: his rejection of human memory, for example, is remarkable and, so far as we know, unprecedented. A great deal of what he has to say, however, arises out of well-established themes, such as the transience of human existence and the limitations placed on human knowledge by divine sovereignty.

The presentation and affinities of the book certainly give us no good grounds to detach it from existing Near Eastern literature, for all its unusual features. When it deals with transience and authority, it does not seem to do so in a way that suggests any signs of engagement with emergent Greek philosophical traditions or concerns. Indeed, although the monologue offers a coherence of overall theme which probably would have been unusual, it also contains enough that is tangential and disconnected to inhibit us from claiming that it is in any useful sense an argument or treatise. In its structure, it reveals its continuing relationship with more traditional advice literature, and in aspects of its content it also shows both a concern with literary expression and links with other traditions of poetry. Qohelet's ideas are not the only aspect of the work important to the author, and they are not always its most distinctive aspect.

If we do boil it down to its beliefs, however, then the scepticism exhibited by the monologue is mostly of the blue-cheese variety: it seems doubtful that anyone else would have expected to take a profit from their life, in Qohelet's sense, would have regarded human understanding as untrammelled, or would have expected to exercise control over their life without the possibility of divine interference.[49] That Qohelet states

---

49. So, similarly, Fischer, *Skepsis oder Furcht Gottes? Studien zur Komposition und Theologie des Buches Kohelet* (BZAW 247; Berlin: de Gruyter, 1997), 239, denies that Qohelet can be detached from existing wisdom traditions: "Obwohl

certain ideas in an unusually strong way does not make them more sceptical, or make it more likely that the corresponding, contrary beliefs were widely held. It is in its more positive statements about the nature of the world that the monologue seems genuinely distinctive, perhaps, but these seem again to have been extrapolated, at least in part, from more common perceptions.

I am not trying to suggest for a moment that the views put forward by Qohelet would all have been shared by all of his contemporaries, but rather that these views seem not principally to be directed against other, more widely supported understandings. Qohelet's speech, to put it another way, does not seem first and foremost to be an expression of scepticism about ideas which were commonly held, whatever else it may be. In such matters as his assertion of divine judgment, indeed, we might be more inclined to see Qohelet as a defender of orthodoxy, and any who rejected it as the sceptics—but then, as we saw earlier, scepticism can be a matter of perspective, and Qohelet appears to view his contemporaries as, to say the least, confused about the issue. Even if we take scepticism in a more restricted, epistemological sense, it is not clear that scepticism is really the best way to characterize what is being said in the mono-logue. It is not just that we cannot easily establish a link between Qohelet and the Greek philosophers on this: whether he is appealing to experi-ence in an empirical way or making what seem to be more dogmatic statements, Qohelet rarely if ever shows himself to be in any doubt about the possibility of knowledge *per se*, or the reliability of the senses. What he does doubt is the ability of humans to know certain things, not on epistemological grounds, but simply because those things are concealed by nature, divine purpose, or human transience. This is not scepticism in the philosophical sense, and it leads him not to express doubt, but to enunciate with confidence a view of the world in which humans base their actions upon poor information and false assumptions.

There may be some heuristic value in describing Qohelet as a sceptic, and an attempt to pin down his scepticism offers a useful way, at least, to explore the relationships between his monologue and other literature.

Kohelet das in der Gesamtheit der Wirklichkeit verborgene Handeln Gottes schärfer und radikaler als die sapientielle Literatur formuliert, lassen sich schon im Prov-erbienbuch eine ganze Reihe von Sprüchen nachweisen, die ebenfalls den Anspruch des Menschen zurückweisen, als könne er die Absicht Gottes ergründen und dadurch seinem Tun den Erfolg sichern." He goes on to conclude that Qohelet cannot be viewed as a "skeptischer Einzelgänger," but must be seen as a typical wisdom teacher, whose speech does not constitute a sceptical, fundamental critique of the possibility of human knowledge. It is problematic, if not outright misleading, to describe Qohelet as "einen erkenntnistheoretischen Skeptiker" (p. 240).

It seems more doubtful, however, that the description can really be used to define him without giving an altogether misleading impression of those relationships. Even to speak of him more loosely as a pessimist raises similar issues, if we take his pessimism to stand in opposition to some more optimistic stance. To be sure, insofar as he focuses on such things as human transience and loss, Qohelet certainly seems pessimistic, but this is more a product of his subject matter than of his opinions: we may reasonably presume that his more cheerful contemporaries tried to ignore their mortality, not to celebrate it, and it is hard to imagine what would constitute a normative optimism in such matters. If this is true of his major themes, it is no less so of the minor ones: when Qohelet talks of oppression, for instance, in 4:1–3 and 5:7–8 (ET 5:7–9), he may or may not have had particular political circumstances in mind, but even if these statements were polemical in their original context, they were neither sceptical nor pessimistic—oppression of the poor was universally condemned in the ancient world, even if it was widely practised. There is a great deal of negativity in much that Qohelet says, but much less that might have been recognized as a radical rejection of established belief.

Perhaps a more profitable approach might lie in accepting what seems to be Qohelet's own understanding of his position, as a rejection of delusion. The human motives which he rejects as *hebel* are not founded on intellectual positions, but on such emotions as greed, or on misperceptions of death and judgment arising from the invisibility of consequence. If we describe Qohelet's objections as scepticism, we turn these things by implication into beliefs, when in reality they are nothing so carefully thought out. The man who works endlessly in 4:7, for instance, does so because he has not stopped to ask what he is doing, and in 2:14, Qohelet's own investment in wisdom proves deluded because he had not considered how little difference it would make ultimately to his fate. The humans criticized by Qohelet in such passages are wasting effort or harming themselves through a lack of clear thought, not because they adhere to some alternative set of ideas.

It is not scepticism or even pessimism that characterizes Qohelet's ideas, then, so much as a sense that humans are missing the point, and he presents himself as a man seeking to steer others away from the false expectations and disappointment which he experienced himself, by opening their eyes to the reality of their situation. If his analysis is largely negative, that is because, in a world of illusion, there is value in disillusion.

CONCLUDING REMARKS:
QOHELET AND HIS CREATOR

I have tried to suggest throughout this study that Qohelet's ideas cannot be detached from the presentation of his personality and experience: the monologue is spoken not by a disembodied voice, but by a character who takes trouble to explain what has driven him to the position he adopts, and whose personality is fleshed out for us by the content and manner of his speech. In the first chapter, however, we left open the question of the relationship between this character and the author of the book that contains his words: the answer to that question, I suggested, could not profoundly affect the way in which we understand the content of those words. The issue becomes very important, however, when we try to understand not their content but their significance, and the way in which the book was intended to be read. Without claiming that we can reach a definitive answer on the evidence available, I want to close by exploring that question a little further.

There is little to be gained, I think, by trying to assess the historicity of Qohelet as an individual. The claims that he makes to extraordinary wisdom, wealth and experience may raise some reasonable doubts, but are not falsifiable—at least if we set aside the broader historical questions entailed in the Solomonic attribution. Accordingly, we cannot positively exclude the possibility that the monologue originated as a factual account of experience, although such an evaluation would need to take into account its many apparent links with other literature: to some extent or another this appears to be a deliberate literary composition, not a journal. In the form that we have it, however, which is the only form in which we know it to have circulated, the monologue is framed by an introduction and epilogue which speak of Qohelet in the third person. So far as this presentation is concerned, it really does not matter whether Qohelet originally spoke and breathed, or whether he was invented out of whole cloth: he is a character speaking in a book.

1. *The Epilogue (12:9–14)*

It is more fruitful to ask how the author of the book intended us to regard that character—even if the author actually was Qohelet, presenting himself as a character—but in order to address that question, we need also to look at those parts of Ecclesiastes where the voice which we hear is that of a narrator. When we turn to those parts, however, we risk becoming embroiled immediately in redactional problems surrounding the epilogue, which many commentators believe to have been supplemented by different hands, possibly over a long period. Those theories, moreover, do not simply complicate discussions about the relationship between author and character, but present a whole different way of looking at the situation, in which differences of emphasis or perspective between the monologue and the epilogue serve as criteria for differentiating redactional layers.[1] We can hardly deny on principle that there may have been additions to the text, but it is difficult to find a methodological *via media* between a redaction-critical and a final-form reading of the text.

It does not offer a solution to the problem, but it may help us to pick our way around it if we speak, for the moment, simply of an epilogist—without prejudice to questions about the authenticity of the epilogue's contents, or the number of different viewpoints that they might incorporate. On that basis, the epilogist's words may be broken into three sections: 12:9–10 offer further information about Qohelet, apparently portraying him as an arranger of sayings, a writer of pleasing and true words, and a teacher of the people; 12:11–12 then talk about advice literature, portraying the work of an individual writer as being like a shepherd's goad, into which individual sayings are stuck like nails—correspondingly, it may be unwise to go beyond that work, since the production of books is endless, and each tears the flesh; finally, 12:13–14 decree an end to the book, urging the reader to fear God and keep his commandments, since God will bring every action into judgment.[2]

---

1. Although it should be observed that attention has turned from redaction-critical to canonical concerns in some quarters, with the epilogue being viewed as a way of interpreting or re-interpreting the book. See, for example, G. T. Sheppard, "The Epilogue to Qoheleth as Theological Commentary," *CBQ* 39 (1977): 182–89; Gerald H. Wilson, "'The Words of the Wise': The Intent and Significance of Qohelet 12:9–14," *JBL* 103 (1984): 175–92.

2. The epilogue and its relationship with the monologue is explored in C. L. Seow, "'Beyond Them, My Son, Be Warned': The Epilogue of Qoheleth Revisited," in Barré, ed., *Wisdom, You Are My Sister*, 125–41. He regards 12:9–13a as quite compatible with the rest of the book, and probably original, while 12:13b–14, although not actually incompatible, are probably to be regarded as secondary.

Whoever wrote them, each of these sections is curious in its own way. The first may not be an inaccurate representation of Qohelet as a composer in some technical sense, but it is a strange sequel to the monologue, and especially to the intense imagery of the preceding verses. It seems so wilfully to miss the point, indeed, that it is almost like the old joke, "Apart from that, Mrs Lincoln, how did you enjoy the play?" The second sounds more like Qohelet, not least in its (perhaps humorously grotesque) depiction of wisdom literature as painful, but it also seems more like a health-warning than a book blurb.[3] The last is, likewise, more in line with Qohelet's thinking than is commonly allowed: the fear of God and divine judgment are, as we have seen, important components in the monologue. If it is supposed to serve as a final summary, however, it is strange that this section should so belatedly introduce the subject of divine commandments, which is broached nowhere in the monologue, and is probably difficult to reconcile with its thought. The previous closing comments in 11:7–12:1, moreover, included references to joy, which is surely Qohelet's key positive recommendation, and those are entirely lacking here.

Considered together, in fact, the most striking thing about these materials is their almost complete lack of sympathy with the ideas and sentiments of the monologue: the epilogist seems concerned not to reflect or commend what Qohelet has just said, but, in turn, to normalize it, to warn against it, and to extract from it a more conventionally pious viewpoint. I doubt that all of this is the work of the original author, but if any is, then it seems to reflect a certain lack of warmth in the narrative voice of the epilogue toward the words that have preceded in Qohelet's monologue. Whether he also created the character of Qohelet or not, whoever created the epilogue shows no overt sign of support for that character's views.[4]

---

3. Christianson, *A Time to Tell*, 113–14, rightly comments, "The inherent irony in a warning against the composition of many books in the epilogue of a book can hardly be overstated. It is a clever deconstructive turn that one could imagine even Qoheleth would admire... [O]ne can easily assume that the warning is an ill-concealed dissent from Qoheleth's own way of knowing." It is interesting to observe, though, that it also sits comfortably with Qohelet's own apparent reluctance to place any value in the opinions of others.

4. Fox, *A Time to Tear Down*, 372, suggests that "The caution the epilogue expresses is a public, protective stance, intended to ease acceptance of Qohelet's pungent words... The distance the epilogist sets between himself and Qohelet is basically protective rather than polemical." Although Fox takes the epilogue to be original (with the possible exception of 12:13–14, which he views as a postscript), his position, therefore, is not wholly dissimilar to that of many scholars who regard

2. *Qohelet as a Straw Man*

We cannot place too much weight on the epilogue, given the problems, but it does raise the intriguing possibility that Qohelet is something more than an adopted or fictionalized mouthpiece for the author, and that the book as a whole is not trying to sell the same ideas as its protagonist. If that sounds too complicated to be plausible, then we might consider for a moment what is going on in the book of Job, where a series of different characters give voice to separate and contradictory opinions, even though each is actually a persona of the book's author. As we noted earlier, this is a technique for exploring an issue that is obvious when it appears in a dialogue—and the Middle Kingdom *Dialogue Between a Man Tired of Life and His Ba* even sets different aspects of one individual to debate with each other.[5] In principle, though, it is not a technique which requires more than one character and voice, even if it is more difficult for us to recognize when criticism is being invited rather than stated in ancient texts.

This possibility has been explored by Martin Shields, who sees the portrayal of Qohelet as a deliberately troubling attack on an existing wisdom movement, set on the lips of a character who is an archetypal wise man:

> I have sought to show that it is fundamental to the purpose of Ecclesiastes that Qoheleth's words *did* trouble his audience, and in particular, those who were students or prospective students of the wisdom movement of his day. Although criticism may have been expected to come from outside the wisdom movement...criticism of the movement from within would have had far greater impact upon its students. Qoheleth's honest appraisal of the wisdom movement as largely futile and pointless would have served as a powerful deterrent to anyone considering the pursuit of wisdom.[6]

it as an addition. Andrew Shead, "Ecclesiastes from the Outside In," *Reformed Theological Review* 55 (1996): 24–37, and "Reading Ecclesiastes 'Epilogically'," *Tyndale Bulletin* 48 (1997): 67–91, has adopted a more radical approach, understanding the views of the epilogue to be wholly consonant with those of the monologue, except in terms of emphasis, and arguing that it was intended to serve as a guide to the reading of the book. I think that both approaches focus too much on the content, and too little on the tone of the epilogue, which is better appreciated in Christianson, *A Time to Tell*, 96–117. Salyer, *Vain Rhetoric*, 216, speaks of an "adversarial and mutually subversive relationship" between Qohelet and the frame-narrator, both literary creations.

5. For translations, see Lichtheim, *Ancient Egyptian Literature*, 1:163–69; Parkinson, *The Tale of Sinuhe*, 151–65.

6. Shields, *The End of Wisdom*, 236–37.

That conclusion, however, is surely too precise. It not only rests on a largely speculative reconstruction of a hypothetical wisdom movement and its members, but it also places undue weight on Qohelet's attitudes toward wisdom: these are not the most significant part of his message, they are not without parallel in other, more orthodox advice literature, and they do not specify any particular sort of wisdom that might be associated with the supposed wisdom movement. Although Shields may well be right, furthermore, to suggest that the epilogue invites a critical approach to Qohelet's words, there is some distance between suggesting that these words could be considered troubling, and concluding that they must have had a quasi-polemical function.

If we are seeking something so specific, then it might be helpful to look at the reactions that the book actually did provoke among relatively early readers, even though the evidence is very slight. The relationship between Ecclesiastes and Ben Sira is not especially productive in this respect, but the later Wisdom of Solomon does seem to reflect a critical understanding of Ecclesiastes directly in 2:1–9:[7]

> For they said among themselves, reasoning incorrectly, "It is brief and painful, our life, and neither is there a cure for human death, nor is any-one known who has returned from Hades. For we came into being by chance, and after this will be as though we do not exist—for the breath in our nostrils is smoke, and our reason a spark kindled in the beating of our hearts. When that is put out, the body will end up as ashes, and the spirit be dispersed as empty air. And our name will be lost to forgetfulness in time, and no-one will remember our works, and our life will pass away like the last traces of a cloud, and dispersed like a mist chased away by the rays of the sun, then forced down by its heat. For our time is the passing of a shadow, and there is no return from our death, because it is sealed, and no-one turns back. Come, then, and let us enjoy the good

---

7. See Shields, *The End of Wisdom*, 33–34. C. H. H. Wright, *The Book of Koheleth Commonly Called Ecclesiastes: Considered in Relation to Modern Criticism, and to the Doctrines of Modern Pessimism, With a Critical and Grammatical Commentary and a Revised Translation* (Donnellan Lectures 1880–81; London: Hodder & Stoughton, 1883), 61–62, suggests that the Solomonic attribution in Wisdom—which is itself implied rather than stated—was adopted to counter the promulgation of ideas from Ecclesiastes in the name of Solomon. More recent scholars have tended to be more circumspect about the relationship between the books, although Patrick Skehan, "The Literary Relationship of the Book of Wisdom to Earlier Wisdom Writings," in *Studies in Israelite Poetry and Wisdom* (CBQMS 1; Washington: Catholic Biblical Association of America, 1971), 172–236, esp. 213–36, remains unusual in doubting that there is any attack on Qohelet (and to my mind rests his case too strongly on what Qohelet really meant, not on what later writers might have perceived him to mean).

things that exist, and take proper advantage of creation, as in youth… Let none of us be without a share in our high spirits, let us leave signs of our joy everywhere, for that is our portion, this our share."

In Wisdom, these are the words of the impious, who have allied them-selves with death, and who go on to commit crimes because they see no consequence beyond life. That is clearly not what Qohelet himself is calling for, but the probable allusions here suggest that his message is being taken that way, as a summons to enjoy life at any cost to others. For the author of Wisdom, their error lies principally in a failure to understand that life itself is less significant than the coming afterlife, which is the true site of judgment: since Qohelet's ideas are posited on the absence of any such meaningful afterlife, those who adopt them are inevitably misled into a focus on the presence.

There also seems to be a reference to Qohelet's ideas about death in *1 En.* 102:6–11:

> And when you die, the sinners will say about you: "Just as we have died, so also the righteous have died; and what gain did they have from their works? Behold, they have died as we have, in sadness and darkness; and what advantage is theirs? From now on we will be equal. And how will they arise, and what will they see forever? And behold, they have died, and from now on until eternity they will not see the light." I say to you, you sinners, you are content to eat and to drink and to rob and to sin and to make people naked and to add to wealth and to see good days. You have seen the righteous ones, how their end came about; indeed, there was no wrongdoing found in them until their death, but they were destroyed and became as if they had never existed, and their spirits have descended into Sheol in agony.[8]

Again, a false view is attributed to the sinners, although here they are unaware that there will be a future restoration of the righteous rather than the sort of afterlife envisaged in Wisdom. This time, however, they rest their view not on the brevity of life and the absolute character of death, but on the apparent equality of the righteous and the wicked when they die. The issue is similar, but the reference is to different themes in Qohelet's speech.

It is difficult to say whether Qohelet's views on death were contro-versial when Ecclesiastes was written, and much depends on questions of dating which cannot be resolved on the present evidence. If the book is late enough, and the shifting attitudes within Judaism early enough, then Qohelet's advocacy of a traditional view of Sheol might indeed be

---

8. From the Ethiopic version; the Greek is similar. Translation from Loren Stuckenbruck, *1 Enoch 91–108* (CEJL; Berlin: de Gruyter, 2007), 500.

regarded as partisan, not merely conventional, and this view has been used, in fact, to link Qohelet to Sadducaism.[9] It is important to observe, though, that issues of death and afterlife do not appear early in the monologue, and we have to wait until 9:10, indeed, for Qohelet's key description of Sheol. On balance, it seems difficult to suppose that Qohelet's ideas about death and the need for pleasure were deliberately hung out in order to provoke a reaction, and more likely that they became problematic as the context in which they were read changed around them. Since the Enoch passage is commonly dated to the second century B.C.E., of course, they may not have had to wait very long for such a change.

When we are looking for an aspect of its thought which might have been deliberately troubling or provocative, then, both the critique of wisdom in Ecclesiastes and the ideas of death seem to stumble against the obstacle that neither is given the sort of prominence that we might expect, were it supposed to play such a role. Accordingly, if we are not altogether to abandon the idea that Qohelet is being set up to be criticized, then it may be better to approach the problem from the opposite direction, by looking at just what is emphasized.

3. *Qohelet's Profit and Loss*

From that point of view, the most obvious candidate seems to be something that I have already highlighted several times as strange: Qohelet's demand for a profit out of life, which appears in 1:2 as the first verse of the monologue after the initial motto. As we saw in the first chapter, that demand seems to accord with a more general presentation of Qohelet as a businessman, who measures human activity in terms of profit and loss. For all that his experiences lead him to be critical of futile greed, moreover, and to doubt the real value of material prosperity, property remains a continuing concern to him, whether he is emphasizing the particularly terrible situation of a man with wealth but no happiness from it in 6:1–6 (which might seem less terrible to those without any wealth to find happiness in), or remarking a little mysteriously on the benefits of money with wisdom in 7:12–13. The book gives the task of rejecting materialism to a character who is so fundamentally attached to his wealth, and who feels the lack of his ability to own things so acutely that it drives him to hate his life and work in 2:17–18.

9. See especially Ludwig Levy, *Das Buch Qoheleth. Ein Beitrag zur Geschichte des Sadduzäismus. Kritisch untersucht, übersetzt und erklärt* (Leipzig: Hinrichs, 1912).

Although it is difficult to know whether the conclusions reached by Qohelet actually represent the views of the author of Ecclesiastes, the tension between those anti-materialistic conclusions and Qohelet's materialistic approach suggests that if the author was in sympathy with one, he is unlikely also to have been in sympathy with the other—and if the epilogue does indeed reflect reservations about Qohelet, this may be the source of them. Indeed, that tension remains in the text even when we set the epilogue aside altogether, and if we are to explore it further, then we probably have also to adopt a more definite attitude towards the relationship between author and character not just in the book as a whole, but within the monologue. If Qohelet's speech is a true record of experience, then the tensions within it are psychological in nature, and there is little more we can say. If we are dealing with a creative characterization, on the other hand, then they may be very important.

There are many aspects of the monologue's content and presentation which make it difficult to accept that we are dealing with a genuine personal account, and the nature of Qohelet's characterization is itself one of them. Judging by our earlier discussions of the monologue's affinities, its writer was probably himself steeped in traditions of literature and thought. As a character, on the other hand, Qohelet claims exceptional wisdom, but no formal education; indeed, he asserts no pedigree for his ideas, speaks in a dialect or register which is some way from literary Hebrew, and apparently looks at the world as though it were a balance-sheet. Without going so far as to impose anachronistic stereotypes or social distinctions, we can recognize that there may be a discrepancy here, and that if the character of Qohelet is not an invention, then he is so selective and particular a self-presentation of the author that he might as well be an invention.

That allows us to suggest that the most obviously distinctive aspects of the characterization may be intended to serve a function, and it is not hard to see why an author might have chosen to make Qohelet so materialistic: the message that wealth is useless would sound very different on the lips of a pauper or ascetic, and Qohelet's instinctive attachment to his property is tied up with the book's expression of his heartfelt anguish. It is important to observe, though, that Qohelet's way of reckoning the world by profit and loss has consequences in the monologue that go far beyond his way of speaking and his emotional attachment to his wealth. His assessment of human work and ambition in terms of *hebel* arises, at least in considerable part, from a projection of his own wishes on to others: the acquisition of wealth is not an illusion for those who do not share Qohelet's desire or expectation to pull it out of the world, and

into their own absolute possession. If we do not accept Qohelet's outlook, then we may also find it difficult to accept his analysis, or to share
his despair.[10]

We cannot know for sure how the author expected his readers to react
to Qohelet's desire to turn a profit out of his life, but we have no reason
to suppose that they would have found it any less unusual than would a
modern reader, particularly as it became clear that this desire was for
something that nobody could reasonably expect.[11] It is not the worldview
which Qohelet develops that frustrates his wish, or even the more familiar problem of divine sovereignty, but the simple fact of death forcing
him to relinquish his property—and there is nothing new in suggesting
that you can't take it with you. That is not at all to say that readers would
have found themselves unsympathetic to all of Qohelet's further conclusions: distinctive though some of them are, Qohelet moves, *via* the narrative of his despair, from a position of unrealistic expectation through to a
realistic, if often gloomy, appreciation of human limitations which
embraces a sensible piety, and a familiar call to enjoy what one can.
From seeing no purpose in pleasure, he comes to recognize that there
may be value without purpose. Qohelet, perhaps, becomes more like the
rest of us.

I doubt, then, that the author is holding his character up to be attacked,
but Qohelet may nevertheless be something much more than a mouthpiece for his opinions. There is a narrative in the monologue beyond
Qohelet's own story, in which an exaggerated attachment to wealth and
profit collides with the realities of human transience and divine control.
Through his despair, we can see the inadequacies of Qohelet's materialism, and in his disillusionment we can see why the world appears so

10. Cf. Salyer, *Vain Rhetoric*, 387: "...the protagonist's lack of generosity,
magnificence and magnanimity resulted in a loss of attractiveness and credibility.
For most readers the radically self-centered ethic and deep-seated pessimism/
skepticism of the narrator results in an additional loss of attractiveness."

11. Interestingly, David E. Faust, "A Prophet Attacks Profit," *JAAR* 3 (1935) (or
the *Journal of the National Association of Biblical Instructors* as it was then), 29–31,
reaches a similar conclusion from a very different direction, declaring that "Koheleth
attacks the reward or profit motive as the goal of man's activities... The author
openly declares that, profit, or getting, does not give a true answer to the way of life"
(p. 29), and that "the main value of the book of Ecclesiastes in the progressive
revelation of God to his people is to prove that profit (material blessings) is not a
reward to be expected from God for virtuous conduct or for obedience to His law."
Although he is surely right to appreciate that materialism is an important theme in
the book, however, Faust does not appear to appreciate that it is also something
which Qohelet himself is portrayed as wanting: I think it is something that the
author, not the protagonist, may be attacking.

deceptive to him; indeed, if we venture to look at it from his perspective, then we may share some of that despair and disillusion. The key point, perhaps, is that we are not expected to start where Qohelet starts, and where we appreciate the particular concerns which so trouble him, we may not always feel obliged to follow where he leads. Deliberately, I suspect, the author has given us a character who is not supposed to command assent at every turn from his readers, but whose situation drives him to a provocative, poetic, and sometimes very personal re-evaluation of the world and of human priorities. It may be a measure of the author's success that, more than two thousand years later, Qohelet continues to engage and provoke not just scholars, but a wide range of other readers. In defiance of his own expectation, the character and his motto are still remembered after many, many generations have come and gone.

APPENDIX:
THE NAME QOHELET

1. *The Form of the Word*

The epithet used in the book to describe the protagonist of Ecclesiastes was originally written as *qhlt*, or possibly *qwhlt*.[1] This was vocalized as *qōhelet* in the manuscripts of the Masoretic tradition, and that pronunciation was certainly known earlier.[2] We cannot be certain, however, that it was the original pronunciation, and it may simply rest on an attempt to read *qhlt* as a Hebrew word: *qōhelet* would be the pronunciation of the feminine participle from the verb *qhl* in the Qal stem—if the Qal stem were ever actually attested for that verb.[3] The verb is associated with the

1. This *plene* spelling is used in 12:8, but is only found once, and it is likely that the defective spelling without *waw* is original.

2. Aquila's transliteration suggests a familiarity with this pronunciation, and tends to affirm that it is early: two manuscripts attribute the reading χωλεθ to him at 1:1; a third gives his reading as χωελεθ in 12:8. See Marshall, "Hexaplaric Fragments," 30. The latter accords with the Masoretic קֹהֶלֶת, and the former may do so too. Jerome represents the Hebrew as *coeleth* in his commentary. Eusebius (*Hist. Eccl.* 6.25.2) tells us that Origen also knew a Jewish pronunciation χωελεθ (perhaps a corruption of χωελεθ); cf. Eduard Schwartz, ed., *Eusebius Werke. 2, 2, Die Kirchengeschichte: Die lateinische Übersetzung des Rufinus bearbeitet in gleichen auftrage von Theodore Mommsen. Zweiter Teil: Die Bücher VI bis X über die Märtyrer in Palästina* (Leipzig: Hinrichs, 1908), 574. See E. Podechard, *L'Ecclésiaste* (Etudes Bibliques; Paris: Lecoffre, 1912), 9.

3. Two alternative vocalizations have been proposed by Abraham Kamenetzky. In "Das Koheleth-Rätsel," *ZAW* 29 (1909): 63–69, esp. 66 n. 4, he proposed קְהֶלֶת, in the context of a hypothesis that דברי קהלת originally signified "folk-sayings," or "Worte, die für den allgemeinen Gebrauch bestimmt sind" (p. 66), and was misunderstood by a subsequent redactor. That vocalization is based on no specific evidence, and Kamenetzky abandoned the theory in his subsequent articles, "Die Rätselname Koheleth," *ZAW* 34 (1914): 225–28, and "Die ursprünglich beabsichtigte Aussprache des Pseudonyms קהלת," *Orientalistische Literaturzeitung* (1921), cols. 11–15. However, he developed in these articles a new proposal that the author of the book was particularly influenced by the accounts of David and Solomon addressing assemblies of the people in Chronicles, and so named Solomon using the term קְהֶלֶת, a (defective) plural form from the unusual word for assembly, קהלה, used in Deut 33:4 and Neh 5:7 (to which a different sense has been assigned by

noun *qāhāl*, "an assembly," and in the stems which are actually used it means "to call an assembly" (Hiphil stem) or "to come together as an assembly" (Niphal), so a Qal participle would presumably also have something to do with assemblies. It was probably this understanding that gave rise to the LXX translation ἐκκλησιαστής, which means an "assemblyman"[4] and most subsequent commentators have likewise interpreted *qōhelet* in such terms, often explaining it, as we shall see, in the context of King Solomon's activities.[5] Moreover, even if the absence elsewhere of a Qal stem for QHL makes it difficult to read *qhlt* straightforwardly as a Qal participle, this does not preclude the possibility that *qhlt* was connected with *qāhāl* in another way: some scholars, indeed, understand it as a denominative form derived directly from *qāhāl* itself (just as "assemblyman" is from "assembly" in English), rather than as a participle from the verb.[6] Such a noun is itself unattested, though, so however we try to explain the form, we cannot extrapolate the precise meaning of *qhlt* from other sources.

Whether *qhlt*/*qōhelet* is read as a participle or a noun, furthermore, the final *t* is unexpected: this ending usually indicates a feminine form.[7] Setting aside associations with Solomon, that raises the intriguing possibility that the character is actually a woman, which would dispense with the difficulty, and we do, in fact, find a verb which is apparently used of Qohelet with a feminine ending in 7:27. The reading there presents some particular problems, which we shall look at shortly, but it is true that the words spoken *by* Qohelet, as opposed to those found in the book *about*

some scholars, see below) and in some rabbinic literature (cf. Jastrow ad loc.); in support of such a form, he cites, among other things, the place name מקהלת (Num 33:25–26). See especially "Die ursprünglich beabsichtigte," cols. 12–13.

4.   There are political connotations in the classical usage, and the Greek word probably does not mean just "citizen," as suggested in Seow, *Ecclesiastes*, 95; cf. Françoise Vinel, *L'Ecclésiaste. Traduction du texte grec de la Septante. Introduction et notes* (La Bible d'Alexandrie; Paris: Cerf, 2002), 100.

5.   The absence of any other attestations of the Qal stem offers a certain freedom to such interpretations: we do not know precisely what the verb would have meant in this stem. It would be fair to suppose, though, that the Qal would not have meant the same as the Hiphil, which was apparently well established as the stem to use for *calling* assemblies, so the reading as a Qal participle does not easily lend itself to association with Solomon's calling of assemblies.

6.   So, for example, Fox, *A Time to Tear Down*, 161, citing Benjamin Kedar-Kopfstein, "Semantic aspects of the pattern *qôtēl*," *HAR* 1 (1977): 155–76. See also Schoors, *Pleasing Words*, 2:438–39.

7.   See GKC §80 d; J-M §89. Although nouns with a feminine form may sometimes refer to a man (e.g. מדעת in Ruth 3:2), it is unlikely that a term coined to describe a man or a specifically male role would take a feminine form.

Qohelet, do little directly to exclude the possibility that Qohelet is female. Of course, Hebrew does not distinguish between masculine and feminine in the first person, so none of the many first-person verbs offers any indication of gender. By chance or design, furthermore, the monologue largely avoids using of Qohelet any adjectives or other grammatical forms which are gender-specific. Masculine forms of the participle are twice applied to the speaker, however, where the feminine could have been specified,[8] and these references make it difficult to assume that it is a woman speaking. The epilogue, moreover, uses explicitly masculine forms of the verb in 12:9–10, and certainly presents Qohelet as a man. The difficulty of the "feminine" *t* in *qhlt*, therefore, cannot be explained away just by making Qohelet female.

The problem has led to a search for analogous forms, in the hope of demonstrating that *qhlt* has been formed in accordance with some special pattern, where the *t* is conventional, and not a specific indication of gender. Many commentators have been intrigued, in particular, by the terms "sons of *hassōperet/sôperet*" and "sons of *pōkeret haṣṣĕbāyîm*" which occur in parallel lists in Ezra 2:55–57 and Neh 7:57–59, and which are often considered to indicate that titles could be formed with *t*. These lists are of "the sons of Solomon's servants," divided into separate categories and grouped with the *nĕtînîm*, who are temple functionaries. The various groups are each "sons of so-and-so," and the terms are probably to be considered personal, family names as they stand.[9] It is possible, however, that they were originally titles—respectively, perhaps "the Soperet," who could have been a scribe (cf. *sōper*), and "the Binder of Gazelles." If so, then *sōperet* and *pōkeret* would indeed furnish evidence that certain titles or functions might be described using forms with a final *t*—a "feminine of office." There is a great deal of speculation involved here, however, and it is far from certain that these terms were once titles.[10] At the very best, moreover, while they might conceivably suggest

---

8. ומוצא אני in 7:26 and יודע אני in 8:12; contrast the use of the feminine in 3:21: הירדת היא and העלה היא.

9. MT reads הספרת at Ezra 2:55 and סופרת at Neh 7:57, a distinction which is supported by the LXX witnesses. They do not read the initial ה in Ezra as an article, though, and render consistently as a proper name (Ασεφεραθ, Ασεφοραθ or similar), as does the version of the list in 1 Esd 5:33–35, which has Ασσαφειωθ or Ασωφερεθ. That פכרת הצביים has also been understood as a proper name in LXX seems to be indicated by the frequent insertion of an additional "sons," breaking the expression into two names. The initial ה of הצביים is not reflected in the LXX renderings of Neh 7:59, or in the list of 1 Esdras. The evidence probably suggests the originality of הספרת and הצביים, but it also indicates that scribes were reluctant to read titles here.

10. With regard to הספרת, it is worth noting the personal name which appears as מספרת in Neh 7:7 (although as מספר in Ezra 2:2, perhaps through confusion with the

that some titles were formed with *t* in the distant past, there is no reason to suppose either that this was still true in the period when Ecclesiastes was written, or that the author might have known about it and adopted the formation as an archaism. We may reasonably doubt, moreover, that any link can usefully be made to a purported (and itself dubious) use of feminine forms for titles in Phoenician,[11] or to an occasional use of nouns with a feminine form to represent occupations or professions in much later Hebrew.[12] The formation of titles with -*t* is more scholarly conjecture than established phenomenon, and the presence of the final -*t* in *qhlt* seems more likely to have inhibited than encouraged any reading of the word as a title or description: *qhlt* as a proper name would be odd, but essentially unproblematic; *qhlt* as a title seems to have the wrong gender, and no specific sense of which we are aware.

2. *"Qohelet" or "the Qohelet"?*

It does seem clear, nevertheless, that some early readers understood *qhlt* to be a title, or at least as a noun which *means* something, just as it seems equally clear that others did not. The most obvious manifestation of this

subsequent noun): such a similar formation from the same root suggests that we need not jump to the conclusion that a title is involved. The idea of פכרת הצבײם meaning "binder of gazelles" would also be more persuasive if צבײם were the normal plural of צבי, "gazelle," and were not used elsewhere as a place-name, or if PKR, "bind," were actually used in biblical Hebrew. The root PKR is familiar in this sense from Syriac, but not widely attested even in Jewish Aramaic.

11. This usage is anyway attested only in the case of a single term, and only in Punic texts. So Stanislav Segert, *A Grammar of Phoenician and Punic* (Munich: Beck, 1976), 173 §62:13 claims that: "Some titles of men are expressed by feminine nouns (cf. H. *qōhælæt*)," and cf. Schoors, *Pleasing Words*, 2:438. Segert cites, however, only the titles רבת ממלכאת and רבת מאת, and although the term ממלכת, "kingdom" can be used to mean "king"—a rather different phenomenon—it is not easy to identify any other examples, or so to generalize from the usage of רבת. Donner and Röllig, in *KAI* 2:111, deny that רבת is to be taken as feminine in the two passages cited by Segert, and argue from context (and in one case from the Numidian translation in a bilingual text) that the form is plural. Titles with a formation in -*t* are more securely attested in Arabic, as many scholars have noted, but it is hard to see what relevance those could have to a consideration of Hebrew usage in this period, unless Qohelet is supposed to be an Arab.

12. See Whitley, *Koheleth*, 5; Schoors, *Pleasing Words*, 2:438. Each offers examples only in the plural from mishnaic Hebrew, and the usage is generally as a collective designation; note, however, the singular משוחאה attested in *b. B. Meṣi'a* 107b for the plural משוכות, "surveyors," which both scholars cite from *m. 'Erub.* 4:11. The origin of these rare forms is unclear, but they do not occur early, and they are specifications of occupation or skill, not titles.

split lies in the different treatment of the word by Greek translators: the LXX, as we noted before, chose to render *qhlt* as ἐκκλησιαστής, which is a clear indication that it took it to be a title or similar designation, while Aquila opted simply to transliterate it as κωλεθ or κωελεθ, which is most easily explained if he took it to be a name.[13] The requirements of translation compelled a decision, but within the textual traditions we find evidence of a certain vacillation between the two understandings—and of considerable confusion.

Hebrew, like English, does not use a definite article with personal names, so the appearance of an article should indicate that a word is not a personal name. In the case of *qhlt*, no such article appears in the MT when we find the epithet at 1:1, 2, 12; 12:9, 10, or, as the text stands, in 7:27. However, in 12:8 the text refers to *hqwhlt*, "the Qohelet." In 7:27, furthermore, the apparent feminine verb which we noted above occurs in the expression *'mrh qhlt*, which has been vocalized to mean "Qohelet [she] said";[14] the LXX has apparently divided the text differently, however, to read an article (*'mr hqhlt*— "says the Qohelet"), and most modern commentators follow suit, assuming that the Masoretic reading is an error. There were probably at least two uses of a definite article in the early Hebrew text, therefore, and we should most likely restore a third: 12:8, with its article, is the virtual repetition at the end of the monologue of the motto which began it in 1:2, so we should expect them to match. As it happens, the LXX again has an article in 1:2, and since it is quite a faithful witness in such matters to the Hebrew text from which

---

13. The renderings of the other translators are uncertain. *HALOT* attributes the translation παροιμιάστης to Symmachus, which would suggest that he too understood the epithet to be a title; it gives no source for this, but is probably interpreting the reading of ms. 248 at 12:10, cited in *Origenis Hexaplorum quae supersunt; sive veterum interpretum graecorum in totum Vetus Testamentum fragmenta. Post Flaminium Nobilium, Drusium, et Montefalconium, adhibita etiam versione Syro-Hexaplari, concinnavit, emendavit, et multis partibus auxit Fridericus Field* (2 vols.; Oxford: Clarendon, 1875), 2:404 (and his n. 30 there). See similarly Krüger, *Qoheleth*, 41 n. 13. Here and in ms. 161, however, the reading is apparently an error for παροιμίας, created through assimilation to ἐκκλησιαστής. See Marshall, "Hexaplaric Fragments," 339. Since we have no evidence to the contrary, it is probable that Symmachus and Theodotion rendered the word in the same way as G. Among the later versions, note that the Syriac and the Targum both seem to regard the term as a proper name, and although it can be treacherous to read too much into determination or non-determination of Aramaic nouns from their state, the Targumist makes it explicit that this is a name which Solomon calls himself (cf. 12:9, 10).

14. Interestingly, de Rossi 3:264 cites this as a minor variant reading in 12:8 also; cf. Kennicott 2:561.

it was translated, there are grounds for restoring *hqhlt* here (as *BHQ* suggests).[15] So, MT has an article in 12:8, and the LXX was probably translated from a Hebrew text that had definite articles in 1:2; 7:27 and 12:8: that surely suggests, doesn't it, that *qhlt* must be read as a title, a gentilic, or some other descriptive term?

The problem is, of course, that the lack of a definite article with a title, although not as problematic as the presence of an article with a name, does raise questions of meaning. If we understand *qhlt* to be a title or something similar, then we can certainly translate the occurrence in 12:8, for instance, as "says *the* Qohelet," but should correspondingly translate that in 12:10 as "*a* Qohelet sought to find." Such switching between determination and indetermination just about works in 1:1–2, where the article can be understood simply as a specification ("Words of a Qohelet... That Qohelet said..."). This understanding, however, is very difficult to sustain in 12:9–10, where it is clearly not "*a* Qohelet" who is being described, but "*the* Qohelet" of the preceding speech, and the absence of an article implies very strongly that Qohelet is supposed to be understood there as a personal name. If the word is not a personal name in 1:1, furthermore, then all that follows is strictly just "some words of a Qohelet." Even granted that the use of the article in Hebrew does not always correspond to our expectations, its omission in the first verse, and the subsequent irregularity of its appearance seem very curious, and make the understanding of *qhlt* as a title seem less than straightforward. If some occurrences of Qohelet in the text apparently require that we take the term to be a title or description, others seem to push us no less firmly toward reading it as a name.

This tension makes itself felt in the textual tradition. The MT seems to represent a partial move away from use of the article with *qhlt*, even at the cost of a very strange word-division in 7:27, and Aquila notably has no article even in 12:8 (although it is hard to say whether that is because he found none in his Hebrew source). This probably corresponds to an understanding of *qhlt* as a name, which may have found some affirmation in links made between 1:1 and the titles of other books, such as Jeremiah, where the reference is certainly to a named individual, and

15. For a detailed presentation, see the posthumous article by Joseph Ziegler (edited by Fraenkel), "Der Gebrauch des Artikels in der Septuaginta des Ecclesiastes," in *Studien zur Septuaginta: Robert Hanhart zu Ehren* (ed. D. Fraenkel et al.; Abhandlungen der Akademie der Wissenschaften in Göttingen, Philologisch-Historische Klasse 190; Mitteilungen des Septuaginta-Unternehmens 20; Göttingen: Vandenhoeck & Ruprecht, 1990), 83–120, esp. 94. The LXX translates the epithet using an article in these three places and no others.

which is reflected in Jewish commentary.[16] Although the LXX seems to preserve an earlier situation, however, with three uses of the article to the MT's one, it still lacks the article in places where we should expect there to be one—notably 1:1 and 12, along with 12:9 and 10. It would be entirely speculative, though, to suggest that we are merely seeing in the LXX and the MT different points along a single trajectory, and that the Hebrew text began with articles on *qhlt* throughout, losing them progressively. We can explain why the witnesses differ, but text-criticism offers no ready solution to the basic inconsistency.

Of course, it is possible that the inconsistency is itself a secondary feature, since, with the exception of 1:12, all the apparently original uses of Qohelet without an article seem to have lain in the title or epilogue. Leaving aside other considerations about the relationship between those parts of the work and the main monologue, it would not seem difficult, on the face of it, to suppose that in the section between the two mottoes, 1:2–12:8, "Qohelet" was originally understood as a title, but that the title and epilogue were added by writers who understood the term as a name. On that reckoning, 1:12 could then have been brought into line with that understanding and with 1:1. Such an explanation, however, introduces much complexity, while yet failing to explain why subsequent redactors should have treated "Qohelet" as a name when the text before them presented it quite unambiguously as a title, and when there is no reason to suppose that it was familiar from any other text or tradition. If we prefer to retain the title and epilogue as original parts of the work, then we might speculate similarly that the author chose to assign different

16.　The title is close to such titles as Jer 1:1 ("The words of Jeremiah, the son of Hilkiah"), Prov 30:1 ("The words of Agur, son of Yakeh"), and Neh 1:1 ("The words of Nehemiah, the son of Hakaliah"): readers familiar with such works would almost certainly have presumed that Qohelet was also a name—until, perhaps, they encountered the article in the next verse. An association with the introductions to Amos and Jeremiah is made already in the midrash to Qohelet (at 1:1§2), and there the understanding of Qohelet as a (symbolic) name is explicit. In the Soncino translation, the relevant passage reads: "There were three prophets to whom, because it consisted of words of reproach, their prophecy was attributed personally, viz. '*The words of Koheleth,*' *The words of Amos*…and *The words of Jeremiah*… Why was Jeremiah's name so called? Because in his days Jerusalem became a desolation (*eremiah*). Why was Amos's name so called? R. Phinehas said: Because he was heavy (*'amus*) of tongue… Why was Koheleth's name so called? Because his words were uttered in public (*hikkahel*), as it is stated, *Then Solomon assembled (*yakhel*) the elders of Israel*"; see A. Cohen, "Ecclesiastes," in *Midrash Rabbah*, vol. 8 (ed. H. Freedman and M. Simon; 2d ed.; London: Soncino, 1951), 3. The midrash goes on to list and explain all the names used of Solomon (a tradition which is also picked up in Jerome's commentary on this verse).

understandings of the term to the different voices of those sections and of the monologue, but it is difficult to fathom any reason for him to have done so.

It may be that we should look a bit more closely at the monologue itself, and at least give more weight to another curious but neglected aspect of the problem. It is striking that in 1:2; 7:27, and 12:8, where we have found grounds to suppose that there was a definite article *h*- in early texts, *hqhlt* always followed *'mr* ("says," "said"): we have no evidence that *h*- ever preceded *qhlt* except after this verb, or, conversely, that this verb was ever found originally in the book with *qhlt*, not *hqhlt*, as its subject. If these occurrences of *'mr hqhlt*, "says the Qohelet," are secondary, or are actually to be understood in a different way, then we do not have any original instances of an article with *qhlt*.

Inasmuch as this problem has been addressed at all, the focus has been on 7:27, where the Masoretic version seems curiously to have mis-divided the text. Of course, the same considerations that make it difficult to understand why the Masoretes divided the words to yield a feminine form of the verb, also make it difficult to understand how that could be the intended original reading—if *'mrh* was indeed understood to be a feminine form of the verb. Other ways to understand it, however, are unconvincing: Dahood's suggestion of a perfect *qatala* form here has rightly won little acceptance,[17] and if we try to take *'mrh* as the noun *'mrh* ("word," "speech"), its relationship to *qhlt* becomes unclear— "word of Qohelet" would require the construct *'mrt qhlt*. If there were some way to understand the sequence of characters *'mrhqhlt* other than as "says the Qohelet," then the Masoretic reading *'mrh qhlt* at 7:27 might be taken as original, and the reading *'mr hqhlt* here (by the LXX or its source) and elsewhere as an error which gave rise to the understanding of "Qohelet" as a title. In the absence of any plausible alternative, however, the Masoretic reading must be regarded as a determined attempt to impose a particular interpretation of "Qohelet" as a name, as an inexplicable slip of the pen by some early copyist, or perhaps the consequence of some more profound difficulty in the text.[18] In any case, it does not

17. Schoors, *Pleasing Words*, 1:79–80.

18. It is worth noting a similar difficulty in 8:1, which also involves the assignment of a ה during word-division. Here MT reads כההכם = כ + unsyncopated article ה + חכם. Aquila reads τίς ὦδε σοφός here, which was probably the original reading of G; cf. Sebastian Euringer, *Der Masorahtext des Koheleth kritisch untersucht* (Leipzig: Hinrichs, 1890), 93–94; Alan H. McNeile, *An Introduction to Ecclesiastes: With Notes and Appendices* (Cambridge: Cambridge University Press, 1904), 164; and Marshall, "Hexaplaric Fragments," 227–28. Symmachus similarly reads τίς οὕτως σοφός (if we emend the ουτος of ms. 252, cf. Marshall, Field, *Quae*

give us a reason to understand the *he* in 7:27 as anything other than a definite article.[19] In 1:2 and 12:8, the complications over word-division are lacking, but the conclusions must be essentially the same.

There is no easy way, then, to interpret *'mr hqhlt* without reading the *he* as an article, and the Masoretic treatment of 7:27 is probably irrelevant. It is worth noting, however, that the third-person mention of Qohelet in that verse is both unexpected and unparalleled within the body of the monologue: it is not at all clear why the editorial voice intrudes here. The passage where it does so is notoriously obscure, and the sequence *'mrhqhlt* has to be read parenthetically. Furthermore, in 7:29, within the same section of his discussion, Qohelet uses the expression *r'h zh mṣ 'ty 'šr* ("look at this, I found that…"), and here we find the same expression, but with *'mr* where *'ṣr* stands in the subsequent use. That is hardly definitive, but there are some grounds to be suspicious of the expression's authenticity: the whole reference to Qohelet may have arisen secondarily in a context which was obscure and corrupt, and could conceivably have introduced *hqhlt* into the tradition. This is very thin, but it is not inconceivable that the inconsistencies arose in the first place from corruption or misunderstanding in the text.

Other approaches have been attempted. Remarking on the use of the article in 7:27 and 12:8, Frank Zimmerman summarized the problem long ago: "Commentators pay scant attention to the fact that קוהלת as a name anomalously receives the definite article. If it is argued that קוהלת is an attribute of office or function and, therefore, might tolerate the

---

supersunt, 2:395), and all of these Greek renderings seem to presuppose a division כה חכם. This is also reflected in the text of Jerome's commentary, where he writes, "Septuaginta pro eo quod nos posuimus: *quis ita ut sapiens*, transtulerunt: *quis nouit sapientes*"; this may suggest that he read כה חכם in his Hebrew source, if he was not simply swayed by the hexaplaric readings. It is far from clear that Aquila's reading is merely facilitatory, as Schoors, *Pleasing Words*, 1:43 assumes. Although *BHQ* prefers to retain MT, a number of modern commentators follow the Greek, for example, Fox, *A Time to Tear Down*, 272, and Seow, *Ecclesiastes*, 277. Both readings are probably early, and neither is easy. Abraham Kamenetzky, "Die P'šiṭa zu Koheleth textkritisch und in ihrem Verhältnis zu dem massoretischen Text, der Septuaginta und den andern alten griechischen Versionen," *ZAW* 24 (1904): 181–239, esp. 239, makes the interesting but entirely speculative suggestion that the initial כה arose as a corrupt repetition of the following הכ. The difficulty in 7:27 is not, then, without parallel.

19. Although it would have the virtue of simplicity, incidentally, there is no real evidence to back any supposition that the word was originally not *qhlt* but *hqhlt*, with the *h* dropping out in some passages when it was mistaken for an article attached to a name.

definite article, then it is strange that in the other verses of the book the name appears without the definite article."[20] His own suggestion rested on a hypothesis which has been subjected to much criticism, and is not now commonly held—that the book as a whole was translated rather poorly from Aramaic:[21] he believed that an original Aramaic form *knšh* (equivalent to *qhlt*, and numerologically to *šlmh*, "Solomon") "was interpreted in a moment of confused cerebration" by the translator "to be an Aramaic noun with the determinate ending."[22] As an answer to the problem, that is unsatisfactory on many levels, but Ginsberg does draw attention elsewhere in his argument to a fact that may be pertinent here: the article seems to be used somewhat erratically throughout Ecclesiastes, and so the inconsistency in its use with the epithet "Qohelet" may merely be symptomatic of a broader issue.[23]

20. Zimmerman, "Aramaic Provenance," 44.

21. See the Introduction, above.

22. Zimmerman, "Aramaic Provenance," 44. See similarly Torrey, "Original Language," esp. 156–57. Zimmerman's explanation is broadly supported by Ginsberg also, who argues, however, that the Aramaic original was *qhlh*; both are masculine participles with the emphatic ending ה, which would be identical in form to feminine participles. See Ginsberg, *Studies*, 31–33. Leaving aside more general objections to the Aramaic translation theory, the main problem with this solution is that it presupposes either such a profound ignorance on the part of the translator that he would rather feminize the name in Hebrew than recognize the emphatic ending, or else the influence of some exegetical reason to take the Aramaic epithet as feminine, which is never displayed clearly elsewhere in his rendering. As Dahood, "Canaanite–Phoenician Influence," 197, puts it "Those who support the Aramaic theory...must suppose that Qoheleth wrote in a dialect of Aramaic in which the absolute and the emphatic states fell together, and that the Hebrew translator made 24 mistakes inside the brief scope of 12 chapters and within the specific area of determination and indetermination, which is a wholly incredible hypothesis."

23. See Zimmerman, "Aramaic Provenance," 20–23. He suggests that, "In translating hundreds of determinate nouns, it would not be surprising if a number of slips, even a large number, had been made. A translator would have to be sharply alert in giving determinate forms their correct value and rendition" (p. 23). Ginsberg, *Studies*, 19–20, is more sympathetic to the problems faced by a translator dealing with the many nuances of the emphatic in Aramaic, and sees these, rather than shoddiness, as the root of the (mis)translation. The difficulties with the article are also outlined in Wilelmus C. Delsman, "Zur Sprache des Buches Koheleth," in *Von Kanaan bis Kerala: Festschrift für Prof. Mag. Dr. J. P. M. van der Ploeg O. P. zur Vollendung des siebzigsten Lebensjahres am 4. Juli 1979. Überreicht von Kollegen, Freunden und Schülern* (ed. W. C. Delsman et al.; Alter Orient und Altes Testament 211; Neukirchen–Vluyn: Neukirchener Verlag; Kevelaer: Butzon & Bercker, 1982), 341–65, esp. 358–59, and discussed at length in Schoors, *Pleasing Words*, 1:164–69; cf. Whitley, *Koheleth*, 108–10. Dahood, "Canaanite–Phoenician Influence," 197–201,

It is difficult to evaluate the more general usage of the article in the book. As in any Hebrew text composed initially without vowel points, we cannot tell for certain where the article was intended if the initial *he* has been displaced by another prefix, and the situation is complicated further in Ecclesiastes by the difficulties which surround the proper reading and sense of many passages.[24] In places where the reading is not in doubt, we do sometimes encounter an unexpected article: Ecclesiastes prefers *kl-h'dm*, for instance, to the expected *kl-'dm*—but it uses this expression consistently in 3:13; 5:18; 7:2; 12:13, and the expression is known also from Exod 9:19; Num 16:29, 32; Josh 11:14; Ps 116:11; Jer 31:30. Actual inconsistency is less common, although we may note, say, the instance of *m'śh* without the article in 8:9, which is difficult to explain as different in sense to the instance with the article at 3:17, and the article is indeed used rather variably with that noun in apparently similar contexts. Even if this does not in fact imply changes in nuance, however, any writer may vary their style for less obvious reasons of euphony, or even for the sake of variety. If Ecclesiastes fails to achieve a pure consistency of expression in its use of the article, though, examples of inconsistency in particular expressions are unusual; there are none which might give rise to significant differences in the way a word is understood, as is the case with *qhlt*. The book does not always follow the rules which we would expect, and in that it is hardly unique,[25] but it is not marked by a general randomness or carelessness in its use of the article which might permit us to explain away our problem.

If the form of the word "Qohelet" offers readers of the book no clear guidance, then, as to whether it is a name or title, the subsequent usage serves only to confuse the matter. In early texts of the Hebrew, as in the

also presents the evidence, in pursuit of his own theory that the book is influenced by Phoenician, a language in which use of the article is rather unpredictable.

24. So, for instance, we might expect an article on יוֹדֵעַ in the expression מַה־לֶּעָנִי יוֹדֵעַ at 6:8, usually translated "what is (the advantage) for the poor man who knows" or similar: the MT points לֶעָנִי as determined, and the participle should agree with the noun in this respect. The shortage cannot be readily attributed to the author though, who may have intended "a poor man"; the Masoretic vocalization is supported by the ancient versions, but all are probably influenced by the previous clause. The Hebrew is difficult, moreover, and many emendations have been proposed.

25. Whitley, *Koheleth*, 109, cites numerous examples from biblical Hebrew of variation in the use of the article even within otherwise identical expressions by the same author, or between versions of the same passages in Kings and Chronicles. Schoors, *Pleasing Words*, 1:169, observes increasing irregularity in later Hebrew, and suspects that Aramaic may have been an influence on Ecclesiastes in this respect.

Greek translation, there was probably a marked distinction between "the Qohelet" of the monologue and its mottoes, and "Qohelet" elsewhere in the book. We are not in a position to judge whether this distinction is original on text-critical grounds, although assumptions that "Qohelet" was a name seem to have influenced the subsequent development of the Hebrew text. It is difficult to see why, though, if the author originally made it clear that "Qohelet" was a title or description, it should have been understood as a name by subsequent readers and this understanding imported into certain passages; conversely, of course, it is no easier to see why readings as a title should partially have displaced an authorial presentation of "Qohelet" as a name.

In short, a case could be made, in terms of the textual evidence and usage, for "Qohelet" having started as either a name or a title; indeed, quite a good case could be made for some inconsistency in the usage right from the outset, which would certainly explain the subsequent confusion. If we are to explain the epithet, we need to look more closely at what it might actually have implied.

3. *The Meaning of "Qohelet"*

If "Qohelet" was a name, then it may have had no specific meaning, just as the name "Lemuel" in Prov 31:1 does not necessarily convey any particular significance if we translate it.[26] That is not to say that a name is necessarily without implication, even if it does not convey information explicitly, and it is possible that "Qohelet" would have conveyed to the original readership of the book some nuance of, for instance, class, nationality, or ethnicity. If, on the other hand, "Qohelet" was a title, then we should expect it to have had a meaning, although, again, that meaning might lie in an implication of the title, rather than in its explicit significance: the "Home Secretary" of Great Britain, for instance, is more important than their job-title might suggest, and many titles, ancient or modern, say more about the rank than about the duties of those who hold them. If the author of Ecclesiastes called its protagonist "Qohelet" for a reason, then that reason may have involved an anticipated reaction to the word on the part of the original readership, which had little or nothing to do with any lexical significance of the term. In that case, the significance could easily have been lost even on slightly later readers, and will not be recoverable simply through a lexical or etymological analysis.

---

26. *HALOT* suggests "belonging to God," אל + למו‎, which is of no obvious relevance to the sayings that follow.

Just such an analysis, though, underpins the explanations provided for the epithet by most interpreters from earliest times. These interpreters have tended to associate "Qohelet" with the root QHL, and hence with ideas of "assembly" or "assembling," although there are several different lines of argument involved. So, traditional Jewish explanations are geared to an affirmation of Solomonic authorship, which requires that the use of a name other than "Solomon" be justified. For example, in the explanation for Qohelet's name furnished by the midrash, this is an explicit reference to the identity of Qohelet as Solomon, who "assembled" (*yqhl*) all the leaders of Israel in 1 Kgs 8:1 (and the term *qhl*, "assembly," is prominent throughout the rest of the account in that chapter). Rashi notes that explanation, but offers a different one along the same lines: Solomon is Qohelet "because he assembled (*qhl*) many wise things...and some say that he would speak all his words in an assembly (*bhqhl*)." Similarly Rashbam: "Solomon is called Qoheleth because he gathered wisdom from all the people of the East."[27] Although some more recent scholars, incidentally, have followed the same basic understanding of the word *qhlt* as Rashi, Rashbam and various other early commentators, this is not an easy line to pursue: the root QHL and its derivatives are used in Hebrew of assembling people, not things.[28]

Modern critical commentators are not generally inclined to accept the Solomonic authorship of the book, which was taken for granted by the earlier writers who linked "Qohelet" to Solomon's activities. Correspondingly, they do not seek an explanation for the use of "Qohelet" to describe Solomon in the way that such earlier commentators did: the problem is perceived to be not that Solomon wrote a book in which he mysteriously called himself Qohelet, but that we possess words attributed to Qohelet which their author may or may not have intended readers to associate with Solomon. We have considered the author's intentions in this respect more generally in Chapter 1, but it is important to observe that the link between QHL and Solomon is probably not a two-way street. If we need to understand why Solomon should be described using a term from that root, then 1 Kgs 8 offers an explanation; on the other hand, there is no reason to suppose that a reader encountering some derivative from that root would naturally have thought of Solomon. It does not appear in the Deuteronomistic account of his reign outside that chapter, and is associated slightly more with David than with Solomon in

27. See Japhet and Salters, *Rashbam on Qoheleth*, 90.
28. So, for example, Seow, *Ecclesiastes*, 97, notes the use of the cognate verb in Syriac to refer to compilation of a book, and suggests that "Qohelet probably does mean 'Gatherer' or 'Collector'—whether of wisdom, wealth, or people."

Chronicles. Furthermore, if any single figure is strongly associated with addressing the assembly of Israel in biblical tradition, that figure is surely Moses. Taken in connection with the other information offered about Qohelet in 1:1 and 1:12, the term might have suggested some connection with Solomon to a reader well-versed in the biblical histories, but it is not an especially obvious name or title for him. Correspondingly, it seems unlikely that the author's use of "Qohelet" for his protagonist was supposed primarily to identify the character as Solomon to his audience, whatever his more general intentions in that respect.

It may be that the LXX translator was attempting, like the midrash, to assert the link with Solomon when he used ἐκκλησιαστής to render the Hebrew,[29] but the translation into Greek provides a route for generalization of the sense: it is not just "Solomon who assembled" that we encounter here, but an "assemblyman" or somesuch. Many modern commentators have been inclined to adopt just such a general reference, seeing "Qohelet" as a description of character or occupation, rather than as a specific allusion to "Solomon the Assembler." A few attribute meanings to QHL which are not connected specifically with "assembling," so that Whitley, for example, understands derivatives from the root to connote "indictment" in Neh 5:7 and Job 11:10 and that the Syriac cognate may have the sense "consider": he suggests that Qohelet is "the Sceptic."[30] Ullendorff similarly notes the Nehemiah passage, and a Syriac sense "litigious," calling Qohelet "the arguer," and Zimmermann, in an article which preceded his advocacy of a translation theory, argued that the epithet referred to "reproving."[31] It is not necessary, however, to read that special sense in the passages cited, and there is no other evidence for such a connotation in Hebrew. If such a description of character is intended, moreover, rather than a formal title, any explanation of the final *-t* in *qhlt* based on resort to supposed titular forms becomes not merely weak but wholly inapplicable. Scholarly appeals to languages other than Hebrew and Syriac are less common, although Barag has gone so far as to find a special sense of "old age" or "maturity"

---

29. Since the LXX rendering of 1 Kgs 8:1 uses the compound ἐξεκκλησίασεν, a precise reference to that verse is unlikely (although Vinel, *L'Ecclésiaste*, 100, sees a specific allusion). A more general reference to the uses of ἐκκλησία in the chapter seems possible, however.

30. Whitley, *Koheleth*, 6. He is followed by Diethelm Michel, *Qohelet* (Erträge der Forschung 258; Darmstadt: Wissenschaftliche Buchgesellschaft, 1988), 8.

31. Edward Ullendorff, "The Meaning of קהלת," *VT* 12 (1962): 215; Frank Zimmerman, "The Root *KAHAL* in Some Scriptural Passages," *JBL* 50 (1931): 311–12. Zimmermann does not cite the passage from Job, but to Neh 5:7 adds Deut 33:4 and Sir 7:7.

through analogy with a supposed Arabic cognate; this is entirely speculative.[32] Most commentators have retained some connection with "assembling" or "assemblies," and so essentially align themselves with the LXX
understanding.

This connection, however, is often handled rather loosely. As we have
noted already, the Hebrew QHL is used strictly to connote assemblies of
people, and so we cannot understand Qohelet just to be a "collector" of
sayings or wealth. The "assemblies" of people, however, are not just any
groups. Michael Fox has claimed that "The *qahal* is not necessarily a
formal assembly. It can be an informal, non-institutional gathering, such
as a *qahal* of peoples (Gen 28:3) or of ghosts (Prov 21:16). We might
imagine him [Qohelet] speaking to any gathering of people."[33] It is not
clear that this is entirely true, however. In the passage which Fox cites
from Genesis, the point of the noun is that it represents a large multitude:
"And may El Shaddai bless you, and make you fruitful, and make you so
many that you become a (whole) assembly of peoples"; similar expressions are used in Gen 35:11 and 48:4. In Proverbs, we are not told that "a
man straying from the path of prudence will rest in *a group of ghosts*":
this is a mythological reference, and he is going to sleep in the "assembly
of the Rephaim"—the shades of the dead who dwell in Sheol (compare
the "assembly of holy ones" in Ps 89:6 [ET 89:5]). All the biblical usage
for *qāhāl*, "assembly," is with reference to large public communities and
assemblies, or, in these few cases, with mythological or metaphorical
assemblies that can be understood in similar terms. This is essentially the
use in later Hebrew as well.[34] Correspondingly, it is difficult to infer from

---

32. Gershon Barag, "קהלת"? היא מה" ("What is 'Qoheleth'?"), *Tarbiz* 21
(1950): 101–5 (Hebrew). He derives this sense from the development of nominal
forms from the root كهل, and consequently translates 1:1 as "words 'from the son of
David's old age (or discernment in old age)'" (103). Subsequent uses of "Qohelet"
are then secondary, and reflect a misunderstanding. See the comments of Schoors,
Pleasing Words, 2:433.

33. Fox, *A Time to Tear Down*, 161.

34. So Paul Joüon, "Sur le nom de 'Qoheleth'," *Biblica* 2 (1921): 53–54. In
response to Podechard's claim (*L'Ecclésiaste*, 134) that the "assembly" mentioned in
Sir 38:33 and 39:10 was an assembly of sages (cf. Schoors, *Pleasing Words*, 2:439),
he notes correctly that "Malheureusement, dans les textes indiqués et dans d'autres
qu'on pourrait alléguer…l'assemblée (קהל, ἐκκλησία) est bien plutôt une assemblée
nombreuse, une assemblée populaire, l'assemblée de la communauté. En fait, le mot
קהל soit dans l'hébreu biblique, soit dans la langue postérieure s'emploie presque
toujours pour désigner une assemblée nombreuse et populaire. Pour désigner une
réunion de savants, une académie, on emploie en néo-hébreu יְשִׁיבָה" (p. 53). This is
affirmed by the citations in Levy, to which he refers, and Jastrow.

"Qohelet" any connection with some much smaller group, such as a philosophical school or academy.[35]

It is also important to observe that QHL and its derivatives have no specific implication of speech. As we saw earlier, the verb is used of assembling or of calling an assembly: it nowhere refers in itself to addressing an assembly. Even if we connect "Qohelet" with the noun *qāhāl*, rather than the verb, that by itself gives us no licence to make Qohelet a "public speaker," or "preacher."[36] In this context, the description of Qohelet furnished by the epilogue is often invoked: we are told there that Qohelet "...taught the people knowledge, and he heard (or 'weighed'), sought out, and and set in order a great many sayings. Qohelet sought to find words that give pleasure, and a proper writing of words that convey truth" (12:9–10).[37] If that is read as a description of Qohelet as a "public teacher,"[38] then it does not seem unreasonable, on the face of it, to suppose that his link with public assemblies involved teaching their members in some way. Qohelet's teaching of the people,

---

35. That connection has been asserted by a number of scholars in the past; cf. Schoors, *Pleasing Words*, 2:435. Among current commentators, it is affirmed by Lohfink on the basis not of Hebrew but of Greek usage: "Das dem hebräischen *qāhāl* 'Versammlung' entsprechende griechische Wort ἐκκλησία bezeichnete bisweilen auch philosophische Zirkel, und ein ἐκκλησιάστης = *qōhælæt* könnte dann auch Gründer und Leiter eines solchen Kreises gewesen sein." See N. Lohfink, *Kohelet* (6th ed.; Die Neue Echter Bibel; Würzburg: Echter, 2009), 11–12; ET of first edition *Qoheleth: A Continental Commentary* (Continental Commentaries; Minneapolis: Fortress, 2003), 10. Certainly, the Greek usage more readily allows such a sense, but this idea presumes that the author is, to some extent, "thinking in Greek and speaking in Hebrew," as Alain Bühlmann puts it in a different context ("The Difficulty of Thinking in Greek and Speaking in Hebrew [Qoheleth 3:18; 4:13–16; 5:8]," *JSOT* 90 [2000]: 101–8), and that degree of hellenization in the book does not seem probable. Building on Lohfink's ideas, Robert Michaud, *Qohélet et l'hellénisme: La Littérature de sagesse: Histoire et Théologie*, vol. 2 (Lire le Bible 77; Paris: Cerf, 1987), 119, envisages Qohelet strolling round the market-place, surrounded by his pupils, in earnest discussion with the traders: his innovative imitation of the Greek philosophers bears fruit, and "le nombre des auditeurs ainsi rassemblés grossit de jour en jour. On peut croire que c'est cette manière originale de diffuser son enseignement qui valut au professeur non conformiste le titre de 'Rassembleur'." That is not at all what קהל seems to signify in biblical usage (Michaud also suggests in a footnote that the Hebrew term can mean "cercle philosophique," an opinion presumably inherited from Lohfink, but presented simply as a fact).

36. So similarly Podechard, *L'Ecclésiaste*, 130–31.

37. The various lexical and text-critical problems in these verses have given rise to much discussion, but they do not affect the basic sense, at least with regard to our present discussion.

38. Fox, *A Time to Tear Down*, 161.

however, seems to reside in his compilation of sayings, and the subsequent 12:11 seems to make clear that the epilogue understands this in literary terms. Even if we divide the activities, so that Qohelet's teaching is separate from his writing, it is difficult to imagine what real context might be envisaged in a description of Qohelet holding forth regularly to some large public assembly, and such a description does not seem to correspond to anything else in the book.

In the end, we need not go so far as to speculate that "Qohelet" might be an acronym or a cryptogram,[39] or even that it was "just a nickname [of the real author], which was probably understood by those in the know at that time,"[40] but the sense of which is now unrecoverable. We cannot say much more, however, than that if the author troubled to assign it to his protagonist, the epithet was supposed to impart some meaning to readers of the book. If it was an existing or invented title, we can get no further to it through a lexical or etymological approach than to suggest that it implies some association with public assemblies. Even though these play no significant part in Qohelet's monologue, such a title could, of course, be an affirmation of status and no more—like, say, "The words of (the) Congressman." If it was a name, on the other hand, the form might similarly have had some implication of class or ethnicity.

---

39. So E. Renan, *L'Ecclésiaste traduit de l'hébreu avec une étude sur l'age et le caractère du livre* (Oeuvres Complètes de Ernest Renan, édition définitive établie par Henriette Psichari 7; Paris: Calmann-Lévy, 1955), 534–36 (originally published in 1882). He believes that it conceals the name "Solomon."

40. "…war es vielleicht nur ein Spitzname, der vielleicht den Eingeweihten in jener Zeit bekannt war": Graetz, *Kohélet*, 17.

BIBLIOGRAPHY

Ackroyd, P. R. "The Meaning of Hebrew דּוֹר Considered." *JSS* 13 (1968): 3–10.

Albright, William Foxwell. "Some Canaanite–Phoenician Sources of Hebrew Wisdom." Pages 1–15 in *Wisdom in Israel and in the Ancient Near East.* Edited by M. Noth and W. Winton Thomas. VTSup 3. Leiden: Brill, 1955.

Alexander, Philip et al. *Qumran Cave 4 XXVI Miscellanea, Part 1.* DJD 36. Oxford: Clarendon, 2000.

Allgeier, A. *Das Buch des Predigers oder Koheleth. Übersetzt und erklärt.* Die Heilige Schrift des Alten Testamentes 6/2. Bonn: Hanstein, 1925.

Alster, Bendt. *The Instructions of Suruppak: A Sumerian Proverb Collection.* Mesopotamia 2. Copenhagen: Akademisk, 1974.

———. *Wisdom of Ancient Sumer.* Bethesda: CDL, 2005.

Anderson, William H. U. "Ironic Correlations and Scepticism in the Joy Statements of Qoheleth?" *SJOT* 14 (2000): 67–100.

———. "The Poetic Inclusio of Qoheleth in Relation to 1,2 and 12,8." *SJOT* 12 (1998): 203–13.

———. "What is Scepticism and Can It Be Found in the Hebrew Bible?" *SJOT* 13 (1999): 225–57.

Annus, Amar, and Alan Lenzi. *Ludlul bēl nēmeqi: The Standard Babylonian Poem of the Righteous Sufferer: Introduction, Cuneiform Text, and Transliteration with a Translation and Glossary.* Publications of the Foundation for Finnish Assyriological Research 2. State Archives of Assyria Cuneiform Texts 7. Helsinki: The Neo-Assyrian Text Corpus Project, 2010.

Archer, Gleason L. "The Linguistic Evidence for the Date of Ecclesiastes." *Journal of Evangelical Theological Society* 12 (1969): 167–81.

Arnaud, D. *Recherches au Pays d'Aštata. Emar VI.4 Textes de la Bibliothèque: Transcriptions et traductions.* Synthèse 28. Paris: Editions Recherche sur les Civilisations, 1987.

Assmann, Jan. "Weisheit, Loyalismus und Frömmigkeit." Pages 11–72 in *Studien zu altägyptischen Lebenslehren.* Edited by E. Hornung and O. Keel. OBO 28. Freiburg: Universitätsverlag. Göttingen: Vandenhoeck & Ruprecht, 1979.

Backhaus, F. J. *"Den Zeit und Zufall trifft sie alle": Studien zur Komposition und zum Gottesbild im Buch Qohelet.* Bonner Biblische Beiträge 83. Frankfurt am Main: Hain, 1993.

Barag, Gershon. "מה היא ״קהלת״?" ("What is 'Qoheleth'?"). *Tarbiz* 21 (1950): 101–5 (Hebrew).

Barnes, Jonathan. "L'Ecclésiaste et le scepticisme Grec." *RThPh* 131 (1999): 103–14.

Barré, Michael L., ed. *Wisdom, You are My Sister: Studies in Honor of Roland E. Murphy, O.Carm., on the Occasion of His Eightieth Birthday.* CBQMS 29. Washington: The Catholic Biblical Association of America, 1997.

Bartholomew, Craig. *Ecclesiastes*. Baker Commentary on the Old Testament Wisdom and Psalms. Grand Rapids: Baker Academic, 2009.

Barton, George A. *A Critical and Exegetical Commentary on the Book of Ecclesiastes*. ICC. Edinburgh: T. & T. Clark, 1908.

Barucq, André. *Ecclésiaste. Qohéleth. Traduction et Commentaire*. Verbum Salutis. Paris: Beauchesne, 1968.

Bellia, Giuseppe, and Angelo Passaro, eds. *Il Libro del Qohelet. Tradizione, redazione, teologia*. Cammini nello Spirito. Biblica 44. Milan: Paoline, 2001.

Bianchi, Francesco. "The Language of Qohelet: A Bibliographical Survey." *ZAW* 105 (1993): 210–23.

Black, Jeremy, Graham Cunningham, Eleanor Robson, and Gábor Zólyomi. *The Literature of Ancient Sumer*. Oxford: Oxford University Press, 2004.

Blenkinsopp, Joseph. "Ecclesiastes 3.1–15: Another Interpretation." *JSOT* 20 (1995): 55–64.

Braun, Rainer. *Kohelet und die fruhhellenistische Popularphilosophie*. BZAW 130. Berlin: de Gruyter, 1973.

Brenner, Athalya. Some Observations on the Figurations of Woman in Wisdom Literature." Pages 50–66 in *A Feminist Companion to Wisdom Literature*. Edited by Athalya Brenner. The Feminist Companion to the Bible 9. Sheffield: Sheffield Academic, 1995.

Bühlmann, Alain. "The Difficulty of Thinking in Greek and Speaking in Hebrew (Qoheleth 3.18. 4.13–16. 5.8)." *JSOT* 90 (2000): 101–8.

Burkes, Shannon. *Death in Qoheleth and Egyptian Biographies of the Late Period*. SBL Dissertation Series 170. Atlanta: SBL, 1999.

Burkitt, F. C. "Is Ecclesiastes a Translation?" *JTS* (os) 23 (1921): 22–28.

Caminos, Ricardo A. *A Tale of Woe: From a Hieratic Papyrus in the A. S. Pushkin Museum of Fine Arts in Moscow*. Oxford: Griffith Institute, 1977.

Carasik, Michael. "Qohelet's Twists and Turns." *JSOT* 28 (2003): 192–209.

Carlebach, Joseph. *Das Buch Koheleth. Ein Deutungsversuch*. Frankfurt am Main: Hermon, 1936.

Castellino, George R. "Qohelet and His Wisdom." *CBQ* 30 (1968): 15–28. Reprinted on pages 31–43 in Zuck, ed., *Reflecting with Solomon*.

Christianson, Eric S. *A Time to Tell: Narrative Strategies in Ecclesiastes*. JSOTSup 280. Sheffield: Sheffield Academic, 1998.

Civil, M. "Enlil and Namzitarra." *AfO* 25 (1974): 65–71.

Clarke, Adam. *The Holy Bible, Containing the Old and New Testaments: The text carefully printed from the most correct copies of the present authorised translation, including the marginal readings and parallel texts: with a commentary and critical notes; designed as a help to a better understanding of the sacred writings*. Vol. 3, *Job to Solomon's Songs*. 2d ed. London: William Tegg, 1854.

Cohen, A. "Ecclesiastes." In *Midrash Rabbah*, vol. 8. Edited by H. Freedman and M. Simon. 2d ed. London: Soncino, 1951.

Cohen, M. "ᵓAššūrênû ʿattâ sᵉbābûnî (Q. sᵉbābûnû) (Psaume XVII 11A)." *VT* 41 (1991): 137–44.

Corré, Alan D. "A Reference to Epispasm in Koheleth." *VT* 4 (1954): 416–18.

Crenshaw, James L. "The Birth of Skepticism in Ancient Israel." Pages 1–19 in *The Divine Helmsman: Studies on God's Control of Human Events, Presented to Lou H. Silberman*. Edited by James L. Crenshaw and Samuel Sandmel. New York: Ktav, 1980.

——. *Ecclesiastes: A Commentary*. Old Testament Library. Philadelphia: Westminster, 1987. London: SCM, 1988.

——. "Qoheleth's Quantitative Language." Pages 1–22 in *The Language of Qohelet in Its Context: Essays in Honour of Prof. A. Schoors on the Occasion of His Seventieth Birthday*. Edited by A. Berlejung and P. van Hecke. OLA 164. Leuven: Peeters and Department of Ooesterse Studies, Leuven, 2007.

——. "Qoheleth's Understanding of Intellectual Inquiry." Pages 205–24 in Schoors, ed., *Qohelet in the Context of Wisdom*.

Dahood, Mitchell. "Canaanite–Phoenician Influence in Qoheleth." *Biblica* 33 (1952): 30–52, 191–221.

——. "Canaanite Words in Qoheleth 10,20." *Biblica* 46 (1965): 210–12.

——. "The Language of Qoheleth." *CBQ* 14 (1952): 227–32.

——. "Northwest Semitic Philology and Three Biblical Texts." *JNSL* 2 (1972): 17–22.

——. "The Phoenician Background of Qoheleth." *Biblica* 47 (1966): 264–82.

——. "The Phoenician Contribution to Biblical Wisdom Literature." Pages 123–52 in *The Role of the Phoenicians in the Interaction of Mediterranean Civilizations: Papers Presented to the Archaeological Symposium at the American University of Beirut. March 1967*. Edited by William A. Ward. Beirut: The American University of Beirut, 1968.

——. "Qoheleth and Northwest Semitic Philology." *Biblica* 43 (1962): 349–65.

——. "Qoheleth and Recent Discoveries." *Biblica* 39 (1958): 302–18.

——. "Scriptio Defectiva in Qoheleth 4,10a." *Biblica* 49 (1968): 243.

——. "Three Parallel Pairs in Eccl. 10:18. A Reply to Prof. Gordis." *JQR* 62 (1971): 84–87.

D'Alario, Vittoria. *Il Libro del Qohelet. Struttura letteraria e retorica*. Supplementi all Rivista Biblica 27. Bologna: Dehoniane, 1992.

Davila, James R. "Qoheleth and Northern Hebrew." *MAARAV* 5–6 (1990): 69–87.

Delitzsch, Franz. *Biblischer Commentar über die poetischen Bücher des Alten Testaments*. Vol. 4, *Hoheslied und Koheleth. Mit Excursen von Consul D. Wetzstein*. Leipzig: Dörffling & Franke, 1875.

Delkurt, Holger. *"Der Mensch ist dem Vieh gleich, das vertilgt wird": Tod und Hoffnung gegen den Tod in Ps 49 und bei Kohelet*. Biblisch-theologische Studien 50. Neukirchen–Vluyn: Neukirchener Verlag, 2005.

Dell, Katherine. J. "The Cycle of Life in Ecclesiastes." *VT* 59 (2009): 181–89.

Dell, Katherine. J., and Margaret Barker, eds. *Wisdom: The Collected Articles of Norman Whybray*. SOTS Monograph Series. Aldershot: Ashgate, 2005.

Delsman, Wilelmus C. "Zur Sprache des Buches Koheleth." Pages 341–65 in *Von Kanaan bis Kerala: Festschrift für Prof. Mag. Dr. J. P. M. van der Ploeg O.P. zur Vollendung des siebzigsten Lebensjahres am 4. Juli 1979. Überreicht von Kollegen, Freunden und Schülern*. Edited by W. C. Delsman et al. Alter Orient und Altes Testament 211. Neukirchen–Vluyn: Neukirchener Verlag. Kevelaer: Butzon & Bercker, 1982.

Diels, Hermann. *Die Fragmente der Vorsokratiker: Griechisch und Deutsch*. 2d ed. Berlin: Weidmannsche Buchhandlung, 1906.

Diesel, Anja A., Reinhard G. Lehmann, Eckart Otto, and Andreas Wagner, eds. *"Jedes Ding hat seine Zeit…" Studien zur israelitischen und altorientalischen Weisheit. Diethelm Michel zum 65. Geburtstag*. BZAW 241. Berlin: de Gruyter, 1996.

Dietrich, M. "Der Dialog zwischen Šupe-ameli und seinem 'Vater'. Die Tradition babylonischer Weisheitssprüche im Westen. Anhang von G. Keydana: Die hethitische Version." *UF* 23 (1991): 33–74.

———."'Ein Leben ohne Freude...' Studie über eine Weisheitskomposition aus den Gelehrtenbibliotheken von Emar und Ugarit." *UF* 24 (1992): 9–29.

Díez Merino, Luis. *Targum de Qohelet. Edición Príncipe del Ms. Villa-Amil no. 5 de Alfonso de Zamora*. Bibliotheca Hispana Bíblica 13. Madrid: Consejo Superior de Investigaciones Científicas, 1987.

Dillon, E. J. *The Sceptics of the Old Testament: Job, Koheleth, Agur: With English Text Translated for the First Time from the Primitive Hebrew as Restored on the Basis of Recent Philological Discoveries*. London: Isbiser & Co., 1895.

Driver, G. R. "Problems and Solutions." *VT* 4 (1954): 225–45.

Ehlich, Konrad. "Hebel–Metaphern der Nichtigkeit." Pages 49–64 in Diesel et al., eds., *"Jedes Ding hat seine Zeit..."*.

Ellermeier, Friedrich. *Qohelet. Teil 1 Abschnitt 1. Untersuchungen zum Buche Qohelet*, Herzberg am Harz: Erwin Jungfer, 1967.

Euringer, Sebastian. *Der Masorahtext des Koheleth kritisch untersucht*. Leipzig: J. C. Hinrichs, 1890.

Faust, David E. "A Prophet Attacks Profit." *JAAR* 3 (1935): 29–31.

Fernández, A. "Es Ecclesiastes una Versión?" *Biblica* 3 (1922): 45–50.

Field, Frederick. *Origenis Hexaplorum quae supersunt; sive veterum interpretum graecorum in totum Vetus Testamentum fragmenta. Post Flaminium Nobilium, Drusium, et Montefalconium, adhibita etiam versione Syro-Hexaplari, concinnavit, emendavit, et multis partibus auxit Fridericus Field*. 2 vols. Oxford: Clarendon, 1875.

Fischer, Alexander Achilles. *Skepsis oder Furcht Gottes? Studien zur Komposition und Theologie des Buches Kohelet*. BZAW 247. Berlin: de Gruyter, 1997.

Fischer, Stefan. *Die Aufforderung zur Lebensfreude im Buch Kohelet und seine Rezeption der ägyptischen Harfnerlieder*. Wiener alttestamentliche Studien 2. Frankfurt am Main: Lang, 1999.

———. "Qohelet and 'Heretic' Harpers' Songs." *JSOT* 26 (2002): 105–21.

Fox, Michael V. "Frame-Narrative and Composition in the Book of Qohelet." *HUCA* 48 (1977): 83–106.

———. "The Identification of Quotations in Biblical Literature." *ZAW* 92 (1980): 416–31.

———. "The Meaning of *Hebel* for Qohelet." *JBL* 105 (1986): 409–27.

———."Qohelet 1.4." *JSOT* 40 (1988): 109.

———. *Qohelet and His Contradictions*. JSOTSup 71. Sheffield: Almond, 1989.

———. "Qohelet's Epistemology." *HUCA* 58 (1987): 137–55.

———. *The Song of Songs and the Ancient Egyptian Love Songs*. Madison: University of Wisconsin Press, 1985.

———. "A Study of Antef." *Orientalia* 46 (1977): 393–423.

———. *A Time to Tear Down and a Time to Build Up: A Rereading of Ecclesiastes*. Grand Rapids: Eerdmans 1999.

———. "Who Can Learn? A Dispute in Ancient Pedagogy." Pages 62–77 in Barré, ed., *Wisdom, You Are My Sister*.

Fredericks, Daniel C. *Coping with Transience: Ecclesiastes on Brevity in Life*. The Biblical Seminar 18. Sheffield: JSOT, 1993.

————. *Qoheleth's Language: Re-evaluating Its Nature and Date.* Ancient Near Eastern Texts and Studies 3. Lewiston: Edwin Mellen, 1988.

Frydrych, Tomáš. *Living Under the Sun: Examination of Proverbs and Qoheleth.* VTSup 90. Leiden: Brill, 2002.

Galling, Kurt. "Der Prediger." Pages 73–125 in Ernst Würthwein, Kurt Galling, and Otto Plöger, *Die fünf Megilloth.* 2d ed. Handbuch zum alten Testament 1/18. Tübingen: J. C. B. Mohr (Paul Siebeck), 1969.

————. "Kohelet-Studien." *ZAW* 50 (1932): 276–99.

Gammie, John. "Stoicism and Anti-Stoicism in Qoheleth." *HAR* 9 (1985): 169–87.

Gammie, John, W. A. Brueggemann, W. L. Humphreys, and J. M. Ward, eds. *Israelite Wisdom: Theological and Literary Essays in Honor of Samuel Terrien.* Missoula: Scholars Press, 1978.

Garfinkel, Stephen. "Qoheleth: The Philosopher Means Business." Pages 51–62 in *Bringing the Hidden to Light: The Process of Interpretation: Studies in Honor of Stephen A. Geller.* Edited by Kathryn F. Kravitz and Dianne M. Sharon. Winona Lake: Eisenbrauns/Jewish Theological Seminary, 2007.

Gentry, Peter J. "The Role of the 'Three' in the Text History of the Septuagint: II. Aspects of Interdependence of the Old Greek and the Three in Ecclesiastes." *AS* 4 (2006): 153–92.

Gianto, Agustinus. "The Theme of Enjoyment in Qohelet." *Biblica* 73 (1992): 528–33.

Ginsberg, H. Louis. קֹהֶלֶת. A New Commentary on the Torah, the Prophets and the Holy Writings. Tel-Aviv: Newman, 1961 (Hebrew).

————. "The Quintessence of Koheleth." Pages 47–59 in *Biblical and Other Studies.* Edited by Alexander Altmann. Philip W. Lown Institute of Advanced Judaic Studies, Studies and Texts 1. Cambridge, Mass.: Harvard University Press, 1963.

————. *Studies in Koheleth.* Texts and Studies of the Jewish Theological Seminary of America 17. New York: Jewish Theological Seminary of America, 1950.

————. "Supplementary Studies in Kohelet." *PAAJR* 21 (1952): 35–62.

Ginsburg, Christian D. *Coheleth, Commonly Called the Book of Ecclesiastes: Translated from the Original Hebrew, with a Commentary, Historical and Critical.* London: Longman, Green, Longman & Roberts, 1861.

Good, Edwin M. "The Unfilled Sea: Style and Meaning in Ecclesiastes 1:2–11." Pages 59–73 in Gammie et al., eds., *Israelite Wisdom.*

Gordis, Robert. "Koheleth: Hebrew or Aramaic?" *JBL* 71 (1952): 93–109.

————. *Koheleth: The Man and His World: A Study of Ecclesiastes.* 3d aug. ed. New York: Schocken, 1968.

————. "The Original Language of Qohelet." *JQR* 37 (1946–47): 67–84.

————. "Quotations as a Literary Usage in Biblical, Oriental, and Rabbinic Literature." *HUCA* 22 (1949): 157–219.

————. "Quotations in Wisdom Literature." *JQR* 30 (1939–40): 123–47.

————. "The Translation Theory of Qohelet Re-Examined." *JQR* 40 (1949–50): 103–16.

————. "Was Koheleth a Phoenician? Some Observations on Methods in Research." *JBL* 74 (1955): 103–14.

Graetz, Heinrich. *Kohélet* קהלת *oder der Salomonische Prediger. Übersetzt und kritisch erläutert. Nebst Anhang über Kohélet's Stellung im Kanon, über die griechische Uebersetzung desselben und über Graecismen darin und einem Glossar.* Leipzig: Winter, 1871.

Greenberg, Moshe. "נסה in Exodus 20:20 and the Purpose of the Sinaitic Theophany." *JBL* 79 (1960): 273–76.

Gropp, Douglas M. "The Origin and Development of the Aramaic *šallîṭ* Clause." *JNES* 52 (1993): 31–36.

Hagen, Fredrik. "'The Prohibitions': A New Kingdom Didactic Text." *JEA* 91 (2005): 125–64.

Haupt, Paul. "The Book of Ecclesiastes." Pages 242–78 in *Oriental Studies: A Selection of the Papers Read Before the Oriental Club of Philadelphia 1888–1894*. Boston: Ginn & Co., 1894.

———. *The Book of Ecclesiastes: A New Metrical Translation with an Introduction and Explanatory Notes*. Baltimore: The Johns Hopkins University Press, 1905.

———. "Ecclesiastes." *The American Journal of Philology* 26 (1905): 125–71.

———. *Koheleth oder Weltschmerz in der Bible: Ein Lieblingsbuch Friedrichs des Grossen*. Leipzig: Hinrichs, 1905.

Hayman, A. P. "Qohelet and the Book of Creation." *JSOT* 16 (1991): 93–111.

Heinemann, Moses. *Uebersetzung des Koheleth, nebst grammatisch exegetischem Commentar*. Berlin, 1831.

Hertzberg, Hans Wilhelm. "Palästinische Bezüge im Buche Kohelet." *ZDPV* 73 (1957): 113–24.

———. *Der Prediger*. Kommentar zum Alten Testament 17/4. Gütersloh: Gütersloher Verlagshaus Gerd Mohn, 1963.

Homan, Michael M. "Beer Production by Throwing Bread into Water: A New Interpretation of Qoh. XI1–2." *VT* 52 (2002): 275–78.

Humbert, Paul. *Recherches sur les sources égyptiennes de la littérature sapientiale d'Israël*. Mémoires de l'Université de Neuchâtel 7. Neuchâtel: Secrétariat de l'Université, 1929.

Hurowitz, Victor Avigdor. "The Wisdom of Šūpê-amēlī: A Deathbed Debate Between a Father and Son." Pages 37–51 in *Wisdom Literature in Mesopotamia and Israel*. Edited by Richard J. Clifford. SBL Symposium Series 36. Atlanta: SBL, 2007.

Ingram, Doug. *Ambiguity in Ecclesiastes*. LHBOTS 431. New York: T&T Clark International, 2006.

Isaksson, Bo. *Studies in the Language of Qoheleth: With Special Emphasis on the Verbal System*. Studi Semitica Uppsaliensia 10. Uppsala: Uppsala University Press, 1987.

Japhet, Sara. "'Goes to the South and Turns to the North' (Ecclesiastes 1:6): The Sources and History of the Exegetical Traditions." *Jewish Studies Quarterly* 1 (1993–94): 289–322.

Japhet, Sara, and R. B. Salters. *Rashbam on Qoheleth*. Jerusalem: Magnes: Leiden: Brill, 1985.

Jenni, Ernst. "Das Wort ʿōlām im Alten Testament." *ZAW* 64 (1952): 197–248; 65 (1953): 1–35.

Johnston, Robert K. "'Confessions of a Workaholic': A Reappraisal of Qoheleth." *CBQ* 38 (1976): 14–28. Reprinted on pages 133–47 in Zuck, ed., *Reflecting with Solomon*.

Joüon, Paul. "Sur le nom de 'Qoheleth'." *Biblica* 2 (1921): 53–54.

Kaiser, Otto. "Determination und Freiheit beim Kohelet/Prediger Salomo und in der Frühen Stoa." Pages 106–25 in *Gottes und der Menschen Weisheit. Gesammelte Aufsätze*. BZAW 261. Berlin: de Gruyter, 1998. Originally published in *Neue Zeitschrift für systematische Theologie* 31 (1989): 251–70.

Kamenetzky, Abraham. "Das Koheleth-Rätsel." *ZAW* 29 (1909): 63–69.

———. "Die P'šiṭa zu Ḳoheleth textkritisch und in ihrem Verhältnis zu dem massoretischen Text, der Septuaginta und den andern alten griechischen Versionen." *ZAW* 24 (1904): 181–239.

———."Die Rätselname Koheleth." *ZAW* 34 (1914): 225–28.

———. "Die ursprünglich beabsichtigte Aussprache des Pseudonyms קהלת." *Orientalistische Literaturzeitung* (1921): cols. 11–15.

Kedar-Kopfstein, Benjamin. "Semantic Aspects of the Pattern *qôṭēl.*" *HAR* 1 (1977): 155–76.

Klopfenstein, Martin A. "Die Skepsis des Qohelet." *TZ* 28 (1972): 97–109. Reprinted on pages 13–26 in *Leben aus dem Wort. Beiträge zum Alten Testament.* Edited by Walter Dietrich. BEAT 40. Bern: Lang, 1996.

Knobel, Peter Stephan. "The Targum of Qohelet." In *The Aramaic Bible,* vol. 15. Edited by K. Cathcart, M. Maher, and M. McNamara. Edinburgh: T. & T. Clark. Collegeville: Liturgical, 1991.

———. "Targum Qoheleth: A Linguistic and Exegetical Inquiry." Ph.D. diss., Yale University, 1976.

Koh, Y. V. *Royal Autobiography in the Book of Qoheleth.* BZAW 369. Berlin: de Gruyter, 2006.

Krüger, Thomas. *Kohelet (Prediger).* Biblischer Kommentar Altes Testament 19. Neukirchen–Vluyn: Neukirchener Verlag, 2000. ET *Qoheleth: A Commentary.* Hermeneia. Minneapolis: Fortress, 2004.

Kugel, James L. "Qohelet and Money." *CBQ* 51 (1989): 32–49.

Lambert, W. G. *Babylonian Wisdom Literature.* Oxford: Clarendon, 1960.

———. "Some New Babylonian Wisdom Literature." Pages 32–34 in *Wisdom in Ancient Israel: Essays in Honour of J. A. Emerton.* Edited by John Day, Robert Gordon, and Hugh G. M. Williamson. Cambridge: Cambridge University Press, 1995.

Lauha, Aarre. *Kohelet.* Biblischer Kommentar Altes Testament 19. Neukirchen–Vluyn: Neukirchener Verlag, 1978.

Laurent, Françoise. *Les biens pour rien en Qohéleth 5,9–6,6 ou La traversée d'un contraste.* BZAW 323. Berlin: de Gruyter, 2002.

Lee, Eunny P. *The Vitality of Enjoyment in Qohelet's Theological Rhetoric.* BZAW 353. Berlin: de Gruyter, 2005.

Lee, J. A. L. *A Lexical Study of the Septuagint Version of the Pentateuch.* SBL Septuagint and Cognate Studies Series 14. Chico: Scholars Press, 1983.

Levine, Etan. *The Aramaic Version of Qohelet.* New York: Genesis/Sepher-Hermon, 1978.

Levy, Ludwig. *Das Buch Qoheleth. Ein Beitrag zur Geschichte des Sadduzäismus. Kritisch untersucht, übersetzt und erklärt.* Leipzig: Hinrichs, 1912.

Lichtheim, Miriam. *Ancient Egyptian Autobiographies Chiefly of the Middle Kingdom: A Study and an Anthology.* OBO 84. Freiburg: Universitätsverlag. Göttingen: Vandenhoeck & Ruprecht, 1988.

———. *Ancient Egyptian Literature: A Book of Readings.* Vol. 1, *The Old and Middle Kingdoms.* Berkeley: University of California Press, 1973.

———. *Ancient Egyptian Literature: A Book of Readings.* Vol. 2, *The New Kingdom.* Berkeley: University of California Press, 1976.

———. *Ancient Egyptian Literature: A Book of Readings.* Vol. 3, *The Late Period.* Berkeley: University of California Press, 1980.

————. *Late Egyptian Wisdom Literature in the International Context: A Study of Demotic Instructions*. OBO 52. Freiburg: Universitätsverlag; Göttingen: Vandenhoeck & Ruprecht, 1983.

————. "The Songs of the Harpers." *JNES* 4 (1945): 178–212.

Lloyd, G. E. R. *Magic, Reason and Experience: Studies in the Origin and Development of Greek Science*. Cambridge: Cambridge University Press, 1979.

Loader, J. A. *Ecclesiastes: A Practical Commentary*. Text and Interpretation. Grand Rapids: Eerdmans, 1986. ET of *Prediker: Een Praktische Bijbelverklarung*. Texst en Toelichtung. Kampen: Kok, 1984.

————. "Qohelet 3:2–8—A 'Sonnet' in the Old Testament." *ZAW* 81 (1969): 239–42. German version: "Kohelet 3,2–8—Ein 'Sonett' im Alten Testament." Pages 5–8 in J. A. Loader, *Begegnung mit Gott. Gesammelte Studien im Bereich des Alten Testaments*. Wiener Alttestamentliche Studien 3. Frankfurt am Main: Lang, 2001.

Lohfink, Norbert. "Die Wiederkehr des immer Gleichen. Eine frühe Synthese zwischen griechischem und jüdischem Weltgefühl in Kohelet 1,4–11." *Archivo di Filosofia* 53 (1985): 125–49.

————. *Kohelet*. 6th ed. Die Neue Echter Bibel. Würzburg: Echter, 2009. ET of 1st ed. *Qoheleth: A Continental Commentary*. Continental Commentaries. Minneapolis: Fortress, 2003.

————. "Qoheleth 5:17–19—Revelation by Joy." *CBQ* 52 (1990): 625–35. A German translation of the English version appears as "Koh 5,17–19—Offenbarung durch Freude." Pages 151–65 in Lohfink, *Studien zu Kohelet*.

————. *Studien zu Kohelet*. Stuttgarter Biblische Aufsatzbände 26. Stuttgart: Katholisches Bibelwerk, 1998.

————. "War Kohelet ein Frauenfeind? Ein Versuch, die Logik und den Gegenstand von Koh., 7,23–8,1a herauszufinden." Pages 259–87 in *La sagesse de l'Ancien Testament*. Edited by M. Gilbert. BETL 51. Leuven: Leuven University Press, 1979. 2d ed. pp. 417–20. Reprinted on pages 31–69 in Lohfink, *Studien zu Kohelet*.

Longman III, Tremper. *The Book of Ecclesiastes*. NICOT. Grand Rapids: Eerdmans, 1998.

————. *Fictional Akkadian Autobiography: A Generic and Comparative Study*. Winona Lake: Eisenbrauns, 1991.

Loretz, Oswald. "'Frau' und griechisch-jüdische Philosophie im Buch Qohelet (Qoh 7,23–8,1 und 9,6–10)." *UF* 23 (1991): 245–64.

————. "Poetry and Prose in the Book of Qohelet (1:1–3:22. 7:23–8:1. 9:6–10. 12:8–14)." Pages 155–89 in *Verse in Ancient Near Eastern Prose*. Edited by Johannes C. de Moor and Wilfred G. E. Watson. Alter Orient und Altes Testament 42. Kevelaer: Butzon & Bercker. Neukirchen–Vluyn: Neukirchener Verlag, 1993.

————. *Qohelet und der alte Orient: Untersuchungen zu Stil und theologischer Thematik des Buches Qohelet*. Freiburg im Breisgau: Herder, 1964.

Lorton, David. "The Expression *šms-ib*." *JARCE* 7 (1968): 41–54.

Lux, Rüdiger. "'Ich, Kohelet, bin Konig…': Die Fiktion als Schlüssel zur Wirklichkeit in Kohelet 1,12–2,26." *Evangelische Theologie* 50 (1990): 331–42.

Lys, Daniel. *L'Ecclésiaste ou que vaut la vie? Traduction, introduction générale, commentaire de 1/1 à 4/3*. Paris: Letouzey et Ané, 1977.

Machinist, Peter. "Fate, *miqreh*, and Reason: Some Reflections on Qohelet and Biblical Thought." Pages 159–75 in *Solving Riddles and Untying Knots: Biblical, Epigraphic, and Semitic Studies in Honor of Jonas C. Greenfield*. Edited by Ziony Zevit, Seymour Gitin, and Michael Sokoloff. Winona Lake: Eisenbrauns, 1995.

Manns, Frédéric. "Le Targum De Qohelet—Manuscrit Urbinati 1. Traduction et commentaire." *Liber Annuus* 42 (1992): 145–98.

Margoliouth, David Samuel. "Ecclesiastes." Pages 32–34 in *The Jewish Encyclopedia: a Descriptive Record of the History, Religion, Literature, and Customs of the Jewish People from the Earliest Times to the Present Day*. Vol. 5, *Dreyfus-Brisac-Goat*. Edited by Cyrus Adler et al. New York: Funk & Wagnalls, 1903.

Marshall, Philip S. "A Critical Edition of the Hexaplaric Fragments of Ecclesiastes." Ph.D. diss., Southern Baptist Theological Seminary, 2007.

Maussion, Marie. *Le mal, le bien et le jugement de Dieu dans le livre de Qohélet*. OBO 190. Fribourg: Editions Universitaires. Göttingen: Vandenhoeck & Ruprecht, 2003.

McNeile, Alan H. *An Introduction to Ecclesiastes: With Notes and Appendices*. Cambridge: Cambridge University Press, 1904.

Michaud, Robert. *Qohélet et l'hellénisme: La Littérature de sagesse: Histoire et Théologie*, vol. 2. Lire le Bible 77. Paris: Cerf, 1987.

Michel, Diethelm. *Qohelet*. Erträge der Forschung 258. Darmstadt: Wissenschaftliche Buchgesellschaft, 1988.

———. *Untersuchungen zur Eigenart des Buches Qohelet*. BZAW 183. Berlin: de Gruyter, 1989.

Miller, Douglas B. *Symbol and Rhetoric in Ecclesiastes: The Place of Hebel in Qohelet's Work*. Academia Biblica 2. Atlanta: SBL, 2002.

Min, Y.-J. "How Do the Rivers Flow? (Ecclesiastes 1.7)." *Bible Translator* 42 (1991): 226–30.

Mopsik, Charles. *L'Ecclésiaste et son Double Araméen*. Les Dix Paroles. Rieux-en-Val: Verdier, 1990.

Müller, Hans-Peter. "Kohelet im Lichte der frühgriechischen Philosophie." Pages 67–80 in *Weisheit in Israel. Beiträge des Symposiums "Das Alte Testament und die Kultur der Moderne" anlässlich des 100. Geburtstags Gerhard von Rads (1901–1971), Heidelberg, 18.–21. Oktober 2001*. Edited by David J. A. Clines, Hermann Lichtenberger, and Hans-Peter Müller. Altes Testament und Moderne 12. Münster: Lit, 2003.

———. "Kolloquialsprache und Volksreligion in den Inschriften von Kuntillet ʿAǧrūd und Ḥirbet el-Qōm." *ZAH* 5 (1992): 15–51.

———. "Theonome Skepsis und Lebensfreude. Zu Koh 1,12–3,15." *BZ* 30 (1986): 1–19.

Newsom, Carol. "Job and Ecclesiastes." Pages 177–94 in *Old Testament Interpretation: Past, Present, and Future: Essays in Honor of Gene M. Tucker*. Edited by James L. Mays, David L. Petersen, and Kent H. Richards. Nashville: Abingdon, 1995.

Niccacci, A. "Qohelet. Analisi sintattica, traduzione, composizione." *Liber Annuus* 54 (2004): 53–94.

———. "Qohelet o la gioia come fatica e dono di Dio a chi lo teme." *Liber Annuus* 52 (2002): 29–102.

Nougayrol, Jean. "Textes Suméro-Accadiens des archives et bibliothèques privées d'Ugarit." Pages 1–46 in *Ugaritica V: nouveaux textes accadiens, hourrites et ugaritiques des archives et bibliothèques privées d'Ugarit: commentaires des textes historiques (première partie)*. Edited by Jean Nougayrol, Emmanuel Laroche, Charles Virolleaud, and Claude F. A. Schaeffer. Mission de Ras Shamra 16. Institut français d'archéologie de Beyrouth bibliothèque archéologique et historique 80. Paris: Geuthner, 1968.

Ogden, Graham S. "The Interpretation of *Dôr* in Ecclesiastes 1.4." *JSOT* 34 (1986): 91–92.

———. *Qoheleth*. 2d ed. Readings: A New Biblical Commentary. Sheffield: Sheffield Phoenix, 2007.

Orni, Efraim, and Elisha Efrat. *Geography of Israel*. 3d ed. Jerusalem: Israel Universities Press, 1971.

Pahk, Johan Yeong-Sik. "Qohelet e le Tradiziuoni sapienzali del vicino oriente antico." Pages 117–43 in Bellia and Passaro, eds., *Il Libro del Qohelet*.

Parkinson, Richard B. *The Tale of Sinuhe and Other Ancient Egyptian Poems 1940–1640 BC*. Oxford: Clarendon, 1997.

Perdue, Leo. *Wisdom Literature: A Theological History*. Louisville: Westminster John Knox, 2007.

Perrin, Nicholas. "Messianism in the Narrative Frame of Ecclesiastes?" *RB* 108 (2001): 37–60.

Perry, T. A. *Dialogues with Kohelet: The Book of Ecclesiastes*. University Park: Pennsylvania State University Press, 1993.

Pinçon, Bertrand. *L'enigme du bonheur: Etude sur le sujet du bien dans le livre de Qohélet*. VTSup 119. Leiden: Brill, 2008.

Plumptre, E. H. *Ecclesiastes: Or, the Preacher, with Notes and Introduction*. The Cambridge Bible for Schools and Colleges. Cambridge: Cambridge University Press, 1881.

Podechard, E. *L'Ecclésiaste*. Etudes Bibliques. Paris: Lecoffre, 1912.

Rad, Gerhard von. *Weisheit in Israel*. Neukirchen–Vluyn: Neukirchener Verlag, 1970. ET *Wisdom in Israel*. London: SCM, 1972.

Rainey, A. F. "A Second Look at Amal in Qoheleth." *Concordia Theological Monthly* 36 (1965): 805.

Ranston, Harry. *Ecclesiastes and the Early Greek Wisdom Literature*. London: Epworth, 1925.

———. "Ecclesiastes and Theognis." *AJSLL* 34 (1918): 99–122.

———. "Koheleth and the Early Greeks." *JTS* 24 (1923): 160–69.

Ravasi, Gianfranco. *Qohelet*. 2d ed. La Parola di Dio. Cinisello Balsamo: Paoline, 1991.

Renan, E. *L'Ecclésiaste traduit de l'hébreu avec une étude sur l'age et le caractère du livre*. Oeuvres Complètes de Ernest Renan, édition définitive établie par Henriette Psichari 7. Paris: Calmann-Lévy, 1955.

Riesener, Ingrid. "Frauenfeindschaft im Alten Testament? Zum Verständnis von Qoh 7,25–29." Pages 193–207 in Diesel et al., eds., *"Jedes Ding hat seine Zeit…"*.

Rose, Martin. *Rien de nouveau: nouvelles approches du livre de Qohéleth. Avec une bibliographie (1988–1998) élaborée par Béatrice Perregaux Allisson*. OBO 168. Göttingen: Vandenhoeck & Ruprecht. Fribourg: Editions Universitaires, 1999.

Rudman, Dominic. *Determinism in the Book of Ecclesiastes*. JSOTSup 316. Sheffield: Sheffield Academic, 2001.

———. "A Note on the Dating of Ecclesiastes." *CBQ* 61 (1999): 47–52.

Salters, Robert B. "Notes on the Interpretation of Qoh 6:2." *ZAW* 91 (1979): 282–89.

Salyer, Gary D. *Vain Rhetoric: Private Insight and Public Debate in Ecclesiastes*. JSOTSup 327. Sheffield: Sheffield Academic, 2001.

Schellenberg, Annette. *Erkenntnis als Problem. Qohelet und die alttestamentliche Diskussion um das menschliche Erkennen*. OBO 188. Freiburg: Universitätsverlag and Vandenhoeck & Ruprecht, 2002.

Schoors, Anton. "L'ambiguità della gioia in Qohelet." Pages 276–92 in Bellia and Passaro, eds., *Il Libro del Qohelet*.

———. *The Preacher Sought to Find Pleasing Words: A Study of the Language of Qoheleth*. Part I, *Grammar*. OLA 41. Leuven: Peeters, Department Oriëntalistiek, Leiden, 1992.

———. *The Preacher Sought to Find Pleasing Words: A Study of the Language of Qoheleth*. Part 2, *Vocabulary*. OLA 143. Leuven: Peeters and Department of Oosterse Studies, 2004.

———. "Qoheleth: The Ambiguity of Enjoyment." Pages 35–41 in *The Bright Side of Life*. Edited by Ellen van Wolde. Concilium 2000/4. London: SCM, 2000.

Schoors, A., ed. *Qohelet in the Context of Wisdom*. BETL 136. Leuven: University Press and Uitgeverij Peeters, 1998.

Schwartz, Eduard, ed. *Eusebius Werke. 2, 2, Die Kirchengeschichte: Die lateinische Übersetzung des Rufinus bearbeitet in gleichen auftrage von Theodore Mommsen. Zweiter Teil: Die Bücher VI bis X über die Märtyrer in Palästina*. Leipzig: Hinrichs, 1908.

Schwienhorst-Schönberger, Ludger. *Kohelet*. Herders theologischer Kommentar zum Alten Testament. Freiburg im Breisgau: Herder, 2004.

———. *Nicht im Menschen Gründet das Glück (Koh 2,24): Kohelet im Spannungsfeld jüdischer Weisheit und hellenistischer Philosophie*. Herders Biblische Studien 2. Freiburg im Breisgau: Herder, 1994.

Sciumbata, M. Patrizia. "Peculiarità e motivazioni della struttura lessicale dei verbi della 'conoscenza' in Qohelet. Abbozzo di una storia dell'epistemologia ebraico-biblica." *Henoch* 18 (1996): 235–49.

Segal, J. B. *Aramaic Texts from North Saqqâra: With Some Fragments in Phoenician*. London: Egypt Exploration Society, 1983.

Segert, Stanislav. *A Grammar of Phoenician and Punic*. Munich: Beck, 1976.

Selle, Hendrik. *Theognis und die Theognidea*. Untersuchungen zur antiken Literatur und Geschichte 95. Berlin: de Gruyter, 2008.

Seow, C. L. "'Beyond Them, My Son, Be Warned': The Epilogue of Qoheleth Revisited." Pages 125–41 in Barré, ed., *Wisdom, You are My Sister*.

———. *Ecclesiastes: A New Translation with Introduction and Commentary*. Anchor Bible 18C. New York: Doubleday, 1997.

———. "Linguistic Evidence and the Dating of Qohelet." *JBL* 115 (1996): 643–66.

———. "Qohelet's Autobiography." Pages 275–87 in *Fortunate the Eyes that See: Essays in Honor of David Noel Freedman in Celebration of His Seventieth Birthday*. Edited by Astrid B. Beck, Andrew H. Bartelt, Paul R. Raabe, and Chris A. Franke. Grand Rapids: Eerdmans, 1995.

———. "The Socioeconomic Context of 'The Preacher's' Hermeneutic." *Princeton Seminary Bulletin* 17 (1996): 168–95.

Shead, Andrew G. "Ecclesiastes from the Outside In." *Reformed Theological Review* 55 (1996): 24–37.

———. "Reading Ecclesiastes 'Epilogically'." *Tyndale Bulletin* 48 (1997): 67–91.

Sheppard, G. T. "The Epilogue to Qoheleth as Theological Commentary." *CBQ* 39 (1977): 182–89.

Shields, Martin. *The End of Wisdom: A Reappraisal of the Historical and Canonical Function of Ecclesiastes*. Winona Lake: Eisenbrauns, 2007.

Siegfried, D. C. *Prediger und Hoheslied. Übersetzt und erklärt.* HAT II/3/2. Göttingen: Vandenhoeck & Ruprecht, 1898.

Skehan, Patrick W. "The Literary Relationship of the Book of Wisdom to Earlier Wisdom Writings." Pages 172–236 in *Studies in Israelite Poetry and Wisdom.* CBQMS 1. Washington: Catholic Biblical Association of America, 1971.

Spangenberg, Izak J. J. "Quotations in Ecclesiastes: An Appraisal." *OTE* 4 (1991): 19–35.

Sperber, Alexander. *The Bible in Aramaic: Based on Old Manuscripts and Printed Texts.* Vol. IVA, *The Hagiographa: Transition from Translation to Midrash.* 2d Impression. Leiden: Brill, 1992.

Staples, W. E. "'Profit' in Ecclesiastes." *JNES* 4 (1945): 87–96.

Stuckenbruck, Loren. *1 Enoch 91–108.* CEJL. Berlin: de Gruyter, 2007.

Taradach, Madeleine, and Joan Ferrer. *Un Targum de Qohélet. Ms. M–2 de Salamanca, Editio Princeps. Texte araméen, traduction et commentaire critique.* Le Monde de la Bible 37. Geneva: Labor et Fides, 1998.

Tin-Sheung, Wong. "Qoheleth 1:3–11: Prose or Poetry?" *Jian Dao* 14 (2000): 25–47.

Torrey, Charles C. "The Question of the Original Language of Qoheleth." *JQR* 39 (1948–49): 151–60.

Tur-Sinai, Naftali Herz (= Harry Torczyner). "דברי קהלת" ("The Words of Qoheleth"). Pages 389–408 in הלשון והספר: בעיות יסוד במדע הלשון ובמקורותיה בספרות (*The Language and the Book: Fundamental Issues in the Study of the Language and in its Literary Sources*), vol. 2. Jerusalem: Bialik Institute, 1950 (Hebrew).

———. "Dunkle Bibelstellen." Pages 274–80 in *Vom alten Testament Karl Marti zum Siebzigsten Geburtstage gewidmet von Freunden, Fachgenossen und Schülern.* Edited by K. Budde. BZAW 41. Giessen: Töpelmann, 1925.

Uehlinger, Christoph. "Qohelet im Horizont mesopotamischer, levantinischer und ägyptischer Weisheitsliteratur der persischen und hellenistischen Zeit." Pages 155–247 in *Das Buch Kohelet. Studien zur Struktur, Geschichte, Rezeption und Theologie.* Edited by Ludger Schwienhorst-Schönberger. BZAW 254. Berlin: de Gruyter, 1997.

Ullendorff, Edward. "The Meaning of קהלת." *VT* 12 (1962): 215.

Ulrich, Eugene et al. *Qumran Cave 4 XI Psalms to Chronicles.* DJD 16. Oxford: Clarendon, 2000.

Verheij, Arian J. C. "Words Speaking for Themselves: On the Poetics of Qohelet 1:4–7." Pages 183–88 in *Give Ear to My Words: Psalms and Other Poetry in and Around the Hebrew Bible: Essays in Honour of Professor N. A. van Uchelen.* Edited by Janet Dyk. Amsterdam: Societas Hebraica Amstelodamensis, 1996.

Vinel, Françoise. *L'Ecclésiaste. Traduction du texte grec de la Septante. Introduction et notes.* La Bible d'Alexandrie. Paris: Cerf, 2002.

Volz, Paul. *Hiob und Weisheit (Das Buch Hiob, Sprüche und Jesus Sirach, Prediger). Übersetzt, erklärt und mit Einleitungen versehen.* 2d ed. Die Schriften des alten Testaments 3/2. Göttingen: Vandenhoeck & Ruprecht, 1921.

Walker, Larry L. "Notes on Higher Criticism and the Dating of Biblical Hebrew." Pages 35–52 in *A Tribute to Gleason Archer.* Edited by Walter C. Kaiser, Jr. and Ronald F. Youngblood. Chicago: Moody, 1986.

Weeks, Stuart. *An Introduction to the Study of Wisdom Literature.* T&T Clark Approaches to Biblical Studies. London: T&T Clark International, 2010.

———. *Early Israelite Wisdom.* Oxford Theological Monographs. Oxford: Clarendon, 1994.

———. *Instruction and Imagery in Proverbs 1–9*. Oxford: Oxford University Press, 2007.

Weinberg, J. P. "Authorship and Author in the Ancient Near East and in the Hebrew Bible." *Hebrew Studies* 44 (2003): 157–69.

Wente, Edward F. "Egyptian 'Make Merry' Songs Reconsidered." *JNES* 21 (1962): 118–28.

West, M. L. *Iambi et Elegi Graeci*. 2 vols. 2d ed. Oxford: Clarendon, 1989–92.

Whitley, Charles F. *Koheleth: His Language and Thought*. BZAW 148. Berlin: de Gruyter, 1979.

Whybray, R. N. *Ecclesiastes*. New Century Bible Commentary. Grand Rapids: Eerdmans. London: Marshall, Morgan & Scott, 1989.

———. "Ecclesiastes 1.5–7 and the Wonders of Nature." *JSOT* 13 (1988): 105–12. Reprinted on pages 233–39 in Zuck, ed., *Reflecting with Solomon*, and on pages 153–60 in Dell and Barker, eds., *Wisdom*.

———. "The Identification and Use of Quotations in Ecclesiastes." Pages 435–51 in *Congress Volume: Vienna, 1980*. Edited by J. A. Emerton. VTSup 32. Leiden: Brill, 1981.

———. "Qoheleth, Preacher of Joy." *JSOT* 7 (1982): 87–98. Reprinted on pages 203–12 in Zuck, ed., *Reflecting with Solomon*, and on pages 141–52 in Dell and Barker, eds., *Wisdom*.

———. "Qoheleth the Immoralist? (Qoh 7:16–17)." Pages 191–204 in Gammie et al., eds., *Israelite Wisdom*. Reprinted on pages 93–106 in Dell and Barker, eds., *Wisdom*.

Wildeboer, Gerrit. *Die fünf Megillot (Das Hohelied, Das Buch Ruth, Die Klagelieder, Der Prediger, Das Buch Esther)*. Kurzer Hand-Commentar zum Alten Testament 17. Freiburg im Breisgau: J. C. B. Mohr (Paul Siebeck), 1898.

Wilson, Gerald H. "'The Words of the Wise': The Intent and Significance of Qohelet 12:9–14." *JBL* 103 (1984): 175–92.

Wilson, Lindsay. "Artful Ambiguity in Ecclesiastes 1,1–11: A Wisdom Technique?" Pages 357–65 in Schoors, ed., *Qohelet in the Context of Wisdom*.

Wise, Michael O. "A Calque from Aramaic in Qoheleth 6:12. 7:12. and 8:13." *JBL* 109 (1990): 249–57.

Wright, Addison G. "The Riddle of the Sphinx: The Structure of the Book of Qoheleth." *CBQ* 30 (1968): 313–34.

———. "The Riddle of the Sphinx Revisited: Numerical Patterns in the Book of Qoheleth." *CBQ* 42 (1980): 35–51.

———. "Additional Numerical Patterns in Qoheleth." *CBQ* 45 (1983): 32–43.

Wright, C. H. H. *The Book of Koheleth Commonly Called Ecclesiastes: Considered in Relation to Modern Criticism, and to the Doctrines of Modern Pessimism, With a Critical and Grammatical Commentary and a Revised Translation*. Donnellan Lectures 1880–81. London: Hodder & Stoughton, 1883.

Young, Ian, and Robert Rezetko, with the assistance of Martin Ehrensvärd. *Linguistic Dating of Biblical Texts*. 2 vols. London: Equinox, 2008.

Zapletal, Vincenz. *Das Buch Kohelet kritisch und metrisch untersucht*. 2d ed. Freiburg: Herder, 1911.

———. *Die Metrik des Buches Kohelet*. Freiburg: Universitats Buchhandlung, 1904.

Ziegler, Joseph. "Der Gebrauch des Artikels in der Septuaginta des Ecclesiastes." Pages 83–120 in *Studien zur Septuaginta: Robert Hanhart zu Ehren.* Edited by D. Fraenkel et al. Abhandlungen der Akademie der Wissenschaften in Göttingen, Philologisch-Historische Klasse 190. Mitteilungen des Septuaginta-Unternehmens 20. Göttingen: Vandenhoeck & Ruprecht, 1990.

Zimmerli, Walther. "Das Buch Kohelet: Traktat oder Sentenzensammlung?" *VT* 24 (1974): 221–30.

Zimmerman, Frank. "The Aramaic Provenance of Qohelet." *JQR* 36 (1945–46): 17–45.

———. "The Question of Hebrew in Qohelet." *JQR* 40 (1949–50): 79–102.

———. "The Root *KAHAL* in Some Scriptural Passages." *JBL* 50 (1931): 311–12.

Zuck, Roy B., ed. *Reflecting with Solomon: Selected Essays on the Book of Ecclesiastes.* Grand Rapids: Baker, 1994.

INDEXES

INDEX OF REFERENCES

INDEX OF AUTHORS